365 ALPHABETS

cross stitch all through the year

by Kooler Design Studio

American School of Needlework®, Inc., San Marcos, California

Bobbie Matela, Managing Editor
Carol Wilson Mansfield, Art Director
Jane Cannon Meyers, Creative Director
Ann Harnden, Editor
Pam Nichols, Editorial Assistant
Mary Hernandez, Book Design

Cross stitch charts by: Amy Butzen,
Rick Causee, Pat Hawes, Mary Hernandez,
Betsy Meyers Knight, Nancy Kuelbs,
Cheri Lowry, Terea Mitchell, Pam Nichols,
and Brent Rathburn.

Alphabets designed by Barbara Baatz, Holly
DeFount, Linda Gillum, Jorja Hernandez,
Pam Johnson, Lorna McRoden, Sandy
Orton, Nancy Rossi, and Giana Shaw.

Photographed designs were stitched by:
Kellie Ault, Deanna Baldus,
Penny Boswinkle, Jill Brooks,
Lucile Carlson, Lynda Carlson,
Linda Causee, Barbara Chancy,
Berry Curran, Eva-Lynn DellaGuardia,
Maryann Donovan, Diana Gerety,
Marge Griffith, Ellen Harnden,
Marlene Hommerding, Maxine Meadows,
Margaret Minor, Pam Nichols,
Mary Alice Patsko, Petie Pickwick,
Carly Poggemeyer, Cindy Seal,
Carrie Snider, Lee Ann Tibbals,
Kathy Tregembo, and Nancy Withrow.

For a full-color catalog including books of cross stitch designs, write to:

American School of Needlework®, Consumer Division
1455 Linda Vista Drive, San Marcos, CA 92069

We have made every effort to ensure the accuracy and completeness of these instructions.
We cannot, however, be responsible for human error, typographical mistakes, or variations in individual work.

© 1997 by Kooler Design Studio, Inc.
Published by American School of Needlework®, Inc.;
ASN Publishing, 1455 Linda Vista Drive, San Marcos, CA 92069

Introduction

Never before has there been a collection of creative alphabets like this! Thanks to the wonderful designers at Kooler Design Studio you can personalize your stitching projects from a choice of 365 alphabets!

Our alphabets have been divided into four categories:

Creatures Great And Small. A wide array of the cutest animals ever! From favorite zoo animals to frogs, turtles, butterflies, cats, dogs, mice and more—you're sure to enjoy stitching these unique alphabets.

Alphabet Soup. No matter what you want to say or spell with your stitches, here's a collection of alphabets that puts success at your fingertips. These alphabets range from simple to unusual.

Our Favorite Things. From pretty bows and musical notes to hot air balloons and televisions—look to this section for interesting design directions.

From The Garden. Not only do our garden alphabets present gifts of nature, like pretty flowers, fruits and vegetables—there are also charming visitors like gardening bunnies, song birds, and scarecrows.

We have added several small single-color cross stitch and backstitch alphabets in each category. With this great variety of sizes and styles to choose from, you'll never run out of inspiration. Use this resource for names, initials, samplers, personalization of most anything, or add them to other designs. If you are new to cross stitch, we've included all the basic instruction you'll need to learn, pages 5 to 8.

Although cross stitch is usually done on an evenweave fabric, if you'd like to stitch on some other type of fabric see our waste canvas note, page 5. Learn how to turn most any fabric into a temporary evenweave surface. To choose floss colors, refer to the Master Color Key included on pages 184-185. It translates the names of the colors for the entire book with the major floss brands.

Contents

The charted designs are in numerical order beginning on page 14.

Front Cover

Back Cover

4

Counted Cross Stitch Basics

THE MATERIALS

The materials required for counted cross stitch are few and inexpensive: a piece of evenweave fabric, a tapestry needle, some 6-strand cotton floss, scissors, and a charted design. An embroidery hoop is optional. All of these are readily available at most needlework shops.

FABRICS

For counted cross stitch embroidery we use "evenweave" fabrics which are woven with the same number of horizontal and vertical threads per inch. Cross stitches are made over the intersections of the horizontal and vertical threads, and because the number of threads in each direction is equal, each stitch will be the same size and perfectly square. A fabric is described by the number of threads per inch; that number is called its thread count.

The thread count, and the number of stitches, will determine the finished size of a stitched design. A higher thread count will produce a smaller design (more stitches are worked per inch) and a lower thread count will produce a larger design because there are fewer stitches per inch.

Evenweave fabrics commonly used for cross stitch are Aida cloth, linen, an array of specialty fabrics, and waste canvas. There are also many kinds of pre-made evenweave products.

Aida cloth is a cotton that has groups of four threads woven in a basketweave pattern, making the intersections very easy to see when constructing the stitches. The groups of threads are called squares. Aida is woven in several sizes, measured by the number of squares (therefore stitches) per inch: 11-count (11 stitches per inch), 14-count (14 stitches per inch), 16-count (16 stitches per inch), and 18-count (18 stitches per inch). The most often used Aida is 14-count.

Figs 1 through **4** show a letter (Alphabet #213 on page 104) cross-stitched on the four sizes of Aida so you can see the size change of the one design worked on different thread counts. Refer to the chart on page 6 to determine the approximate height and width of different design sizes worked on various thread counts.

11-count

Fig 1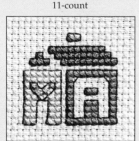

14-count

Fig 2

16-count

Fig 3

18-count

Fig 4

Linen is woven of single round linen threads. Cross stitches are made over two threads in each direction. Linen may be a bit difficult for beginners to use as there are no obvious intersections as on Aida, but a little practice will produce great results.

Linen is available in a variety of thread counts. Because stitches are worked over two threads, the number of stitches per inch will be half the thread count. For example, on 28-count linen, you will work 14 stitches per inch—or the same finished size as if the designs were worked on 14-count Aida cloth.

Specialty Fabrics are woven in the same manner as linen, but may be cotton, linen, synthetic, or a combination of fibers. These fabrics have different thread counts and may be known by different names, depending on the manufacturer.

Waste Canvas can be used should you wish to cross stitch on a non-evenweave surface. It is a temporary evenweave product that is available in a variety of thread counts. Baste a piece of waste canvas onto the surface to be embroidered, work over the canvas threads, then remove the threads when stitching is complete.

Pre-made Products are wonderful if you want to stitch a fingertip towel, a pillow, or perhaps a baby bib, but you don't like to sew. You'll love the many pre-mades available with an evenweave fabric (usually Aida) part of the construction. In addition to those we've mentioned, you'll find table linens, kitchen and bath accessories, afghans, bookmarks, a variety of baby items, and many others.

These accessories have a pre-determined amount of space available for stitching. When working on pre-mades, determine the number of stitches that can be worked in the available space, then choose an alphabet that will fit. For more planning information, refer to page 8.

NEEDLES

A small blunt-tipped tapestry needle, size 24 or 26, will be used for stitching. The higher the needle number, the smaller the needle. The correct size needle is easy to thread with the amount of thread required, but is not so large that it will distort the holes in the fabric. Threaded, the needle should easily slip through the fabric. **Fig 5** will tell you which size needle is appropriate for each size of fabric and suggest the number of floss strands to use.

Fig 5

Fabric	Stitches Per Inch	Strands of Floss	Tapestry Needle Size
Aida	11	3	22 or 24
Aida	14	2	24 or 26
Aida	16	2	24, 26 or 28
Aida	18	1 or 2	26 or 28

THREADS

The most commonly used thread for counted cross stitch is 6-strand cotton embroidery floss. It can be divided to work with one, two, or more strands at a time. Separate the floss into individual strands, then put the required number back together before threading the needle.

These alphabets were cross stitched on 16-count Aida cloth with two strands of floss. This combination allows the true color intensity to show. On 14-count fabrics, the same number of strands is usually used, but the color will be less intense because the background fabric is slightly visible. On 18-count fabrics, one strand is usually used.

We used Anchor floss to stitch the alphabets. Generic color names are given for the floss on the color keys throughout this book, and a Master Color Key on pages 184-185 lists the Anchor, Coats, and DMC embroidery floss number translations for these names. Each company has its own color families, which may not match from brand to brand, so these translations are only suggested substitutions.

Metallic gold can be used to add sparkle to a design. A single strand of Kreinik® #8 (fine) or #4 (very fine) braid can be used for cross stitch or backstitch. If desired, metallic thread can be used instead of the braid; work with the appropriate number of strands of your chosen brand.

SCISSORS

A pair of small, sharp-pointed scissors is necessary, especially for snipping misplaced stitches. You may want to hang your scissors on a chain or ribbon around your neck—you'll need them often.

CHARTED DESIGNS

Counted cross stitch designs are worked from charts. Each square on a chart represents the space for one cross stitch, and a symbol in a square represents the floss color to be used for the stitch. A color key is not shown for an alphabet that requires only one color—choose your desired color.

Decorative stitches are also shown on charts. Straight lines over or between symbols indicate backstitches or straight stitches. Eyelets and lazy daisies are shown by their shape and French knots by dots.

Figs 6 and **7** show the color key and chart for the "A" from Alphabet 213 on page 104. This is the same letter shown stitched on the four different thread counts on page 5.

Fig 6

○	=	very lt pink
●	=	med lt pink
~	=	med lt orange
◇	=	med yellow-green
#	=	med lt green
▲	=	lt blue
│	=	Backstitch: *dk gray*

The color key, **Fig 6**, shows symbols that represent each color to be used for the cross stitches.

The chart, **Fig 7**, shows the placement of the different colors to create the design. You will begin at the top of the design and work one cross stitch on the fabric corresponding to each square with a symbol. When house colors have been stitched according to symbols, use one strand of dark gray to backstitch along the edges of the design as shown by the dark lines.

Fig 7

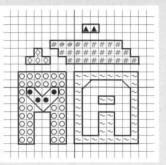

Charts can be foolers: Remember, the size of the charted design is not necessarily the size that your finished work will be. The worked size is determined by the number of threads per inch of the fabric you select. For example, if you work a letter that is 22 stitches wide and 11 stitches high on 11-count Aida, the worked design will be 2" wide and 1" high. When worked on 18-count Aida, the same design will be 1 ¼" wide and about ½" high. Use the chart below, **Fig 8**, as a guide to determine the approximate finished width and height of a stitched design based on your chosen background fabric.

Fig 8

Number of Stitches in Design					
Thread Count	10	20	30	40	50
11-count	1"	1¾"	2¾"	3⅝"	4½"
14-count	¾"	1⅜"	2⅛"	2⅞"	3⅝"
16-count	⅝"	1¼"	1⅞"	2½"	3⅛"
18-count	½"	1⅛"	1⅝"	2¼"	2¾"
(measurements are given to the nearest ⅛")					

GETTING STARTED

Count squares to find the center of a large letter or group of letters. Count threads or fold fabric to find its center. Count up and over to the left on chart and fabric to begin cross stitching.

Cut floss into comfortable working lengths—we suggest about 18". To begin, bring threaded needle to front of fabric. Follow the basic stitch instructions on page 7 to work the design following the chart.

Hold an inch of the end against the back, then anchor it with your first few stitches. To end threads and begin new ones next to existing stitches, weave through the backs of several stitches. Trim thread ends close to fabric. Wherever possible, end your thread under stitches of the same color and toward the center of the design.

THE STITCHES

Note: Unless otherwise noted in the color key, use two strands of floss for cross stitches, eyelets, and French knots; use one strand for backstitches, straight stitches, and lazy daisies.

Cross Stitch

The basic cross stitch is formed in two steps. **Fig 9** shows a single cross stitch on Aida cloth. Follow the numbering and bring needle up at 1, down at 2, up at 3, and down at 4 to complete the stitch. Whenever possible, work horizontal rows of stitches, **Fig 10**. Work half of each stitch (1-2) across the row from left to right; on the return journey from right to left, complete each stitch with the 3-4 sequence.

Fig 9

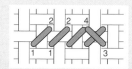

Fig 10

When a vertical row of stitches is appropriate for the design, complete each stitch then proceed to the next as shown in **Fig 11**. No matter how you work the stitches, make sure that all crosses slant in the same direction.

Fig 11

Backstitch

Backstitches are worked after cross stitches have been completed. They may slope in any direction and are occasionally worked over more than one square of fabric. **Fig 12** shows the progression of several stitches; bring thread up at odd numbers and down at even numbers.

Fig 12

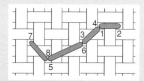

Sometimes you have to choose where to end one backstitch color and begin the next color. As a rule of thumb, choose the object that should appear closest to you. Backstitch around that shape with the appropriate color, then backstitch the areas behind it with adjacent color(s).

Straight Stitch

A straight stitch, **Fig 13**, is made like a long backstitch. Come up at one end of the stitch and down at the other. Be sure to secure thread well at the beginning and ending of a group of straight stitches so they stay taut.

Fig 13

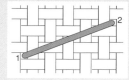

French Knot

Bring thread up where indicated on chart. Wrap floss once around needle, and reinsert needle close to, but at least one thread away, from where thread first came up, **Fig 14**. Hold wrapping thread tightly, close to surface of fabric. Pull needle through, letting thread go just as knot is formed. For a larger knot, use more strands of floss, but wrap only once. More than one wrap produces a loose, unstable knot.

Fig 14

Eyelet

This is a technique that produces a starburst effect; the sizes and shapes of the eyelets may vary. Bring floss up at any point along the outside of the charted shape, **Fig 15**, and stitch down at center. Continue to work around shape as charted, always entering fabric at center of eyelet. Follow the length and position of each stitch shown on chart.

Fig 15

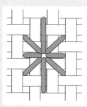

Lazy Daisy Stitch

This stitch creates pointed oval shapes that resemble flower petals. Bring thread up at center hole, 1, **Fig 16**. Loop floss, insert needle in same hole, and bring it out two squares from center, 2, or as indicated on chart, with loop beneath point of needle. Pull needle through, adjusting size and shape of loop. Stitch down over loop, one thread farther from center, to secure it. Repeat for each oval shape. Anchor ending thread especially well on the wrong side.

Fig 16

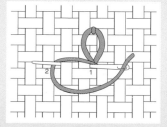

PLANNING A PROJECT

Choosing An Alphabet
The alphabets are worked in a variety of ways on our covers and color pages. These graphic renditions will show you a sampling of letters from each alphabet. You can combine letters for any project you wish. Which ever way you want to use the designs, the planning process will be the same.

Choose an alphabet that you like and decide upon the letters you wish to stitch. The spacing between letters is a matter of taste, and the effect you want to achieve. Choose spacing that looks good to you. For an approximate size of the planned stitching, refer to the chart (**Fig 8**) on page 6. For a more accurate measurement, refer to **Fig 17** below.

Determining Stitched Size
Count the width of the letters then add the squares for the spacing between the letters. To determine the stitched width of the area, divide the total number of stitches in width by the number of stitches per inch of fabric. Round off the number to determine how many inches wide the design will be. Repeat for the height of the design.

For example, let's plan to stitch the word "WELCOME" using little houses: Alphabet 213 on page 104.

1. Count the width of the letters: W = 17, M = 18, and the rest each = 15.

2. Plan the spacing between letters: 3.

3. As you spell the word, count each letter plus the spacing:

Fig 17

W E L C O M E
17 + 3 + 15 + 3 + 15 + 3 + 15 + 3 + 15 + 3 + 18 + 3 + 15 = 128

4. Divide the counted stitch width (128) by the count of the fabric you are using. For 14-count fabric:

   $128 \div 14 = 9''$ wide.

5. For the height, divide the tallest letter (they are all 15 high) by the count of the fabric (14):

   $15 \div 14 = 1''$ high.

This project would be 9" x 1" when stitched on 14-count fabric.

Adding A Border
Once you have determined the letters to be stitched, you may want to add a border. A simple checkerboard treatment has been occasionally used in this book to surround or supplement an alphabet and create a sampler effect. For example, **Figs 18** to **20** show the charts for three stitched borders. The color keys show a light color (▫) and a dark color (×). **Figs 18** and **19** are two-row borders, one with dark corners and one with light corners. **Fig 20** shows a four-row border.

Fig 18

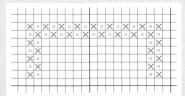

```
▫ = lt color
× = dk color
```

Fig 19

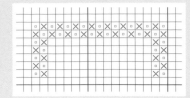

```
▫ = lt color
× = dk color
```

Fig 20

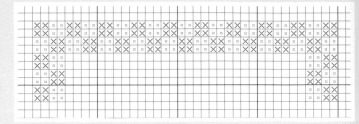

```
▫ = lt color
× = dk color
```

You can widen or lengthen these checkerboard borders to fit a desired space. Choose two colors (or white or black plus a color) that complement the overall design. There are also many variations on the checkerboard theme. You can eliminate one of the colors, leaving the fabric to show, or work single stitches or blocks of stitches for a dotted border effect.

Preparing to Stitch
If you are working on a pre-made item, make sure there is a large enough stitching area available for your planned letters. If you are working on a piece of fabric, determine the stitched size then allow enough additional fabric around the design plus 2" or 3" more on each side for use in finishing and mounting.

Cut your fabric exactly true, right along the holes of the fabric. Some ravelling may occur as you handle the fabric. To minimize ravelling, along the raw edges use an overcast basting stitch, machine zigzag stitch, or masking tape (to be cut away when you are finished).

Ideally, the progression of your work should be from left to right and from the top of the design (and fabric) toward the bottom. With this sequence, you will bring your thread up from the back to the front through unoccupied fabric holes and will stitch down from front to back through already occupied holes, thereby disturbing completed stitches as little as possible.

FINISHING NEEDLEWORK

When you have finished stitching, dampen your embroidery (or, if soiled, wash in lukewarm mild soapsuds and rinse well). Roll in a towel to remove excess moisture. Place face down on a dry towel or padded surface and press carefully until dry and smooth. Make sure all thread ends are well anchored and clipped closely. Proceed with desired finishing.

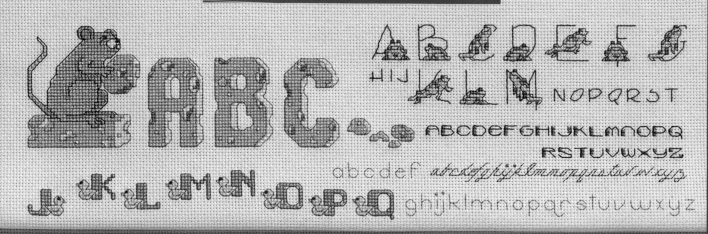

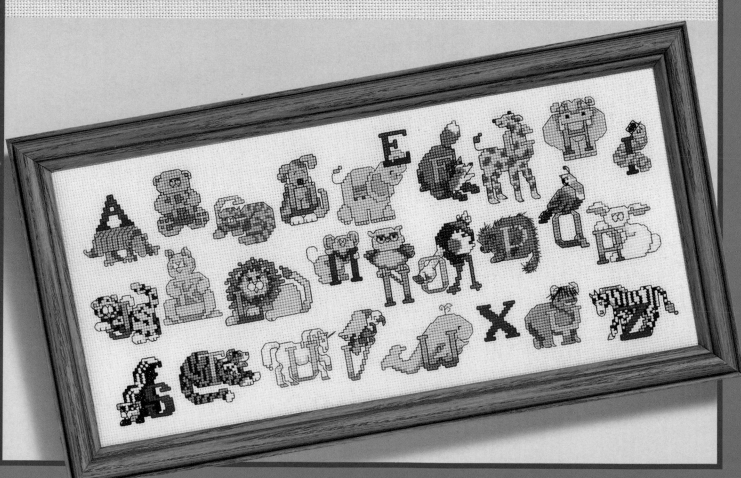

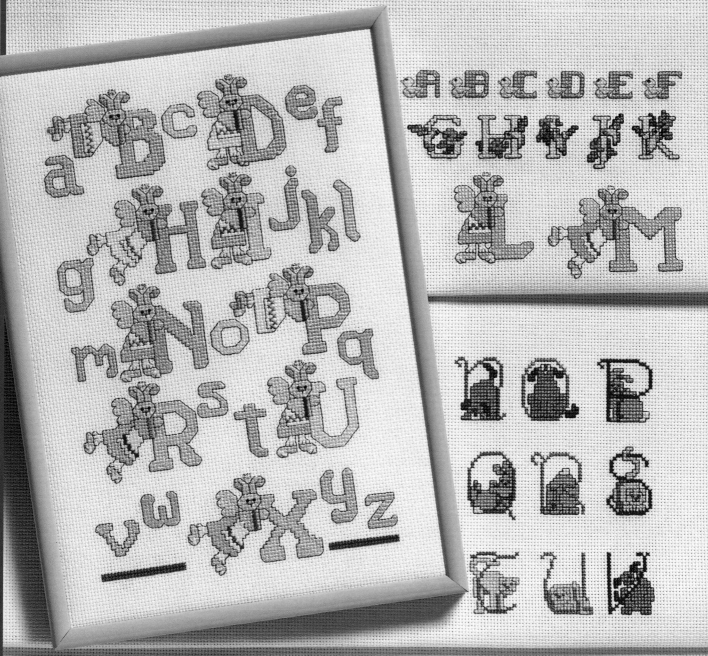

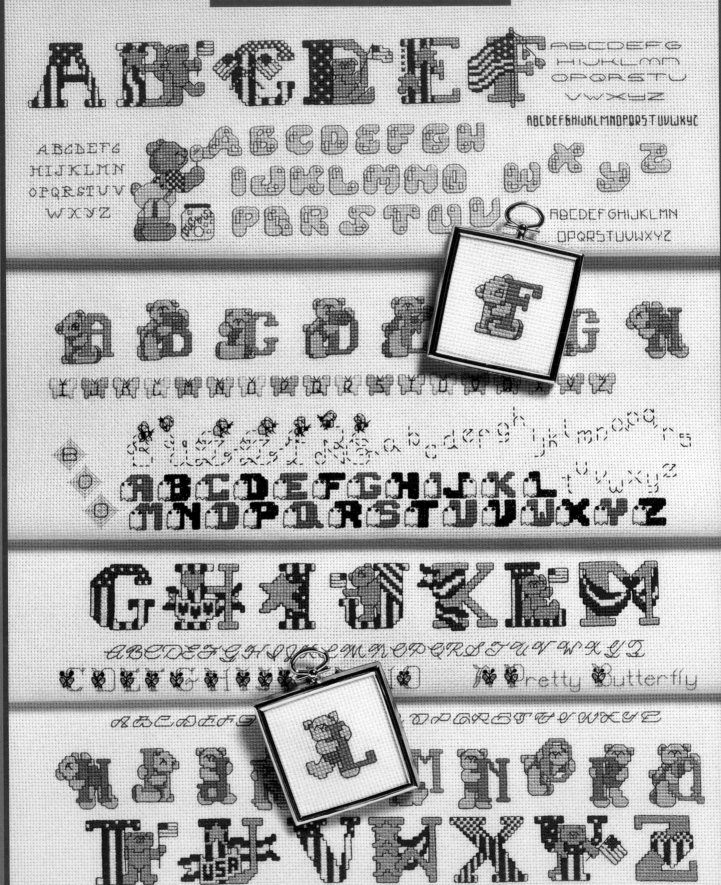

Creatures Great and Small Design Directory

The charts are in numerical order beginning on page 14.

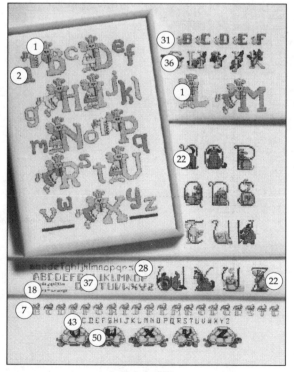

page 9

page 10

page 11

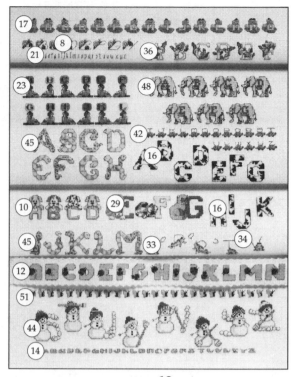

page 12

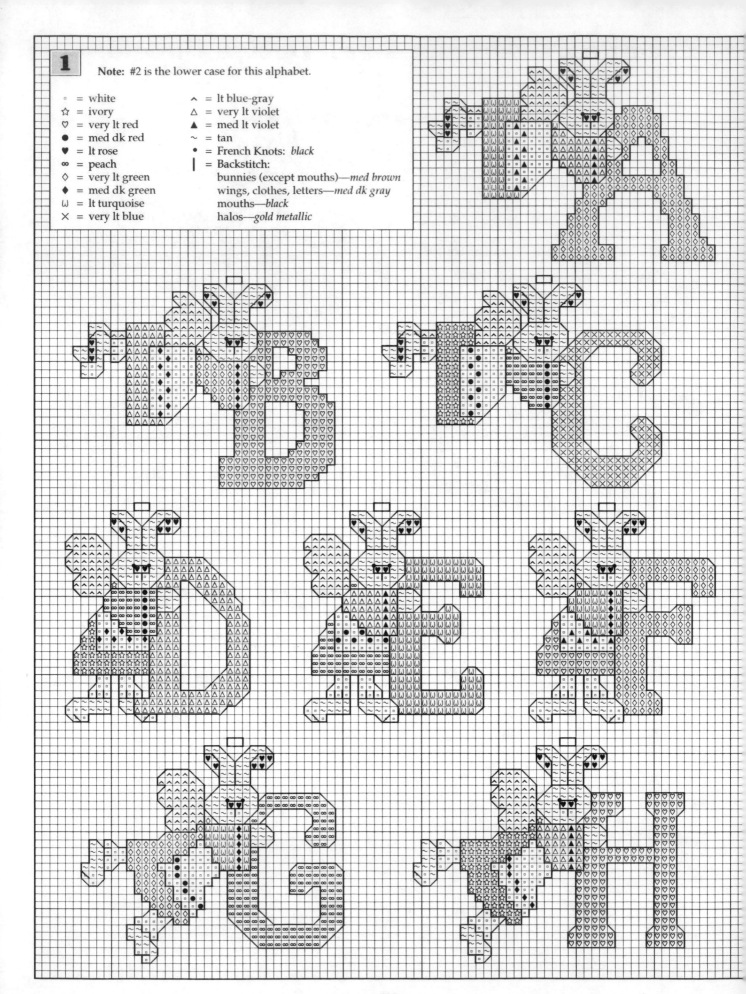

Note: #2 is the lower case for this alphabet.

- □ = white
- ☆ = ivory
- ♡ = very lt red
- ● = med dk red
- ♥ = lt rose
- ∞ = peach
- ◇ = very lt green
- ◆ = med dk green
- ω = lt turquoise
- ✕ = very lt blue
- ∧ = lt blue-gray
- △ = very lt violet
- ▲ = med lt violet
- ∼ = tan
- • = French Knots: *black*
- | = Backstitch:
  - bunnies (except mouths)—*med brown*
  - wings, clothes, letters—*med dk gray*
  - mouths—*black*
  - halos—*gold metallic*

14

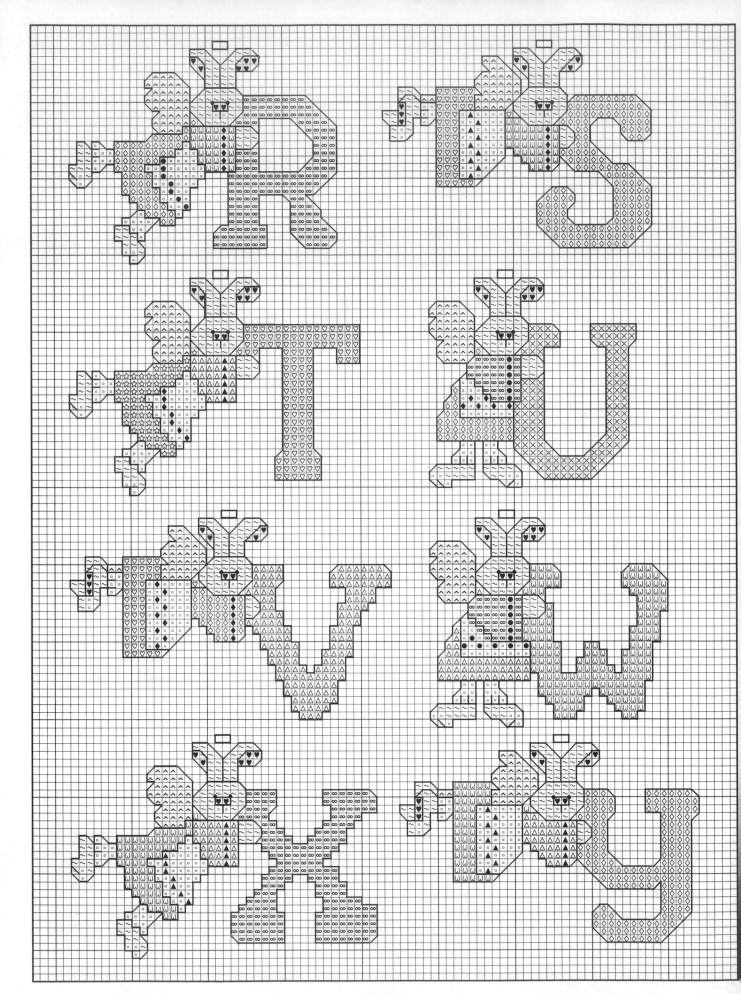

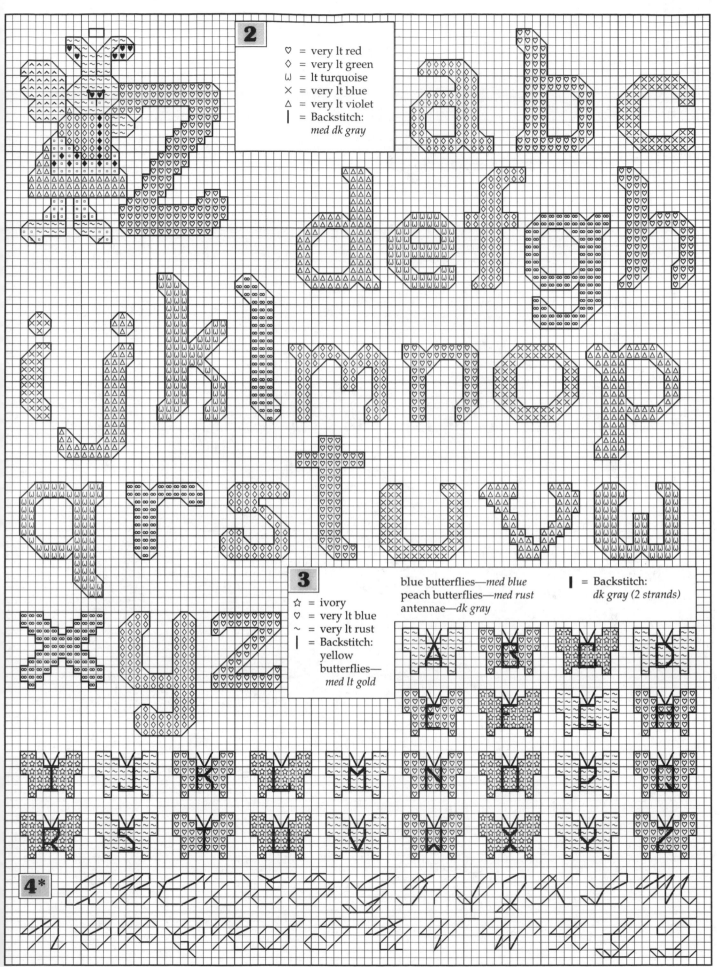

2

♡ = very lt red
◇ = very lt green
ω = lt turquoise
✕ = very lt blue
△ = very lt violet
| = Backstitch:
   med dk gray

3

☆ = ivory
♡ = very lt blue
~ = very lt rust
| = Backstitch:
   yellow
   butterflies—
      med lt gold

blue butterflies—*med blue*
peach butterflies—*med rust*
antennae—*dk gray*

| = Backstitch:
   dk gray (2 strands)

4*

*Use desired color.

17

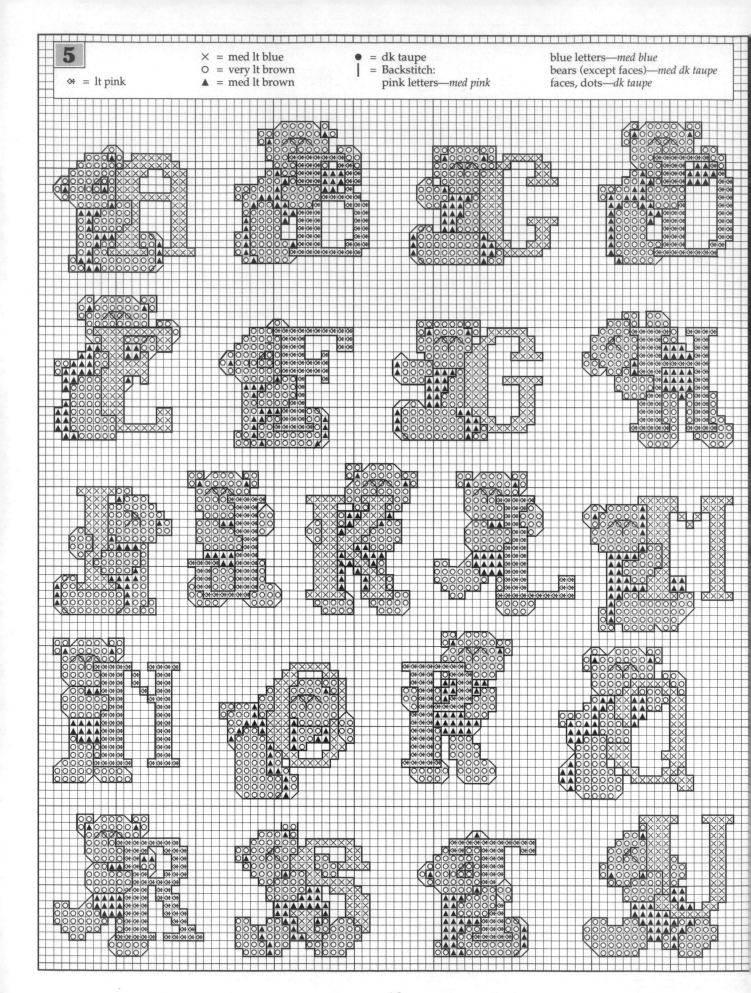

5

× = med lt blue
○ = very lt brown
▲ = med lt brown
✤ = lt pink

● = dk taupe
| = Backstitch:
pink letters—*med pink*

blue letters—*med blue*
bears (except faces)—*med dk taupe*
faces, dots—*dk taupe*

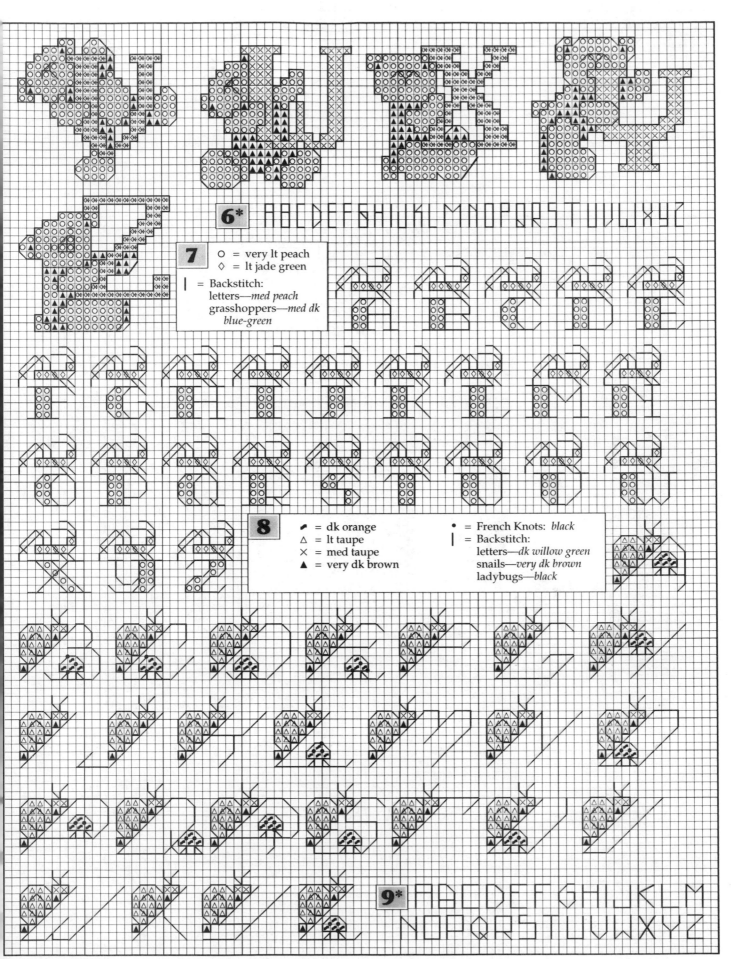

6* ABCDEFGHIJKLMNOPQRSTUVWXYZ

7 ○ = very lt peach
◇ = lt jade green

| = Backstitch:
letters—*med peach*
grasshoppers—*med dk
blue-green*

8 🍂 = dk orange   • = French Knots: *black*
△ = lt taupe | = Backstitch:
✕ = med taupe   letters—*dk willow green*
▲ = very dk brown   snails—*very dk brown*
               ladybugs—*black*

9* ABCDEFGHIJKLM
NOPQRSTUVWXYZ

* Use desired color.

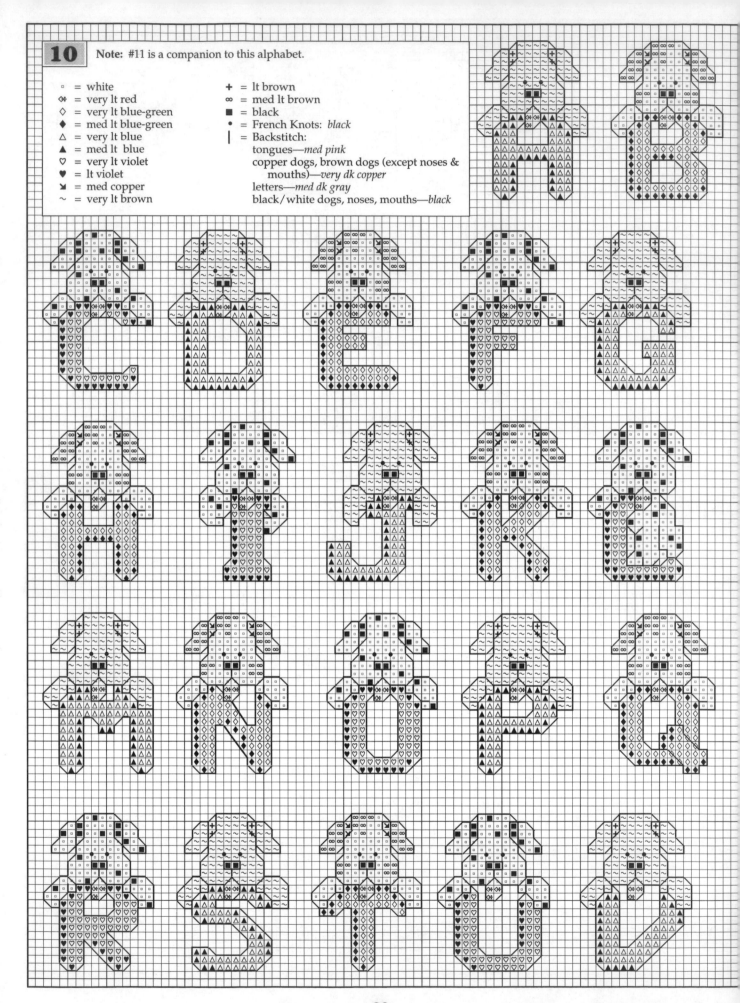

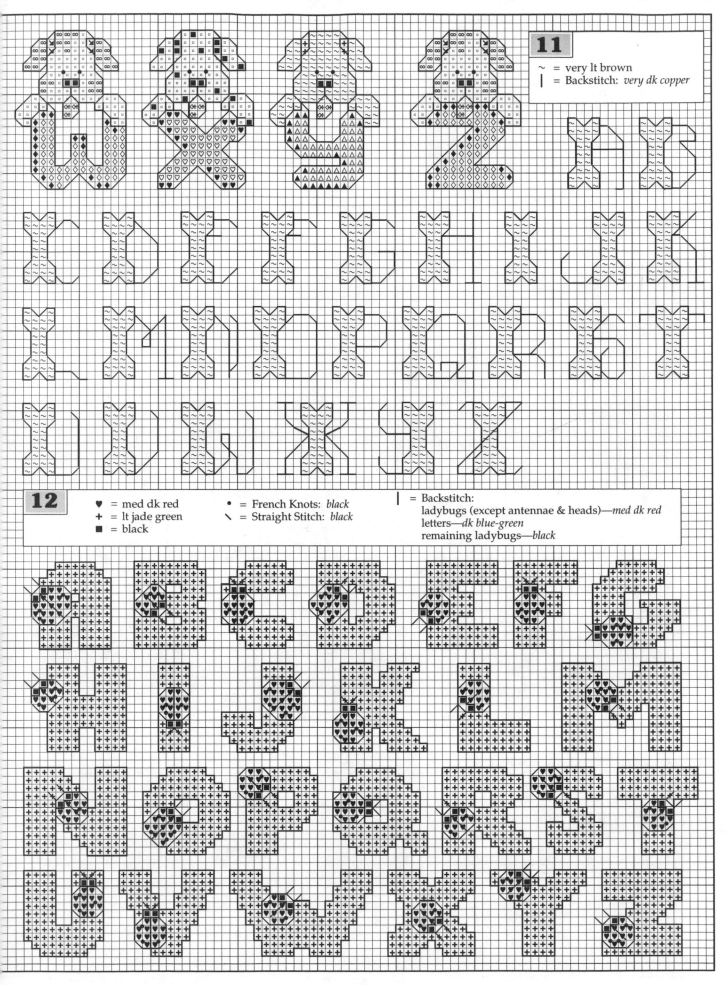

~ = very lt brown
| = Backstitch: *very dk copper*

12

♥ = med dk red
+ = lt jade green
■ = black

• = French Knots: *black*
╲ = Straight Stitch: *black*

| = Backstitch:
ladybugs (except antennae & heads)—*med dk red*
letters—*dk blue-green*
remaining ladybugs—*black*

13

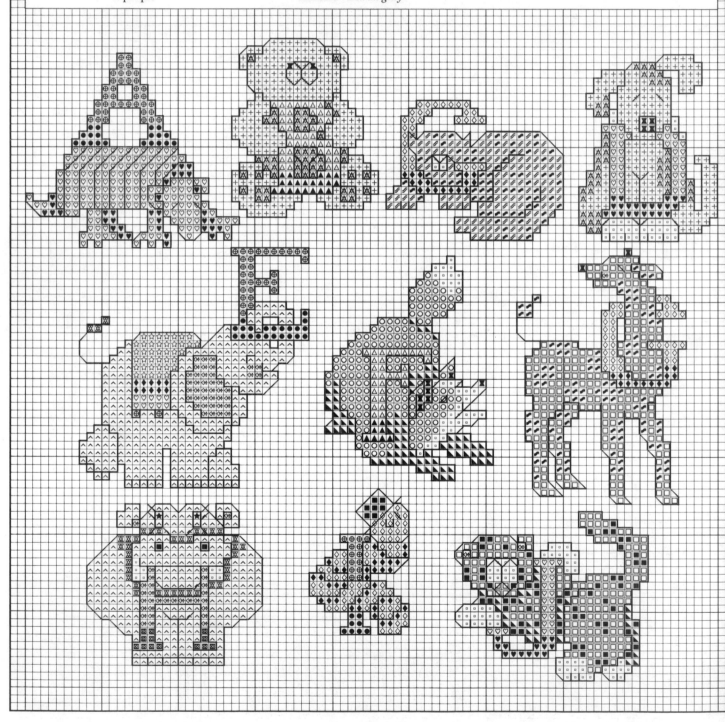

- ▫ = white
- ✾ = lt rose
- ▧ = med rose
- ⊕ = med red
- ● = dk red
- ✐ = lt peach
- ✒ = med peach
- ✳ = med dk yellow
- ◇ = very lt green
- ◆ = med lt green
- ☆ = lt teal blue
- ★ = med teal blue
- △ = lt blue
- ▲ = med blue
- ♡ = lt purple

- ♥ = med purple
- ▢ = very lt brown
- ⊡ = lt brown
- ○ = med lt brown
- ◣ = med dk brown
- + = lt taupe
- ✕ = med taupe
- ✕ = dk taupe
- ∧ = very lt gray
- ▨ = med lt gray
- ■ = black
- ╲ = Straight Stitch:
  - yak—*very dk purple*
  - porcupine—*med dk brown*
  - unicorn—*med dk gray*

- | = Backstitch:
  - rose & red letters—*very dk red*
  - green letters, inchworm (except hat & eye)—*dk green*
  - teal blue letters, whale spout—*med dk teal blue*
  - blue letters—*very dk blue*
  - purple letters—*very dk purple*
  - cat (except eyes)—*med dk brown*
  - jaguar, night owl, all brown & taupe animals, cat eyes—*dk taupe*
  - elephant eye, whale eye—*black*
  - remaining animals—*med dk gray*

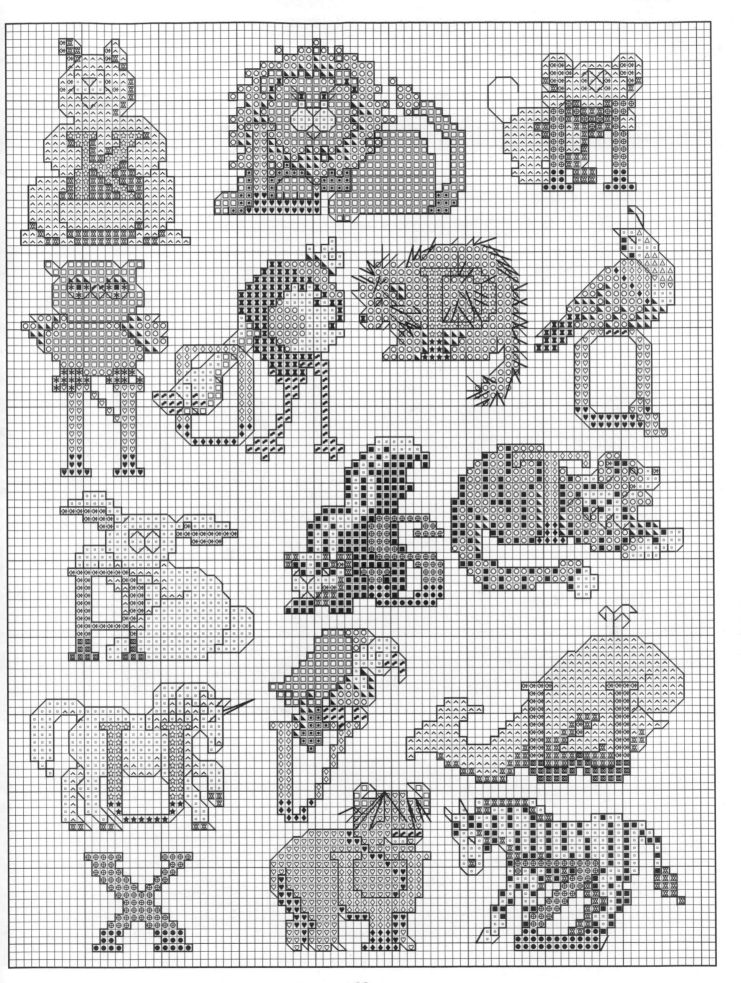

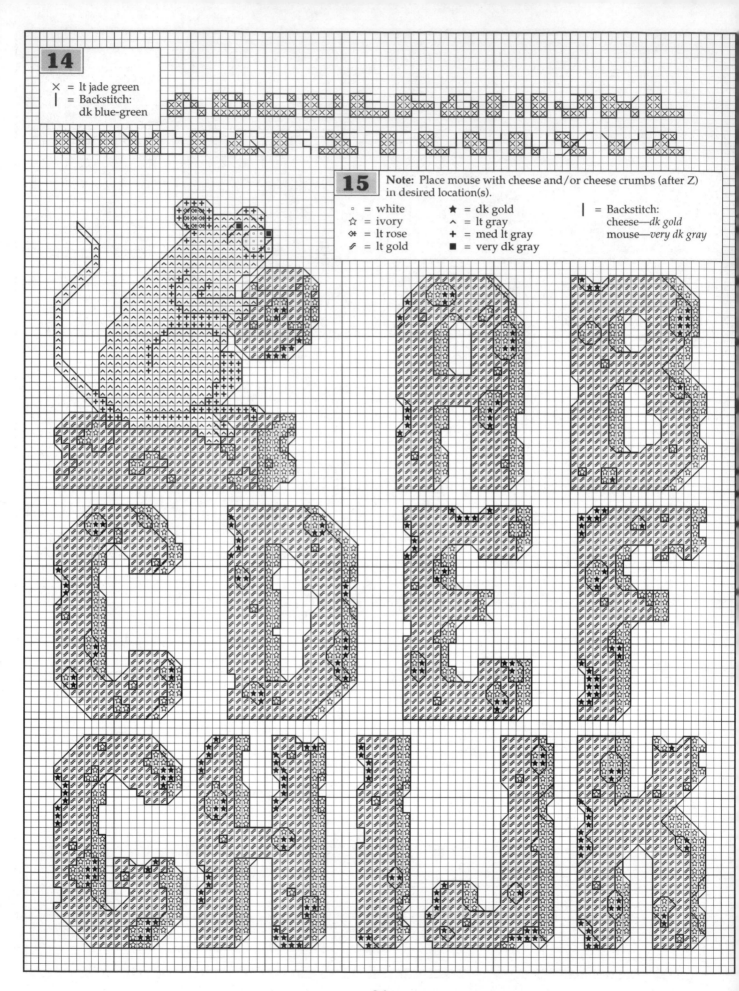

14

× = lt jade green
| = Backstitch:
   dk blue-green

15 Note: Place mouse with cheese and/or cheese crumbs (after Z) in desired location(s).

▫ = white   ★ = dk gold | = Backstitch:
☆ = ivory   ∧ = lt gray   cheese—*dk gold*
✸ = lt rose   + = med lt gray   mouse—*very dk gray*
✐ = lt gold   ■ = very dk gray

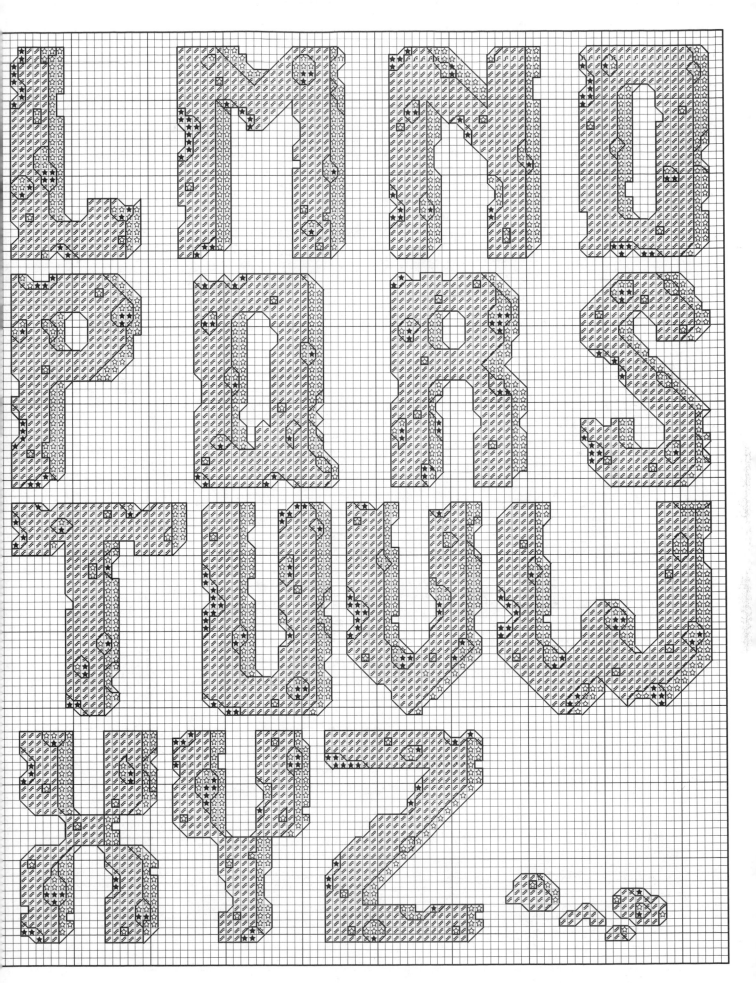

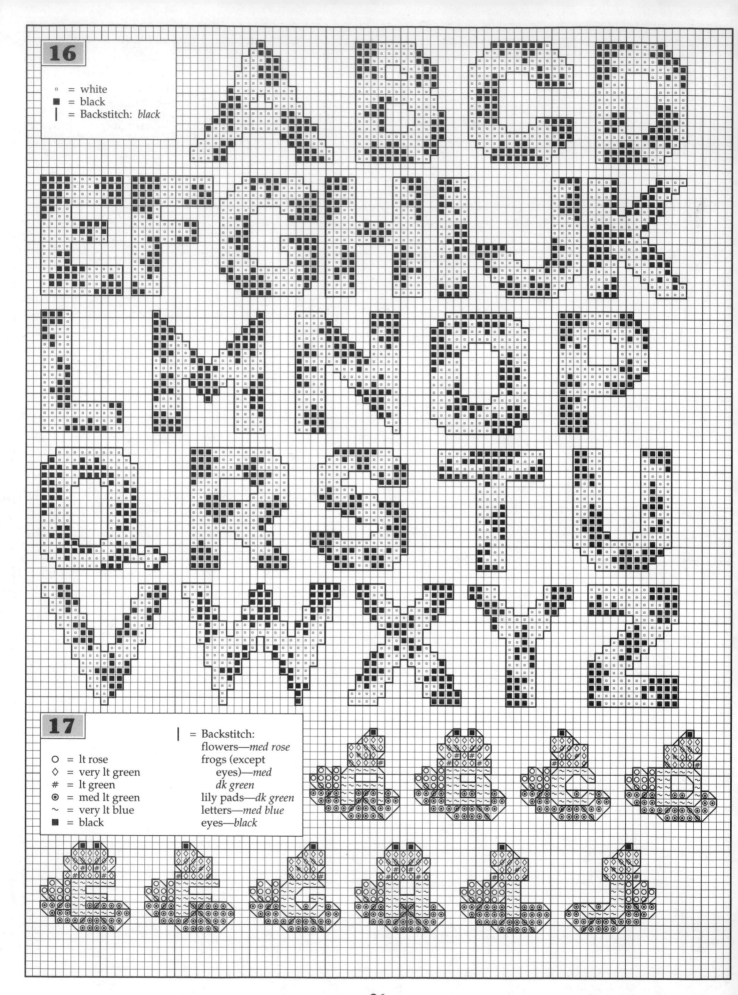

16

 □ = white
 ■ = black
 | = Backstitch: *black*

17

 | = Backstitch:
     flowers—*med rose*
 ○ = lt rose   frogs (except
 ◇ = very lt green   eyes)—*med*
 # = lt green   *dk green*
 ◉ = med lt green   lily pads—*dk green*
 ~ = very lt blue   letters—*med blue*
 ■ = black   eyes—*black*

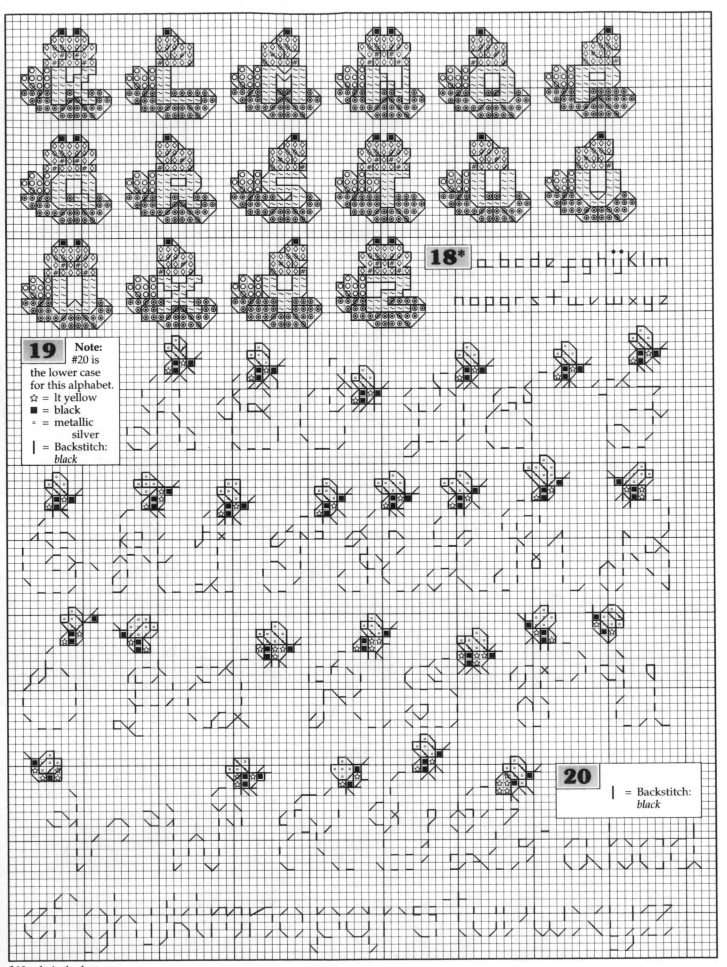

18* a b c d e f g h i j k l m
n o p q r s t u v w x y z

19 Note: #20 is the lower case for this alphabet.
☆ = lt yellow
■ = black
▫ = metallic silver
| = Backstitch: *black*

20
| = Backstitch: *black*

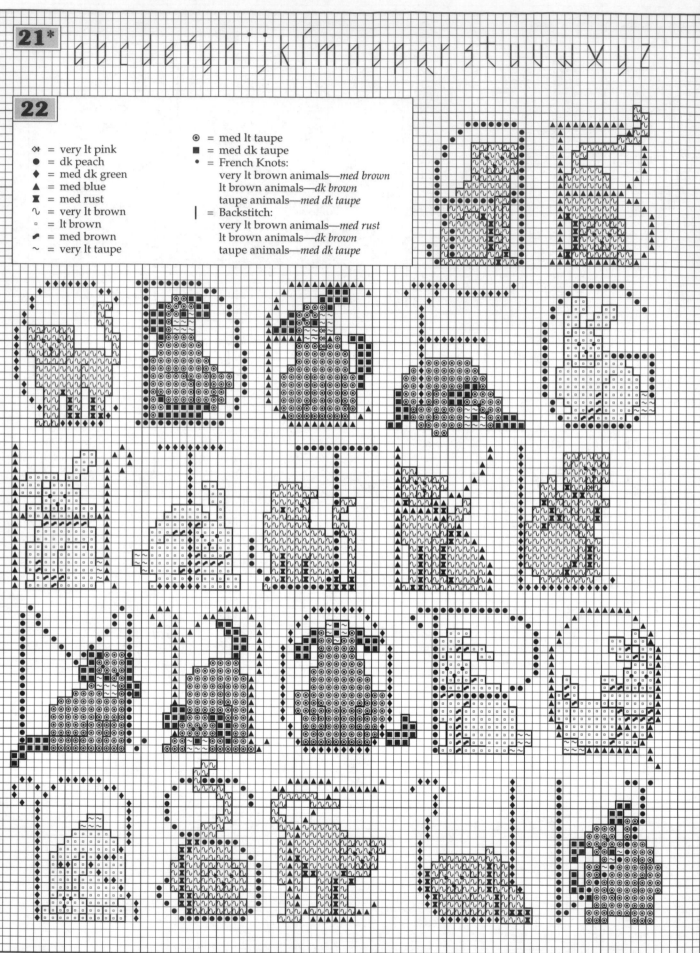

*Use desired color.

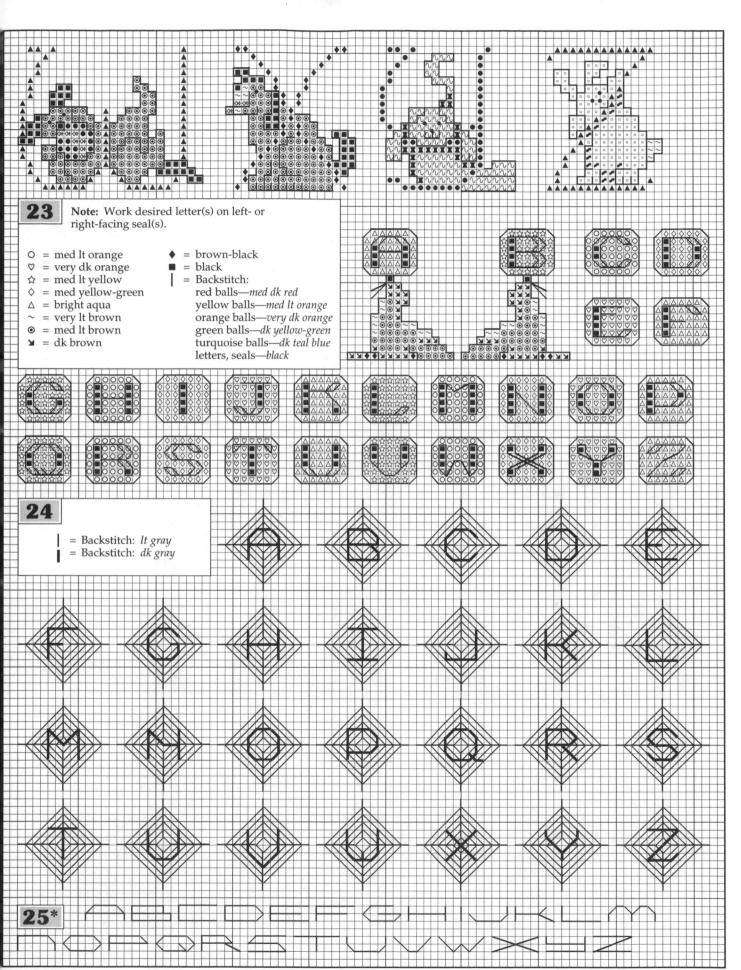

23

Note: Work desired letter(s) on left- or right-facing seal(s).

○ = med lt orange
♡ = very dk orange
☆ = med lt yellow
◇ = med yellow-green
△ = bright aqua
~ = very lt brown
◉ = med lt brown
⅄ = dk brown

♦ = brown-black
■ = black
| = Backstitch:
  red balls—*med dk red*
  yellow balls—*med lt orange*
  orange balls—*very dk orange*
  green balls—*dk yellow-green*
  turquoise balls—*dk teal blue*
  letters, seals—*black*

24

| = Backstitch: *lt gray*
| = Backstitch: *dk gray*

25*

Use desired color.

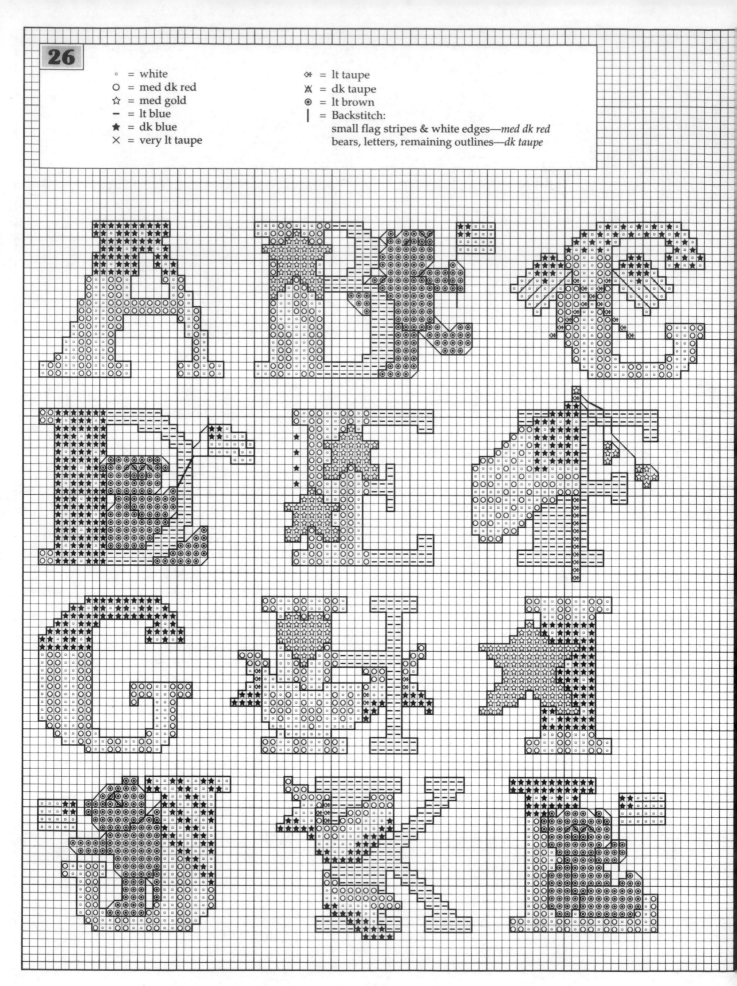

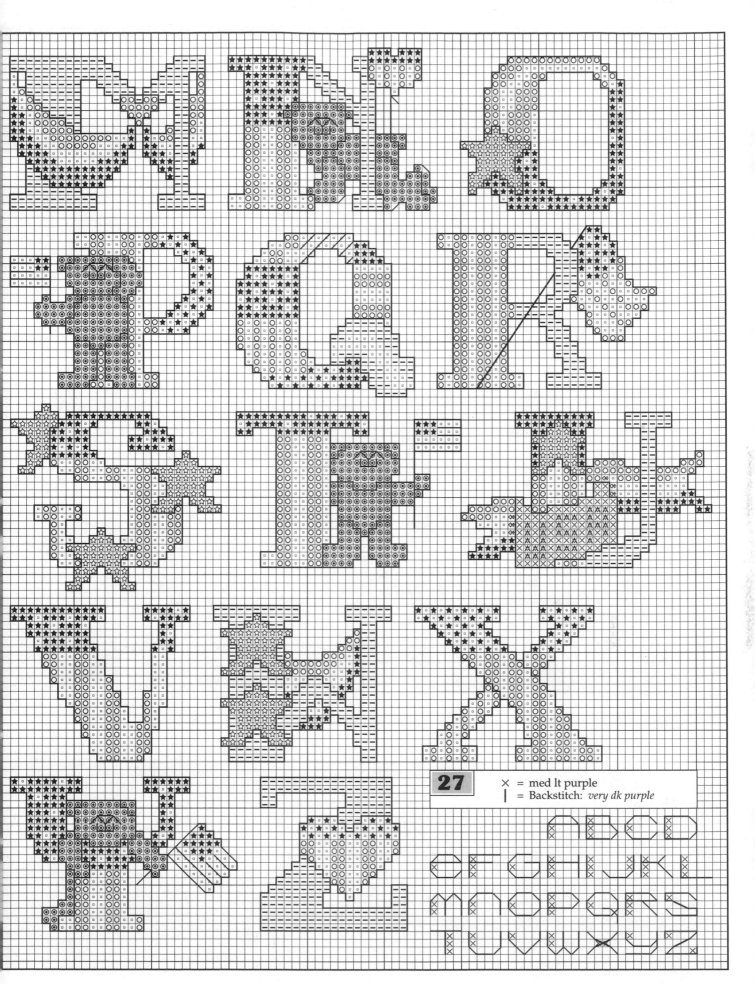

27

× = med lt purple
| = Backstitch: *very dk purple*

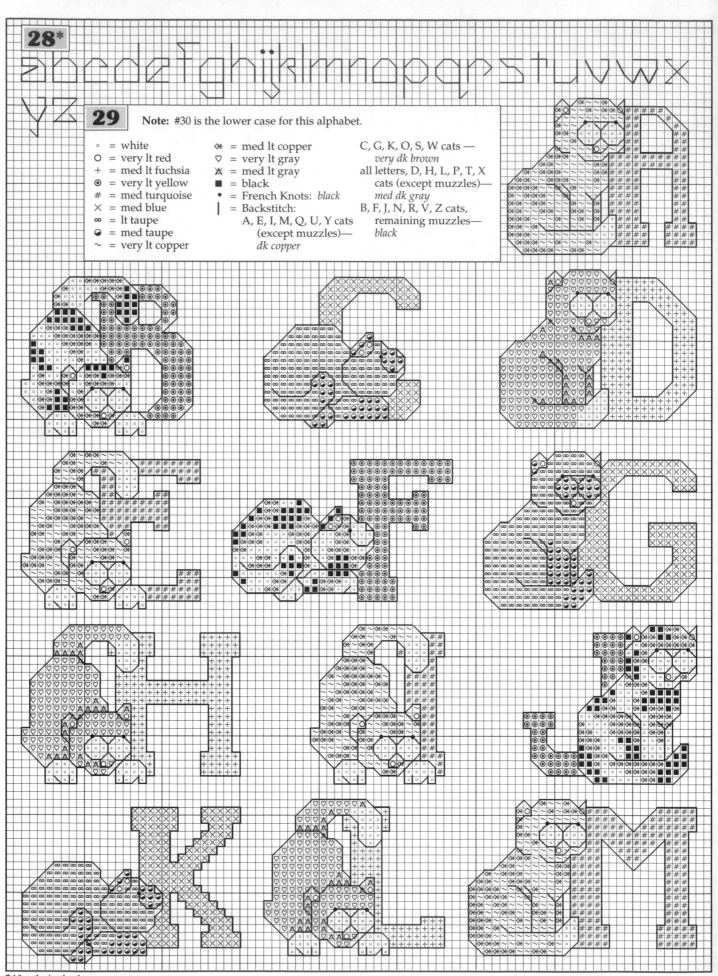

28* abcdefghijklmnopqrstuvwxyz

29 Note: #30 is the lower case for this alphabet.

□ = white	⊕ = med lt copper	C, G, K, O, S, W cats —
○ = very lt red	♡ = very lt gray	*very dk brown*
+ = med lt fuchsia	⋈ = med lt gray	all letters, D, H, L, P, T, X
⊙ = very lt yellow	■ = black	cats (except muzzles)—
# = med turquoise	• = French Knots: *black*	*med dk gray*
× = med blue		= Backstitch:	B, F, J, N, R, V, Z cats,
∞ = lt taupe	A, E, I, M, Q, U, Y cats	remaining muzzles—
◐ = med taupe	(except muzzles)—	*black*
~ = very lt copper	*dk copper*	

*Use desired color.

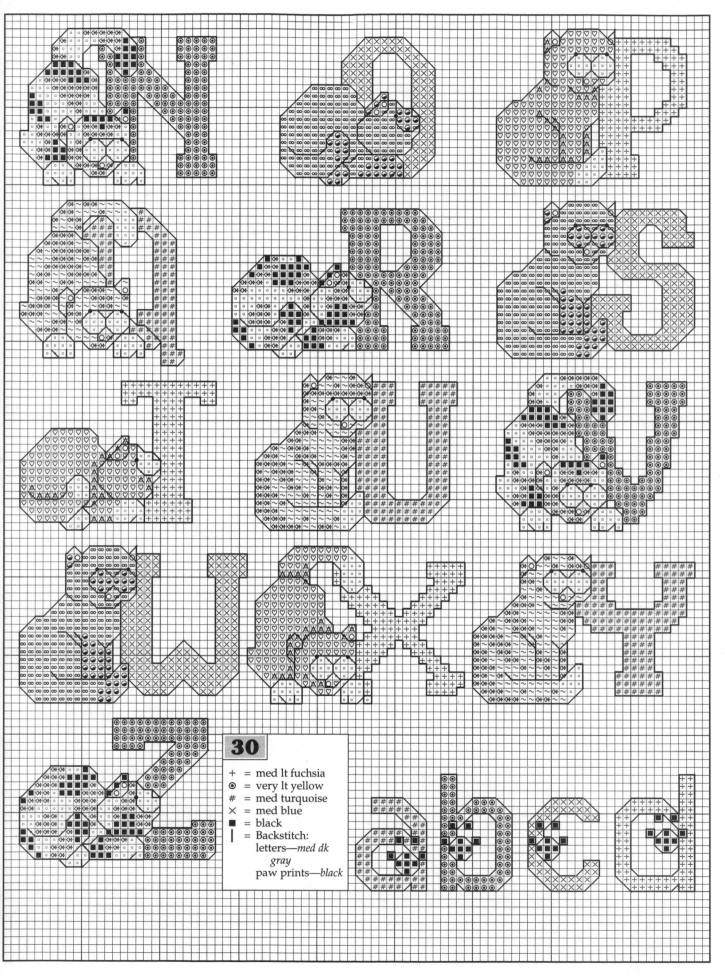

30

+ = med lt fuchsia
⊙ = very lt yellow
= med turquoise
× = med blue
■ = black
| = Backstitch:
   letters—*med dk*
     gray
   paw prints—*black*

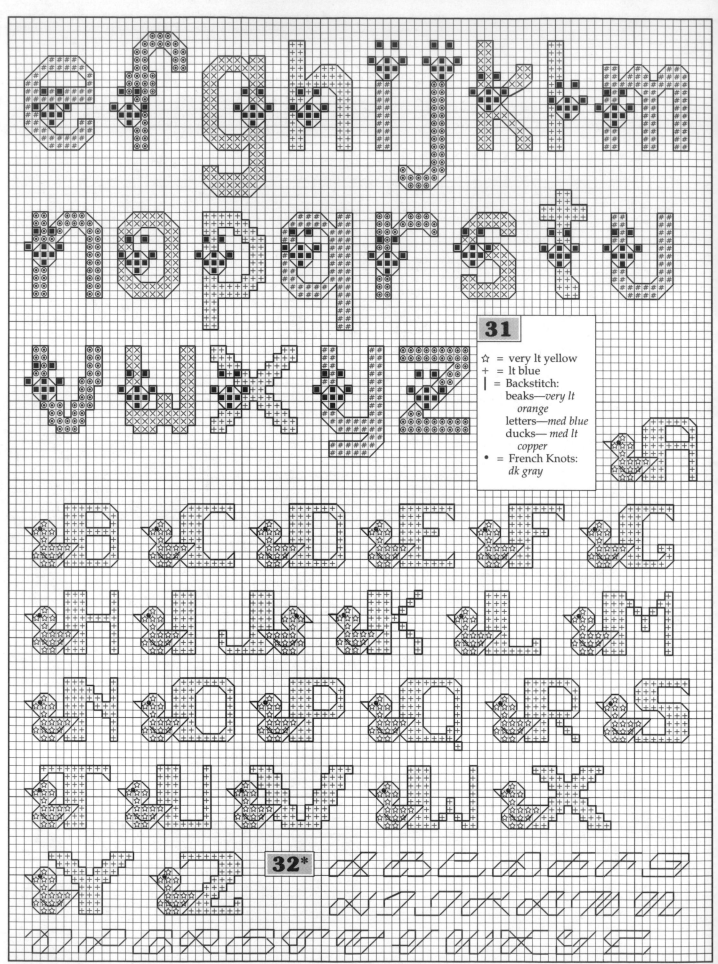

31

☆ = very lt yellow
+ = lt blue
| = Backstitch:
   beaks—*very lt orange*
   letters—*med blue*
   ducks— *med lt copper*
• = French Knots: *dk gray*

32*

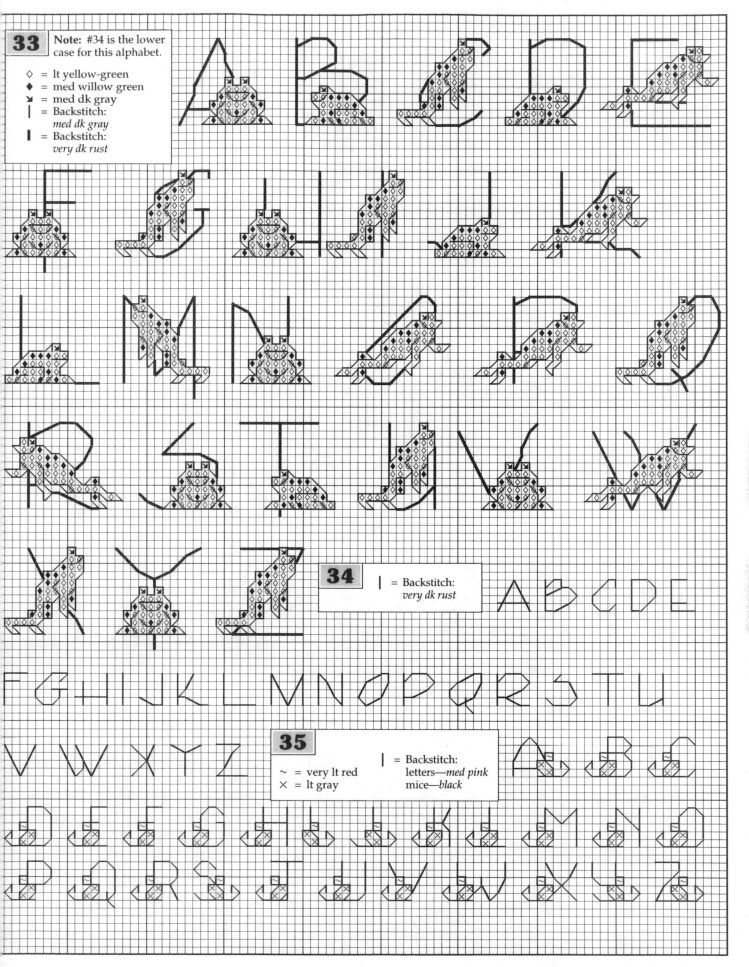

33 **Note:** #34 is the lower case for this alphabet.

◇ = lt yellow-green
◆ = med willow green
⋎ = med dk gray
| = Backstitch: *med dk gray*
| = Backstitch: *very dk rust*

34 | = Backstitch: *very dk rust*

35
~ = very lt red
× = lt gray
| = Backstitch: letters—*med pink* mice—*black*

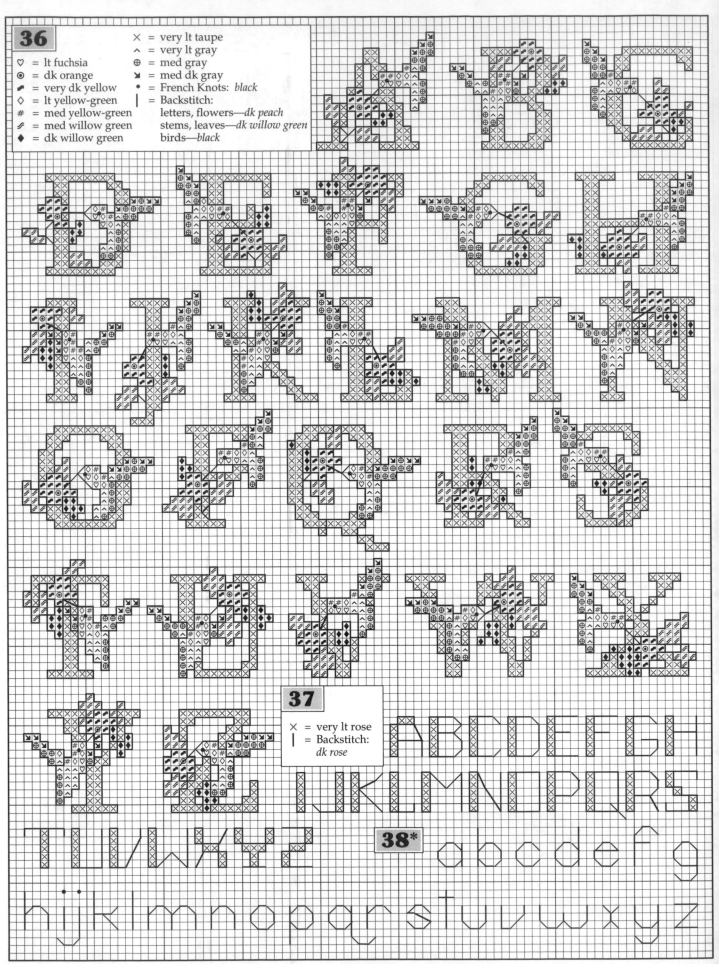

36

♡ = lt fuchsia
⊙ = dk orange
✎ = very dk yellow
◇ = lt yellow-green
= med yellow-green
✐ = med willow green
◆ = dk willow green

× = very lt taupe
∧ = very lt gray
⊕ = med gray
◢ = med dk gray
• = French Knots: *black*
| = Backstitch:
  letters, flowers—*dk peach*
  stems, leaves—*dk willow green*
  birds—*black*

37

× = very lt rose
| = Backstitch:
  dk rose

38*

* *Use desired color.*

36

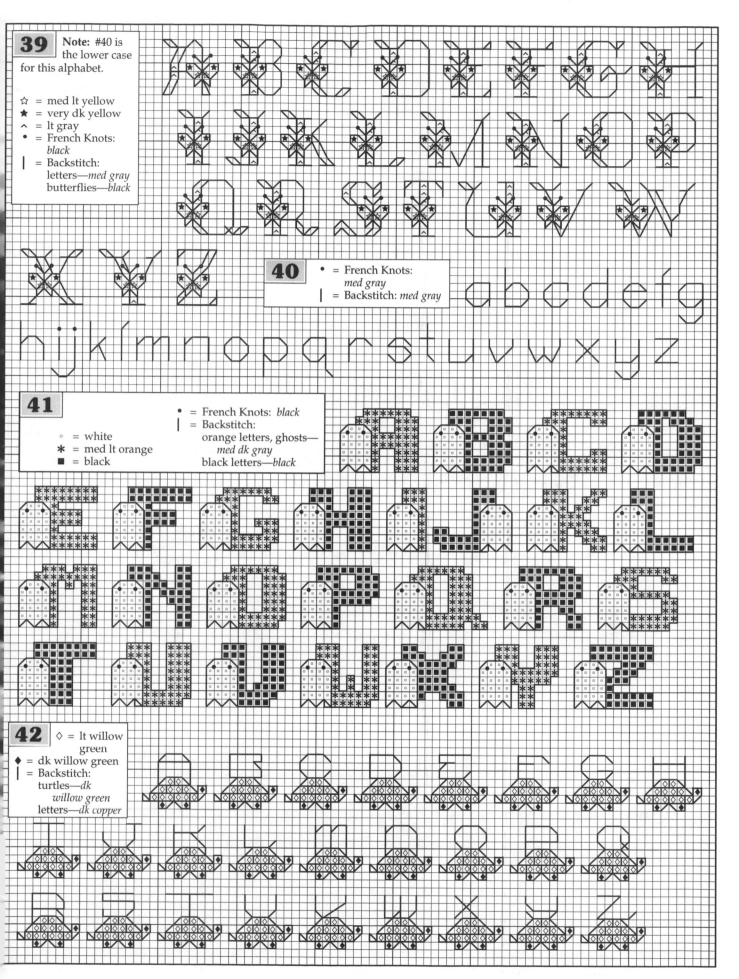

39 **Note:** #40 is the lower case for this alphabet.

☆ = med lt yellow
★ = very dk yellow
^ = lt gray
• = French Knots: *black*
| = Backstitch:
   letters—*med gray*
   butterflies—*black*

40 • = French Knots: *med gray*
| = Backstitch: *med gray*

41
  □ = white
  ✳ = med lt orange
  ■ = black

• = French Knots: *black*
| = Backstitch:
   orange letters, ghosts—
    med dk gray
   black letters—*black*

42 ◇ = lt willow green
◆ = dk willow green
| = Backstitch:
   turtles—*dk willow green*
   letters—*dk copper*

*Use desired color.

45

♡ = med dk yellow
♥ = very dk yellow
◇ = med lt yellow-green
= med green
✳ = med lt turquoise
▲ = med purple
● = French Knots: *med dk gray*
| = Backstitch: *med dk gray*

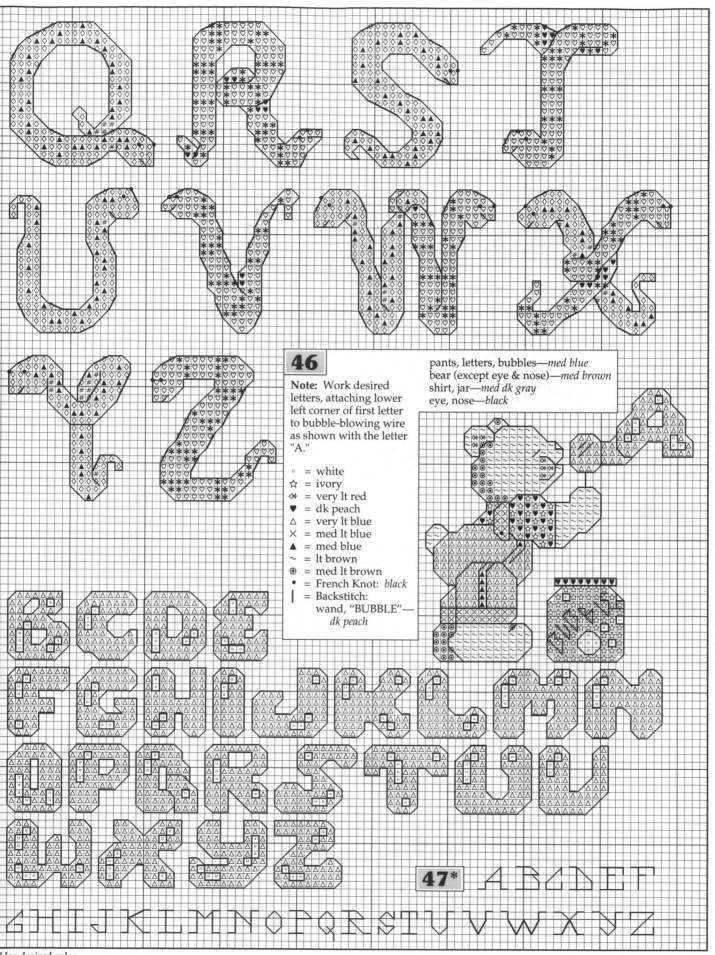

46

Note: Work desired letters, attaching lower left corner of first letter to bubble-blowing wire as shown with the letter "A."

- ▫ = white
- ☆ = ivory
- ✿ = very lt red
- ♥ = dk peach
- △ = very lt blue
- ✕ = med lt blue
- ▲ = med blue
- ~ = lt brown
- ◉ = med lt brown
- • = French Knot: *black*
- | = Backstitch: wand, "BUBBLE"— *dk peach*

pants, letters, bubbles—*med blue*
bear (except eye & nose)—*med brown*
shirt, jar—*med dk gray*
eye, nose—*black*

47*

Use desired color.

41

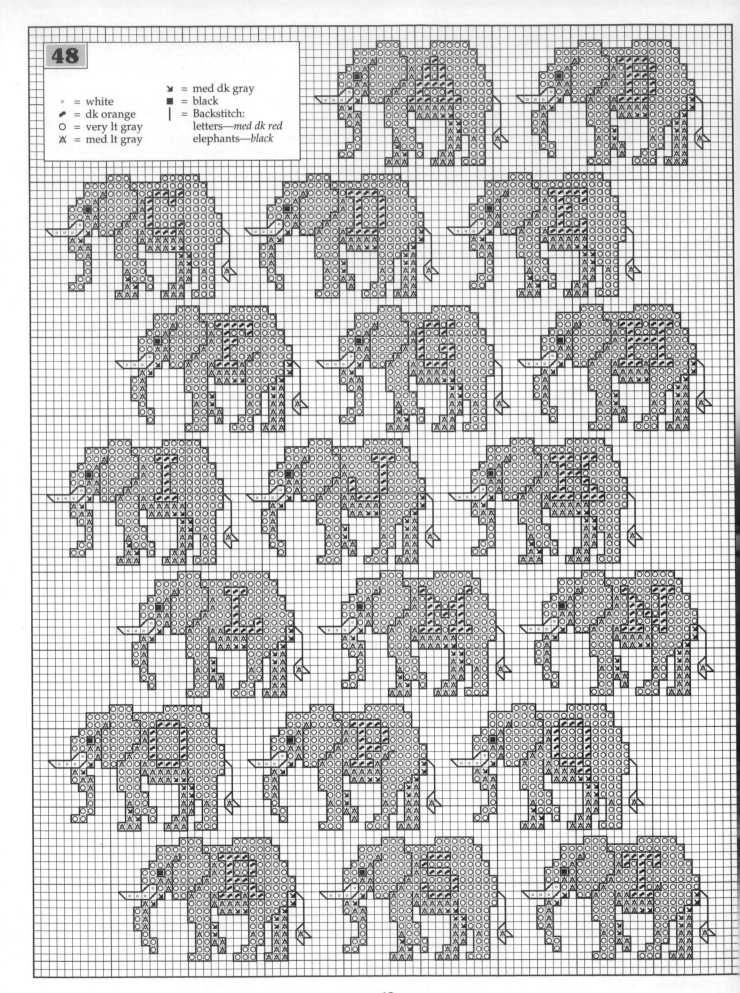

48

- □ = white
- ◢ = dk orange
- ○ = very lt gray
- ✕ = med lt gray
- ◣ = med dk gray
- ■ = black
- | = Backstitch:
  letters—*med dk red*
  elephants—*black*

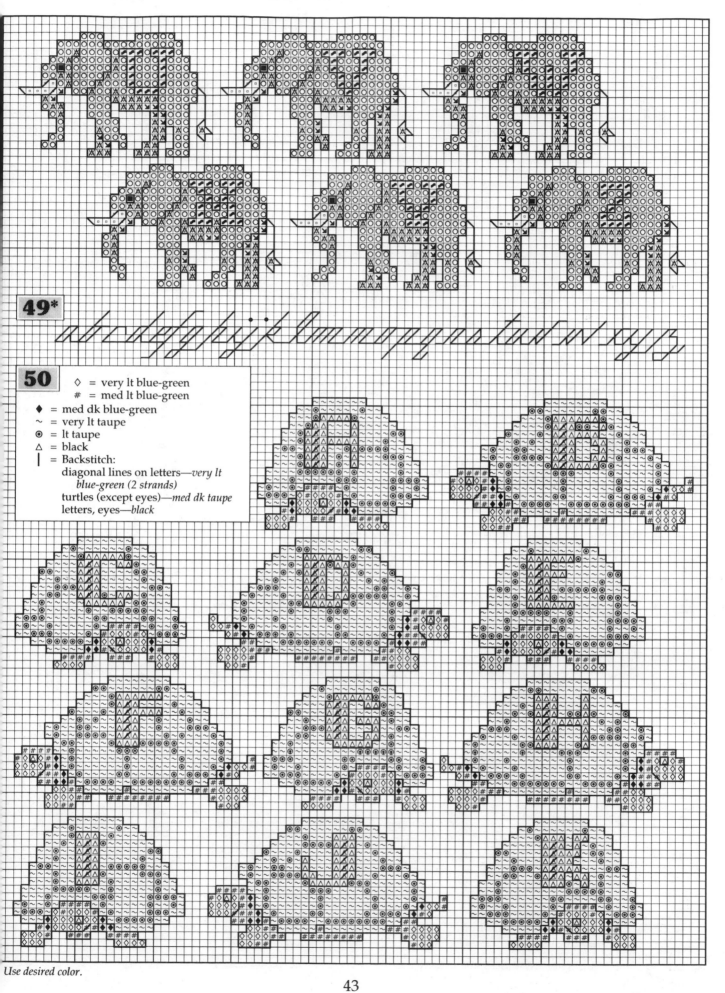

49*

50

◇ = very lt blue-green
= med lt blue-green
♦ = med dk blue-green
~ = very lt taupe
⊙ = lt taupe
△ = black
| = Backstitch:
diagonal lines on letters—*very lt blue-green (2 strands)*
turtles (except eyes)—*med dk taupe*
letters, eyes—*black*

Use desired color.

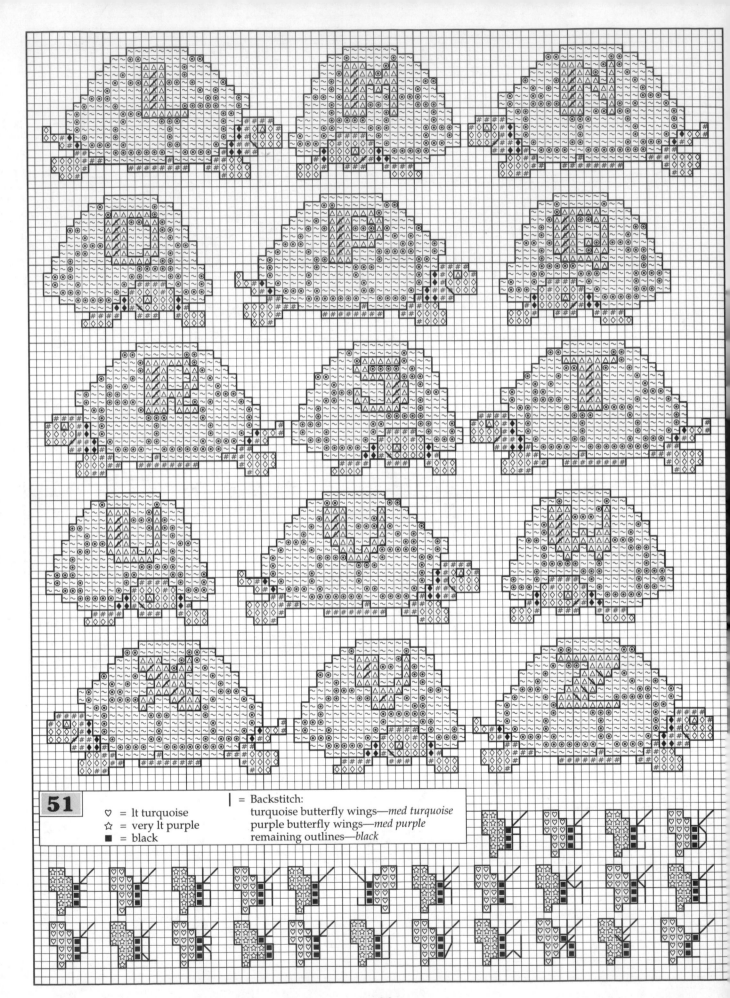

51

♡ = lt turquoise
☆ = very lt purple
■ = black

| = Backstitch:
turquoise butterfly wings—*med turquoise*
purple butterfly wings—*med purple*
remaining outlines—*black*

ABCDEF
ABCDEFGHIJ
klmnop QRSTUV
wxyz
abcdefghijklmnopqrstuvwxyz
abcdefghijklmnopqrstuvwxyz ABCDEF
hijklmnop QRST
ABCDEFGH
IJKLMNO UVWXYZ
PQRSTUV
WXYZ ABCDEFGHIJ
KLMNO pqrstuvwxyz
ABCDEFGHIJKLMN
OPQRSTUVWX
abcdefghijklmn YZ
opqrstuvwxyz

ABCDEFG
HIJKLMNO
PQRSTUV
WXYZ
ABCDEFGHIJKLMNOPQRST UVW
abcdefghijklmnop XYZ
QRSTUVWXYZ
ABCDEFGHIJKLMNOPQRSTUV
LMNOPQ abcdefghijklmnopqrstuvwxyz XYZ
RSTUVWXYZ ABCDEFGHIJKLMNOPQ
rstuvwxyz
ABCDEFGH
IJKLMNOP abcdefghijklmnopqrstuvwxyz
QRSTUV
WXYZ ABCDEFghijklmnopqrstuvwxyz

ABCDEFGHIJKLMNOPQ
AAA BBB CCC DDD EEE FF GGG HHH (I) JJ klmnopqrstuvwxyz

abcdefghij abcdefghijklmnop
qrstuvwxyz
KLMNOP
QRSTUVWXYZ

ABCD
EFGHI
JKLM
NOPQR
STUVW
XYZ

ABCDEFG ABCDEF
GHIJKL
HIJKLM MNOPQ
NOPQRSTUVWXYZ RSTUV
WXYZ
TUVWXYZ
ABCD ABCDEFG
EFGH HIJKLM
IJKLM NOPQRS
NOPQRST TUVW
UVWXYZ XYZ

ABCDEFG
HIJKLMNOPQRSTU
VWXYZ ABCDEFGH
ABCDEFGHIJ klmnopqrstuvwxyz
ABCDEFGHIJKLMNOPQRSTU
ABCDEFGHIJKLMNO VWXYZ
PQRSTUVWXYZ ABCDEFGHIJKLM

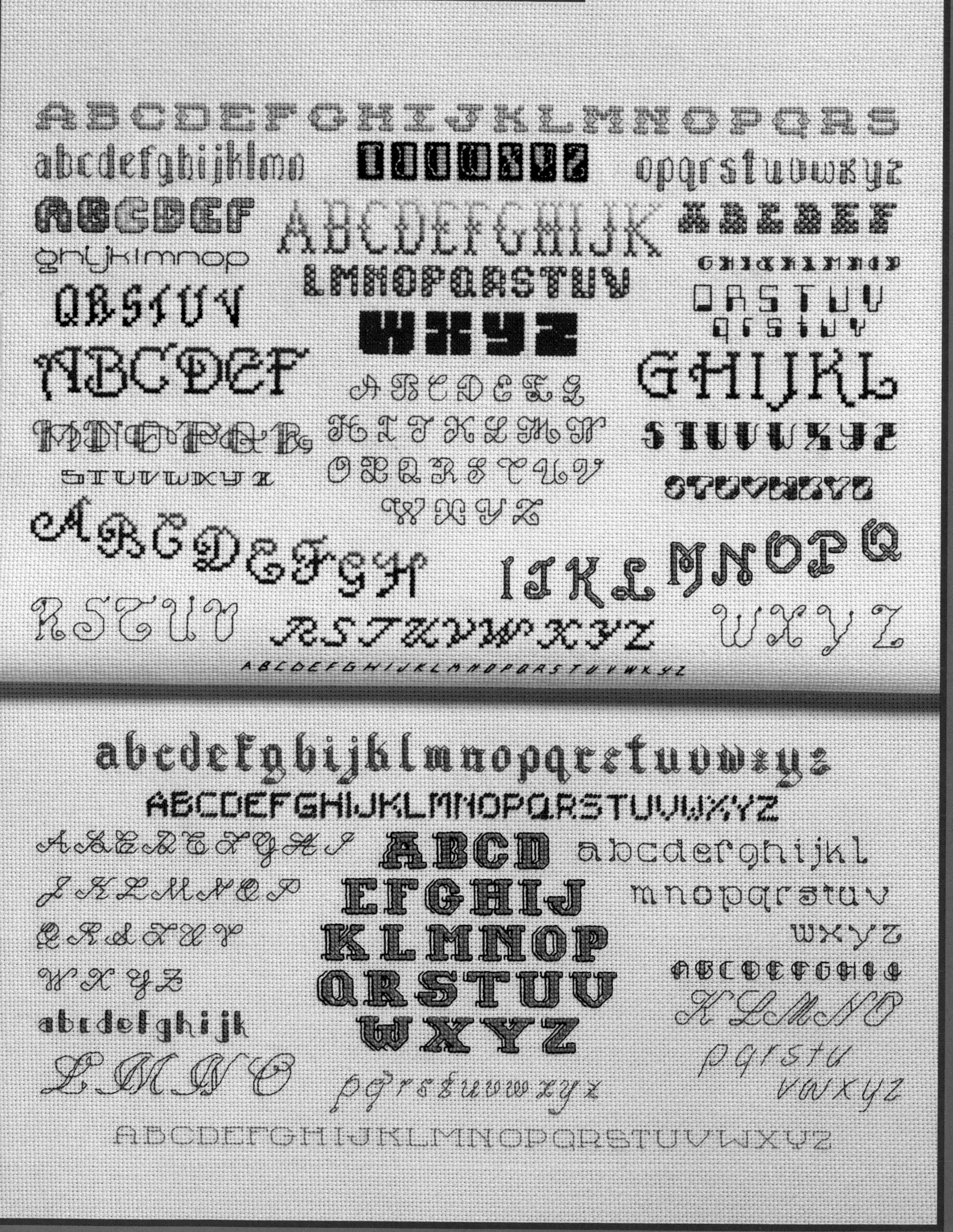

ABCDEFGHIJK

ABCDEFGHI
JK

ABCDEFGH
IJKLMNOPQ
RSTUVW
XYZ

LMNOPQRST
UVWXYZ

ABCDEFGHIJK

LMNOPQRSTUVWXYZ

ABCDEFGHIJ

ABCDEFGHI

ABCDE JKL

abcde FGHIJKL

abcdefghi JKLMNOPQ

abcdefghijklmn
opqrstuvwxyz

MNO PQRSTU

STUVWXYZ

PQRVWXYZ

vwxyz

rstuvwxyz

ABCDEFK hijklmnyqr STUVWXYZ

ABC

XYZ

abcdefghijklmnopqrstuvwxyz

ABCDEFGHIJKLMNOPQRSTUVWXYZ

AaBbCcDdEeFfGgHhIi

abcdefghijklmn

OPQRSTUVWXYZ

abcde
fghijk
lmnopq
rstuv
wxyz

ABCDEFGH

ABCDEFGHIJKLMNOPQR

ABCDEFGHIJKLMN

ABCDEFGH

ABCDEFGHIJKL

ABCDEFGHIJKL

HBC
XYZ

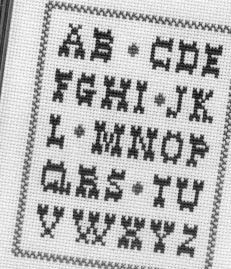

AB · CDE
FGHI · JK
L · MNOP
QRS · TU
VWXYZ

48

Alphabet Soup Design Directory

The charts are in numerical order beginning on page 50.

page 45

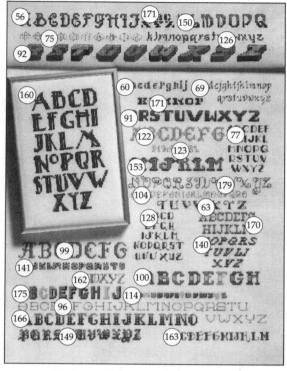

page 46

page 47

page 48

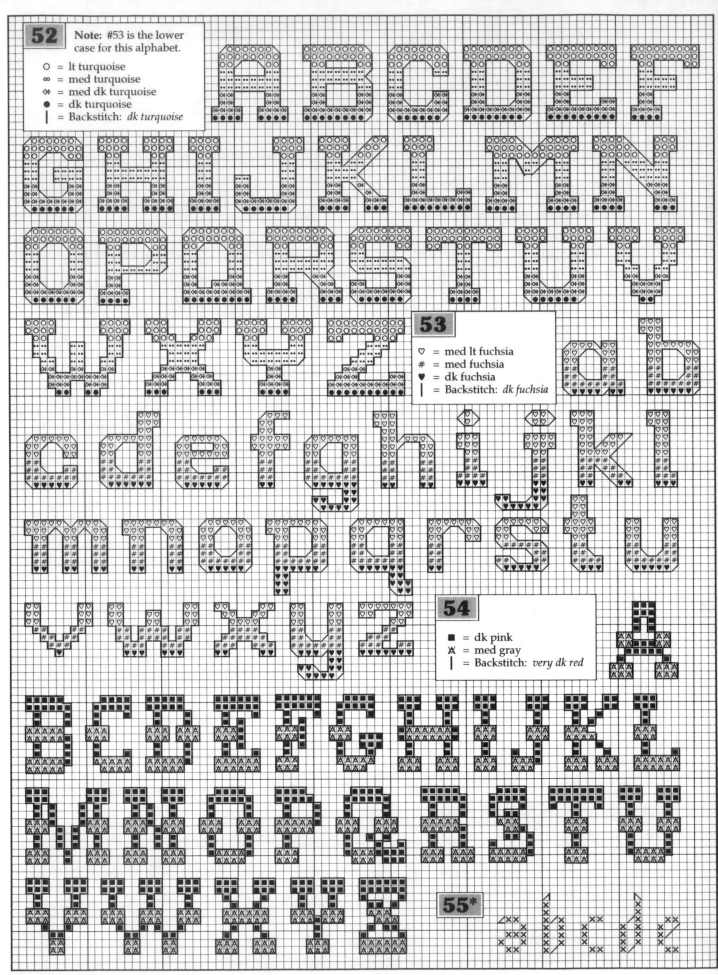

52 Note: #53 is the lower case for this alphabet.

○ = lt turquoise
∞ = med turquoise
✿ = med dk turquoise
● = dk turquoise
| = Backstitch: *dk turquoise*

53

♡ = med lt fuchsia
= med fuchsia
♥ = dk fuchsia
| = Backstitch: *dk fuchsia*

54

■ = dk pink
✕ = med gray
| = Backstitch: *very dk red*

55*

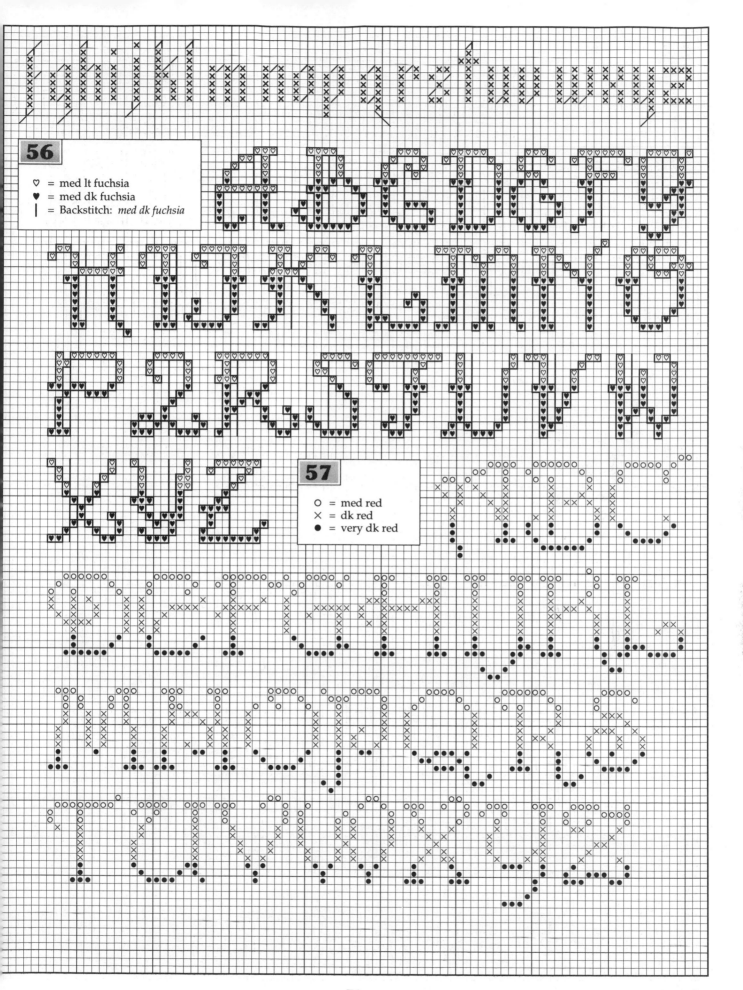

56

♡ = med lt fuchsia
♥ = med dk fuchsia
| = Backstitch: *med dk fuchsia*

57

○ = med red
✕ = dk red
● = very dk red

58*

Note: #59 is the lower case for this alphabet.

59*

60
× = lt blue
| = Backstitch: *med blue*

61
○ = med lt pink
● = very dk rose
| = Backstitch: *very dk rose*

*Use desired color.

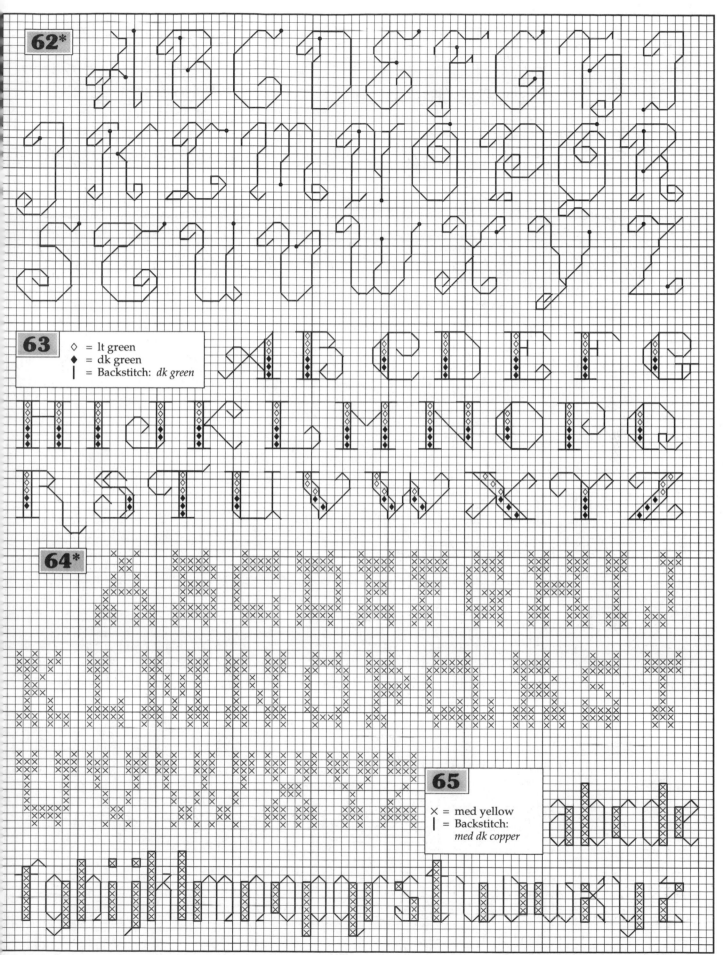

62*

63
◇ = lt green
♦ = dk green
| = Backstitch: *dk green*

ABCDEFG
HIJKLMNOPQ
RSTUVWXYZ

64*

65
× = med yellow
| = Backstitch:
med dk copper

abcde
fghijklmnopqrstuvwxyz

66

× = med dk rose
| = Backstitch: *dk rose*

67*

68

♡ = lt violet
| = Backstitch:
     med dk violet

69*

70*

71*

72*

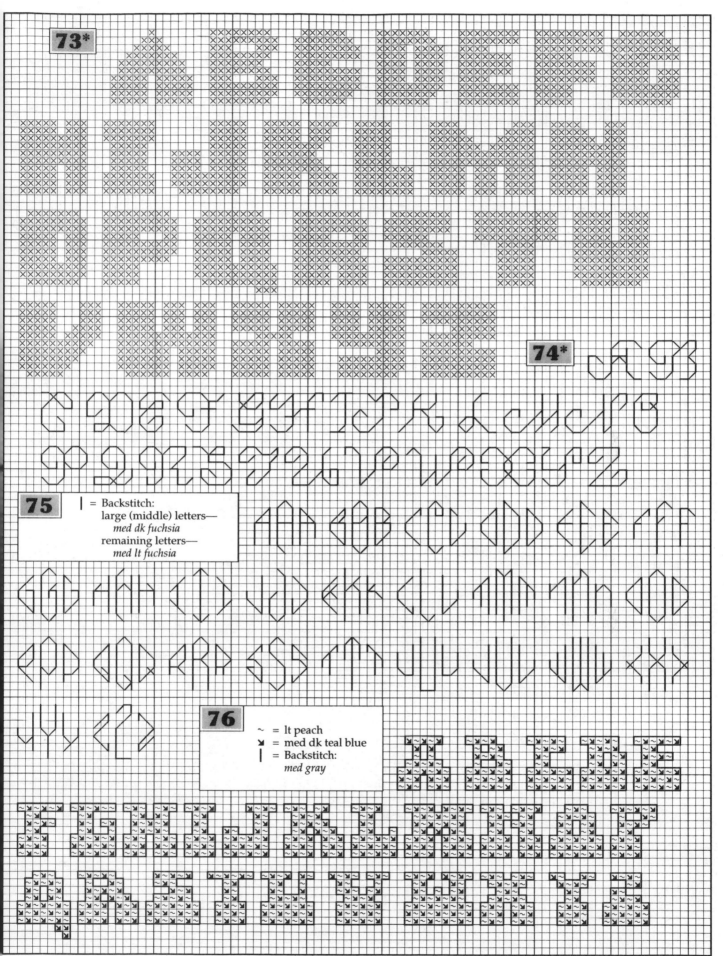

73*

74*

75 | = Backstitch:
large (middle) letters—
med dk fuchsia
remaining letters—
med lt fuchsia

76
~ = lt peach
⋈ = med dk teal blue
| = Backstitch:
med gray

* *Use desired color.*

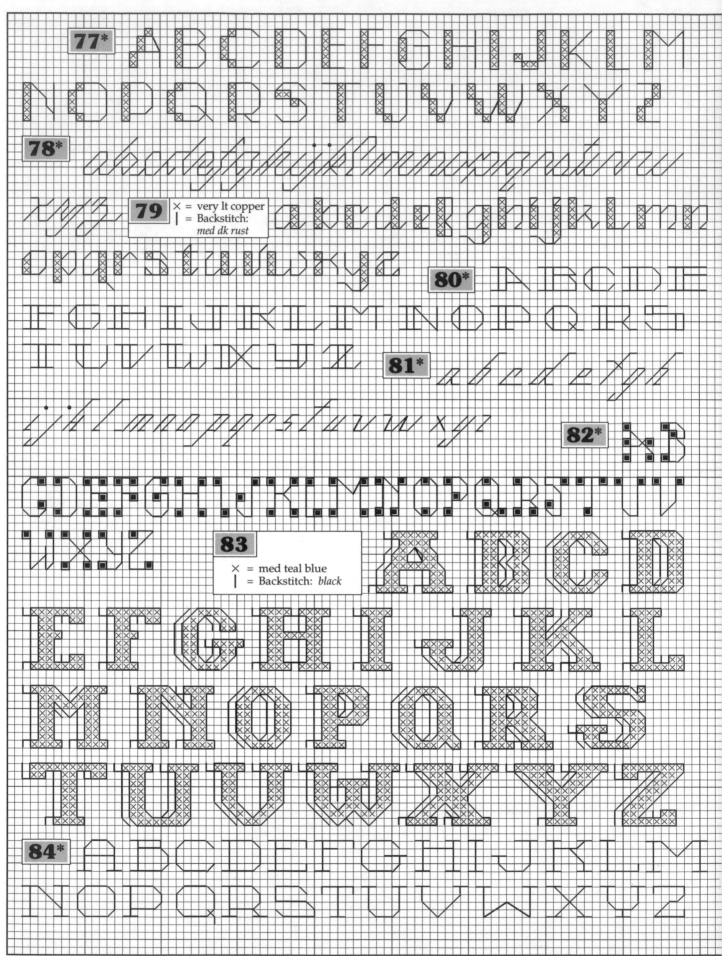

77*

ABCDEFGHIJKLM
NOPQRSTUVWXYZ

78*

abcdefghijklmnopqrstu
vwxyz

79 × = very lt copper
| = Backstitch:
med dk rust

abcdefghijklmn
opqrstuvwxyz

80* ABCDE
FGHIJKLMNOPQRS
TUVWXYZ

81* abcdefghi
jklmnopqrstuvwxyz

82*

ABCDEFGHIJKLMNOPQRSTU
VWXYZ

83

× = med teal blue
| = Backstitch: *black*

ABCD
EFGHIJKL
MNOPQRS
TUVWXYZ

84* ABCDEFGHIJKLM
NOPQRSTUVWXYZ

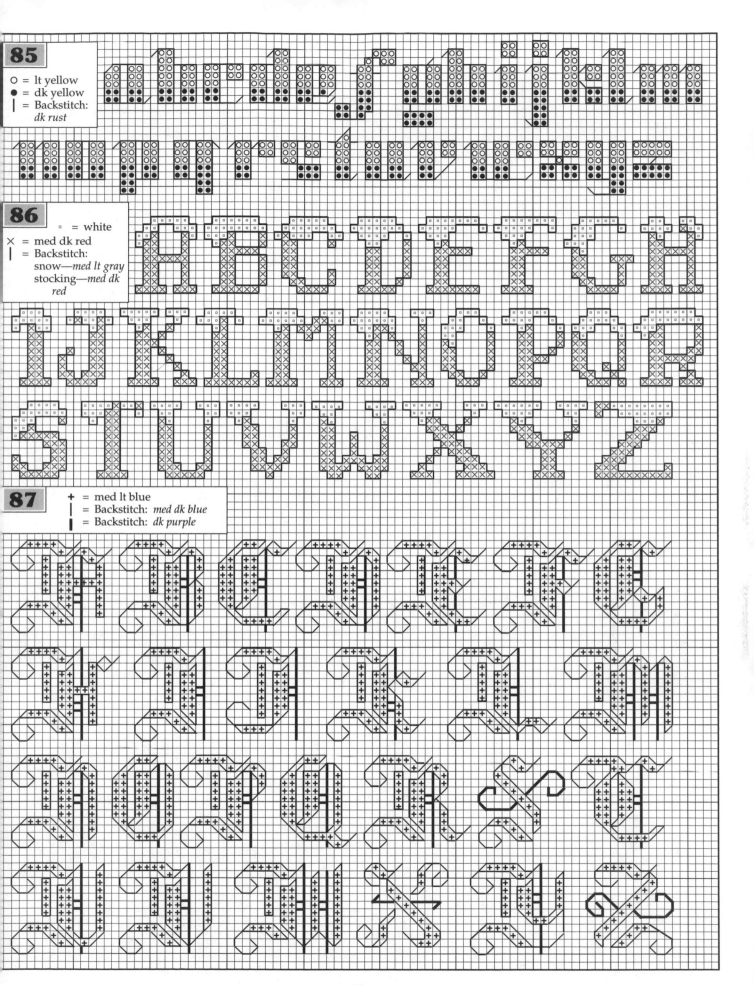

85

○ = lt yellow
● = dk yellow
| = Backstitch: *dk rust*

86

▫ = white
× = med dk red
| = Backstitch:
snow—*med lt gray*
stocking—*med dk red*

87

+ = med lt blue
| = Backstitch: *med dk blue*
| = Backstitch: *dk purple*

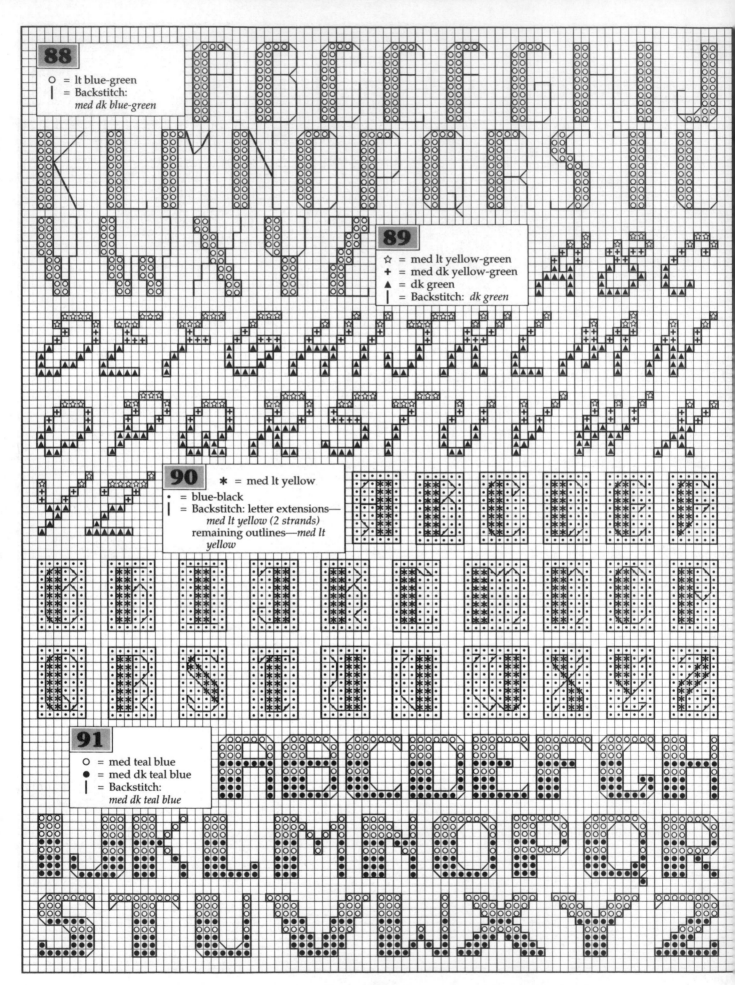

88

O = lt blue-green
| = Backstitch:
med dk blue-green

89

☆ = med lt yellow-green
+ = med dk yellow-green
▲ = dk green
| = Backstitch: *dk green*

90

✱ = med lt yellow
• = blue-black
| = Backstitch: letter extensions—
med lt yellow (2 strands)
remaining outlines—*med lt yellow*

91

O = med teal blue
● = med dk teal blue
| = Backstitch:
med dk teal blue

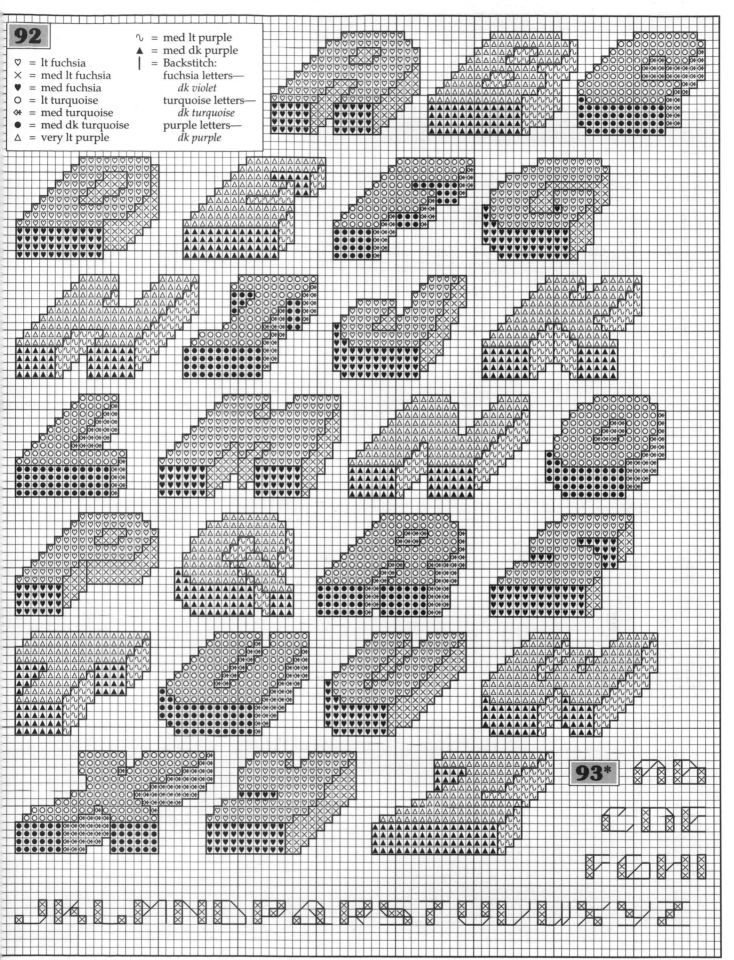

92

♡ = lt fuchsia
✕ = med lt fuchsia
♥ = med fuchsia
○ = lt turquoise
✤ = med turquoise
● = med dk turquoise
△ = very lt purple

∿ = med lt purple
▲ = med dk purple
| = Backstitch:
  fuchsia letters—
    dk violet
  turquoise letters—
    dk turquoise
  purple letters—
    dk purple

93*

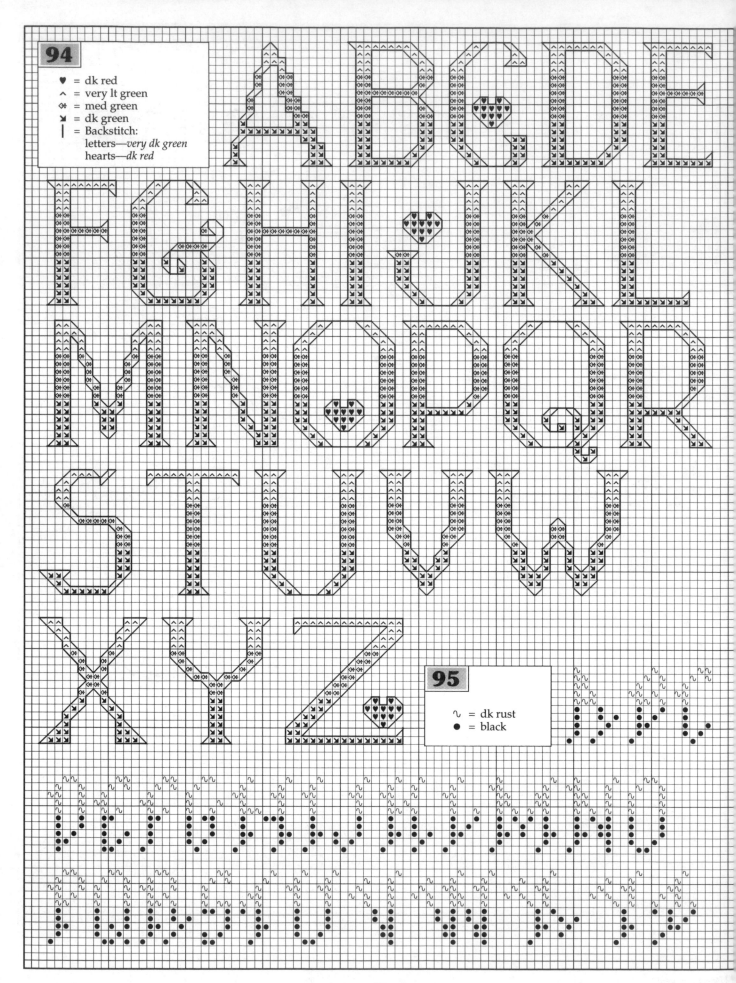

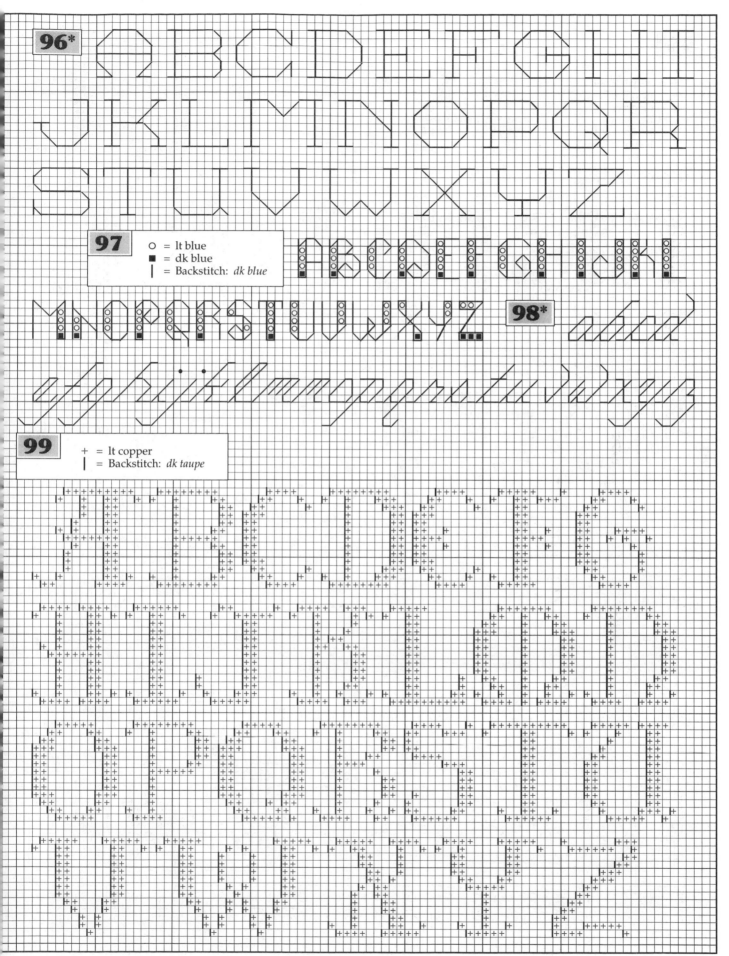

96* ABCDEFGHI JKLMNOPQR STUVWXYZ

97 ○ = lt blue
■ = dk blue
| = Backstitch: *dk blue*

ABCDEFGHIJKL MNOPQRSTUVWXYZ

98*

99 + = lt copper
| = Backstitch: *dk taupe*

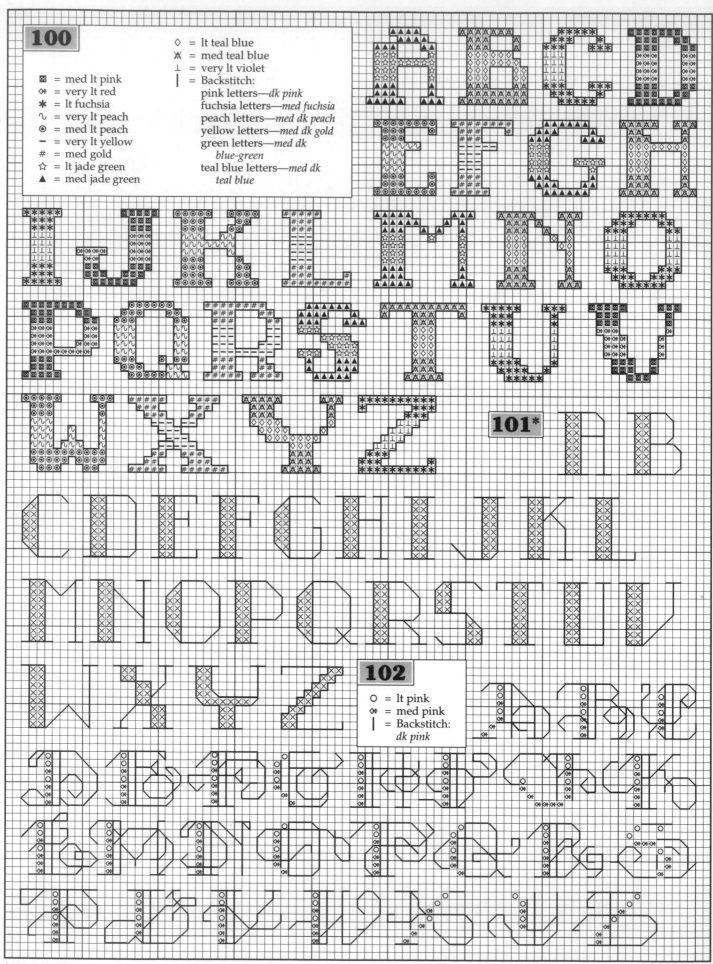

100

⊠ = med lt pink
✧ = very lt red
✳ = lt fuchsia
∿ = very lt peach
⊙ = med lt peach
− = very lt yellow
= med gold
☆ = lt jade green
▲ = med jade green

◇ = lt teal blue
✖ = med teal blue
⊥ = very lt violet
| = Backstitch:
    pink letters—*dk pink*
    fuchsia letters—*med fuchsia*
    peach letters—*med dk peach*
    yellow letters—*med dk gold*
    green letters—*med dk*
      blue-green
    teal blue letters—*med dk*
      teal blue

101*

102

○ = lt pink
✧ = med pink
| = Backstitch:
   dk pink

***** Use desired color.*

103*
abcdefghijklmnopqrst
uvwxyz

104*
abcdefghijk
lmnopqrstuvwxyz

105*

106* ABCDEF
GHIJKLMNOPQRSTUVWXYZ

107*
abcdefghijklm
nopqrstuvwxyz

108*
abcdefghijklmnop
qrstuvwxyz

109

• = French Knots: *med lt green*
| = Backstitch: *med lt green*
| = Backstitch: *very dk green*

ab
cdefghijklmno
pqrstuvwxyz

* Use desired color.

63

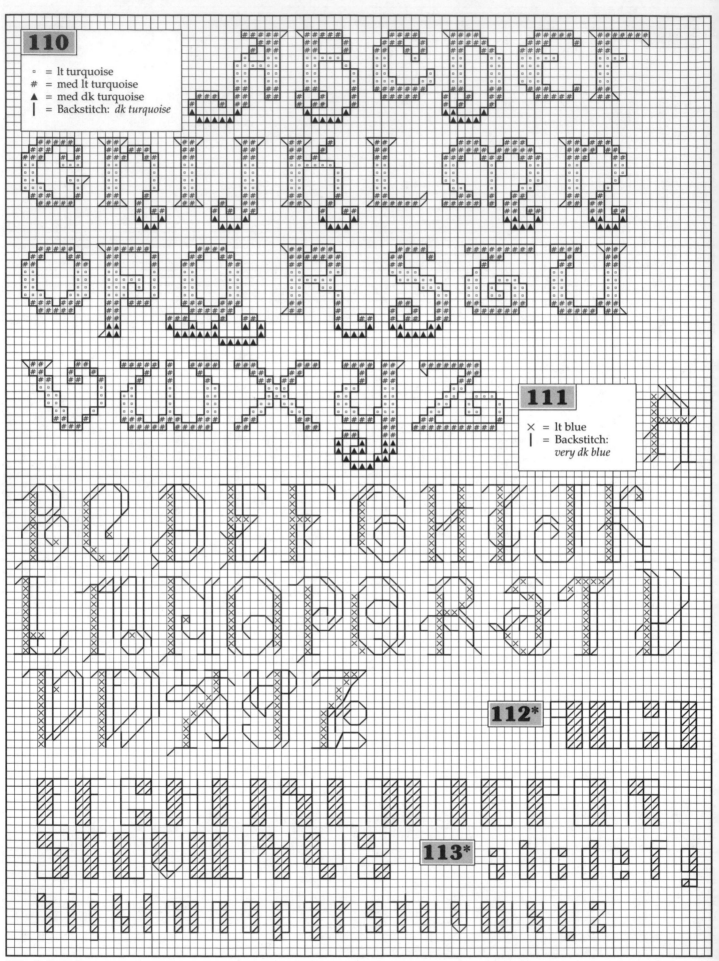

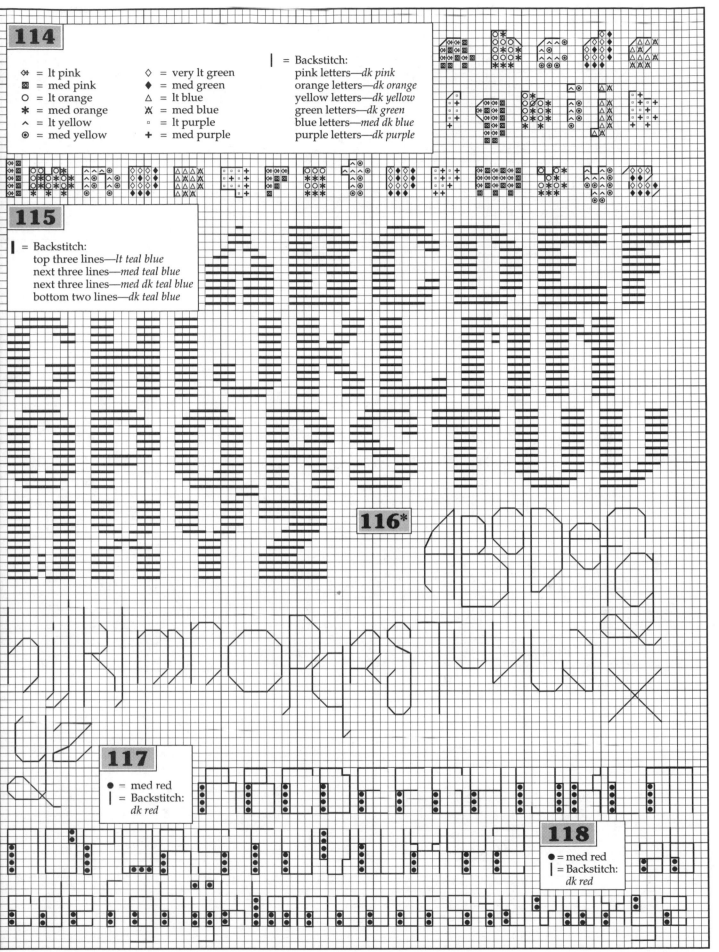

114

⊕	=	lt pink	◇	=	very lt green		=	Backstitch:
⊞	=	med pink	◆	=	med green			pink letters—*dk pink*
○	=	lt orange	△	=	lt blue			orange letters—*dk orange*
✳	=	med orange	✕	=	med blue			yellow letters—*dk yellow*
∧	=	lt yellow	□	=	lt purple			green letters—*dk green*
⊙	=	med yellow	+	=	med purple			blue letters—*med dk blue*
								purple letters—*dk purple*

115

| = Backstitch:
top three lines—*lt teal blue*
next three lines—*med teal blue*
next three lines—*med dk teal blue*
bottom two lines—*dk teal blue*

116*

117

● = med red
| = Backstitch:
dk red

118

● = med red
| = Backstitch:
dk red

Use desired color.

65

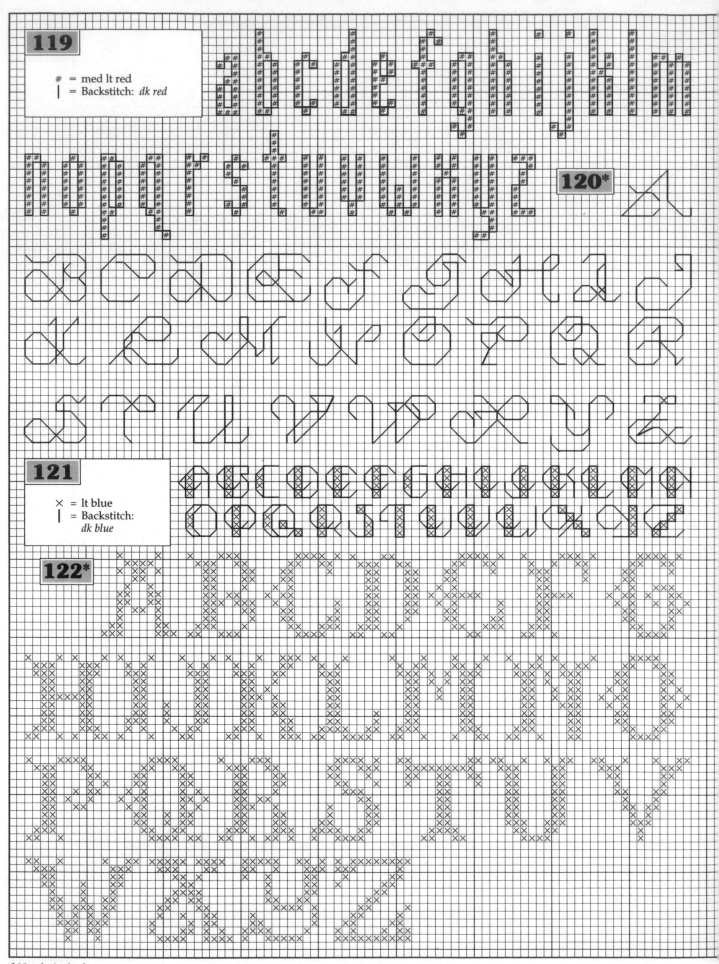

119

= med lt red
| = Backstitch: *dk red*

120*

121

× = lt blue
| = Backstitch: *dk blue*

122*

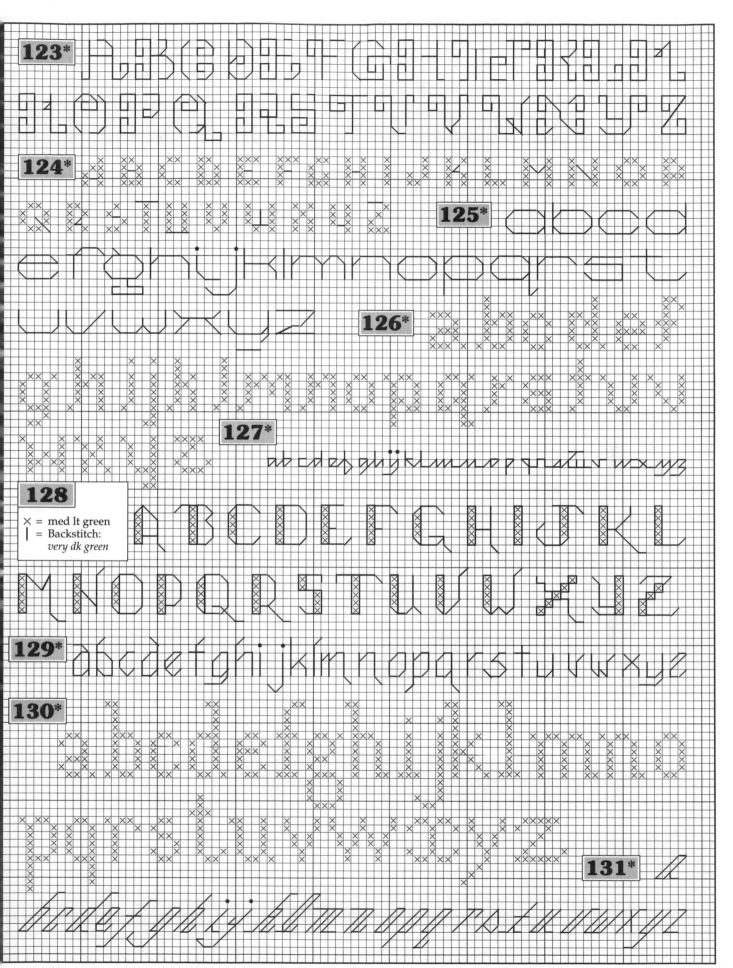

128

× = med lt green
| = Backstitch: *very dk green*

*Use desired color.

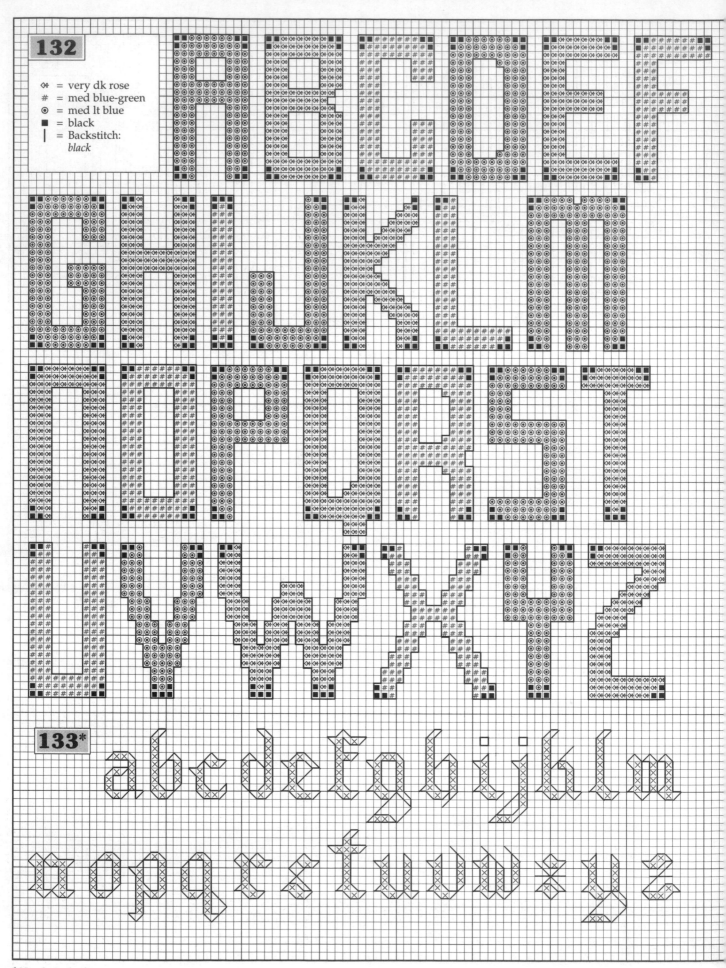

132

⋈ = very dk rose
\# = med blue-green
⊙ = med lt blue
■ = black
| = Backstitch:
black

133*

abcdefghijklm
nopqrstuvwxyz

* Use desired color.

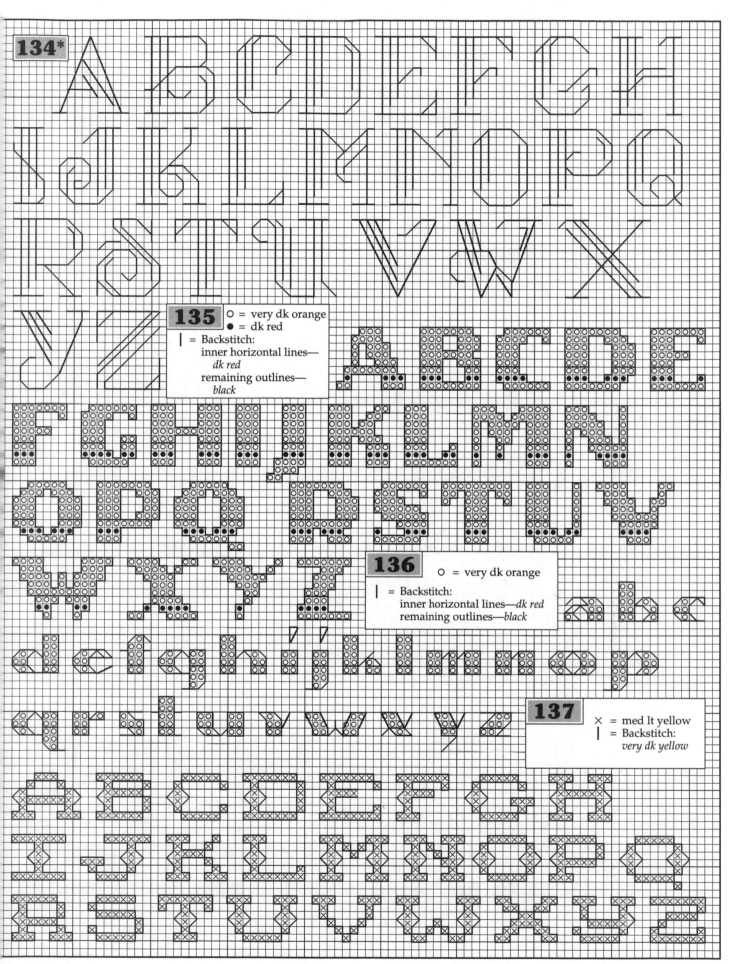

134*

ABCDEFGHIJKLMNOPQRSTUVWXYZ

135   O = very dk orange
• = dk red
| = Backstitch:
inner horizontal lines—
dk red
remaining outlines—
black

136   O = very dk orange
| = Backstitch:
inner horizontal lines—*dk red*
remaining outlines—*black*

137   × = med lt yellow
| = Backstitch:
very dk yellow

Use desired color.

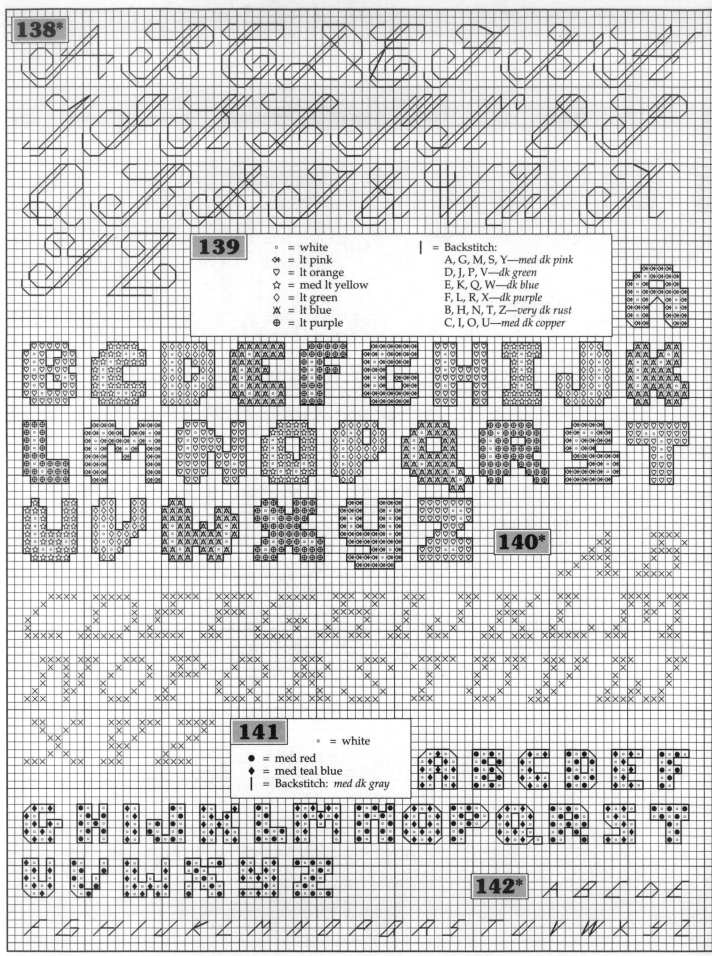

138*

139

▫ = white	| = Backstitch:	
⊕ = lt pink	A, G, M, S, Y—*med dk pink*	
♡ = lt orange	D, J, P, V—*dk green*	
☆ = med lt yellow	E, K, Q, W—*dk blue*	
◇ = lt green	F, L, R, X—*dk purple*	
⋈ = lt blue	B, H, N, T, Z—*very dk rust*	
⊕ = lt purple	C, I, O, U—*med dk copper*	

140*

141

▫ = white	
● = med red	
◆ = med teal blue	
| = Backstitch: *med dk gray*	

142*

*Use desired color.

143

O = med rust
X = dk rust
● = dk taupe
| = Backstitch:
  dk taupe

144*

145

+ = lt violet
| = Backstitch:
  dk purple

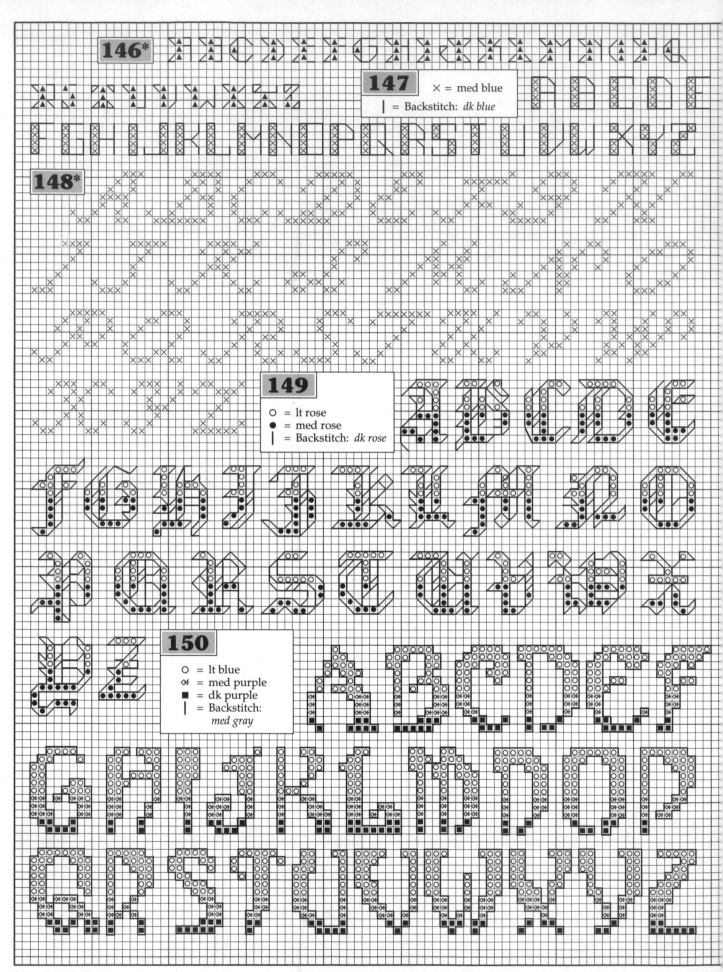

146*

147
×　= med blue
|　= Backstitch: *dk blue*

148*

149
○　= lt rose
●　= med rose
|　= Backstitch: *dk rose*

150
○　= lt blue
⬧　= med purple
■　= dk purple
|　= Backstitch:
　　med gray

* *Use desired color.*

72

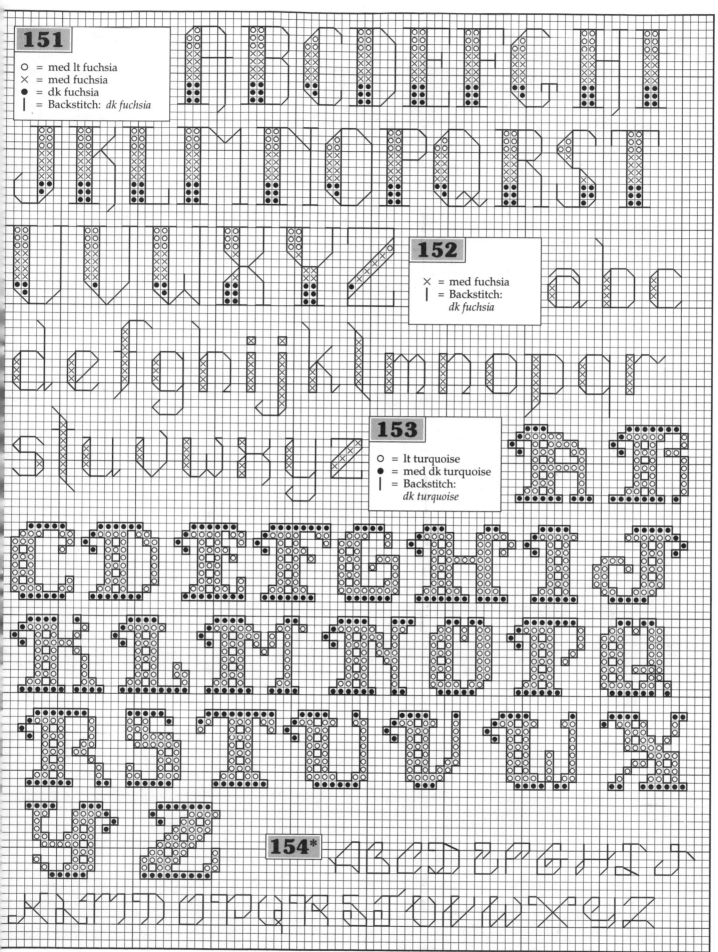

151

○ = med lt fuchsia
✕ = med fuchsia
● = dk fuchsia
| = Backstitch: *dk fuchsia*

152

✕ = med fuchsia
| = Backstitch:
dk fuchsia

153

○ = lt turquoise
● = med dk turquoise
| = Backstitch:
dk turquoise

154*

Use desired color.

73

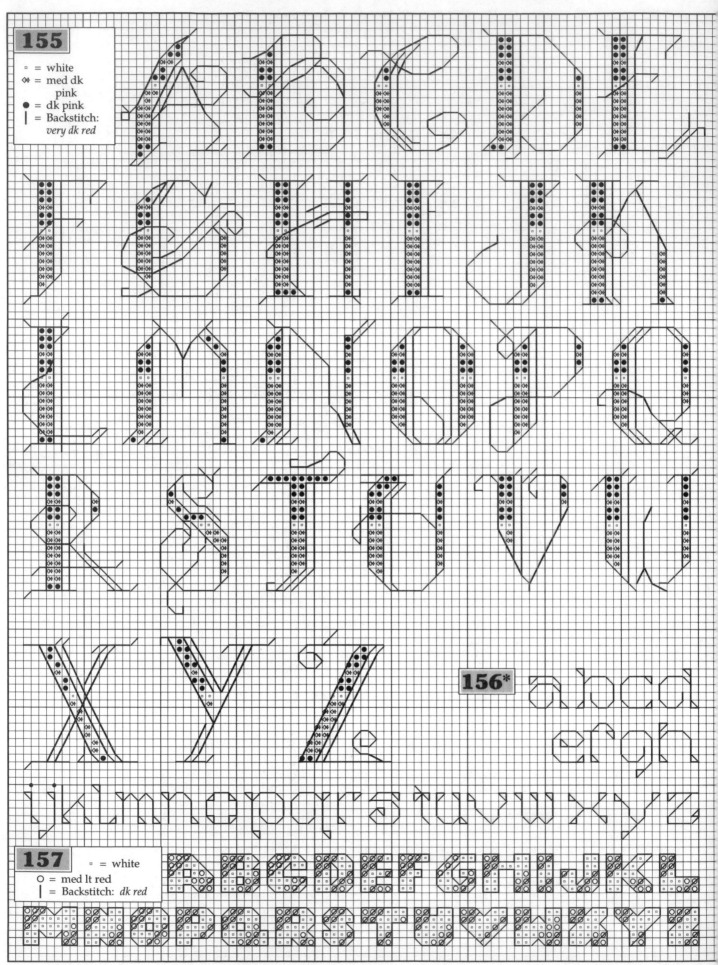

155

- ▫ = white
- ⟐ = med dk pink
- ● = dk pink
- | = Backstitch: *very dk red*

156*

157

- ▫ = white
- ○ = med lt red
- | = Backstitch: *dk red*

**Use desired color.*

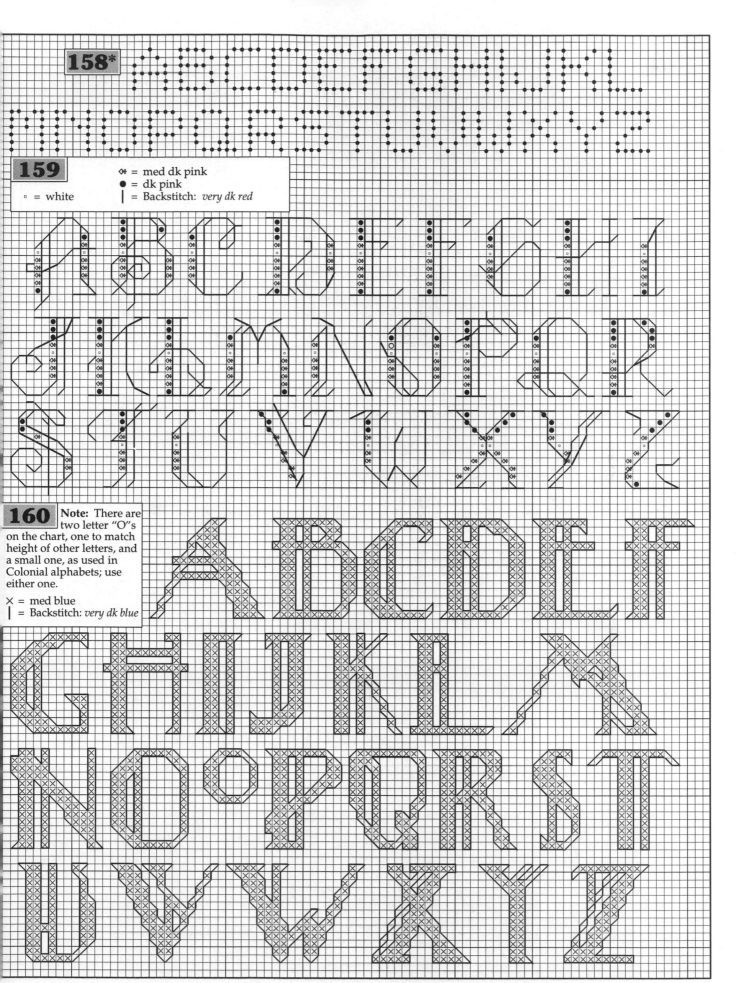

158*

159

◈ = med dk pink
● = dk pink
▫ = white | = Backstitch: *very dk red*

160 **Note:** There are two letter "O"s on the chart, one to match height of other letters, and a small one, as used in Colonial alphabets; use either one.

× = med blue
| = Backstitch: *very dk blue*

Use desired color.

161

× = med lt teal blue
| = Backstitch:
  very dk turquoise

162

× = lt peach
| = Backstitch:
  med dk peach

163

× = med lt pink
| = Backstitch:
  dk pink

164

○ = very lt yellow
✢ = med gold
● = dk gold
| = Backstitch:
  very dk gold

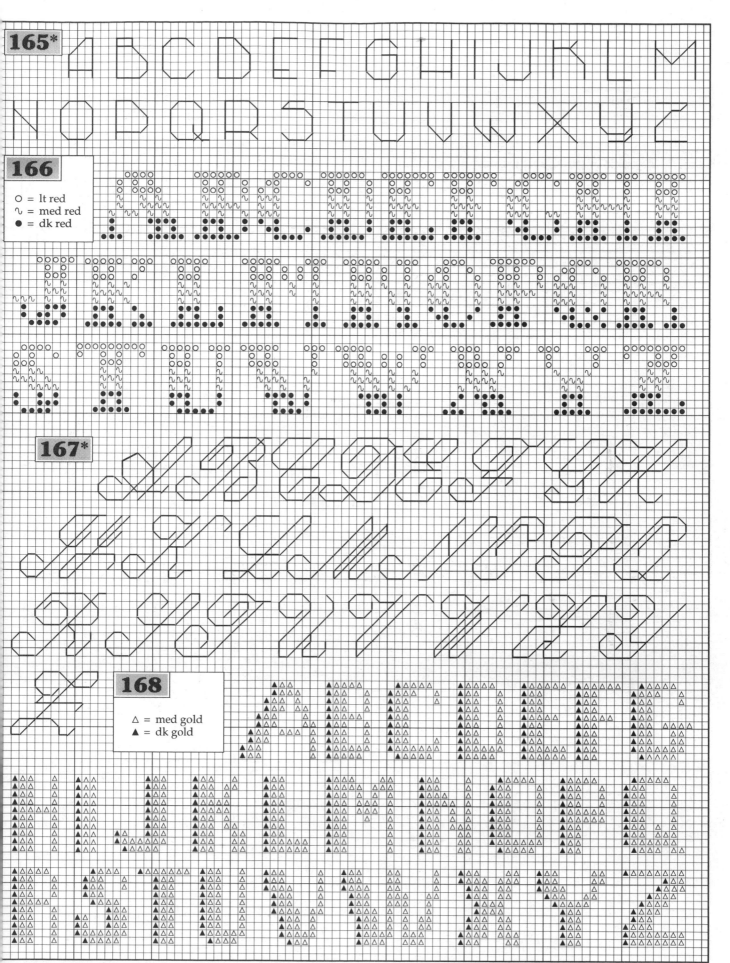

165*

ABCDEFGHIJKLM
NOPQRSTUVWXYZ

166

○ = lt red
∿ = med red
● = dk red

167*

168

△ = med gold
▲ = dk gold

Use desired color.

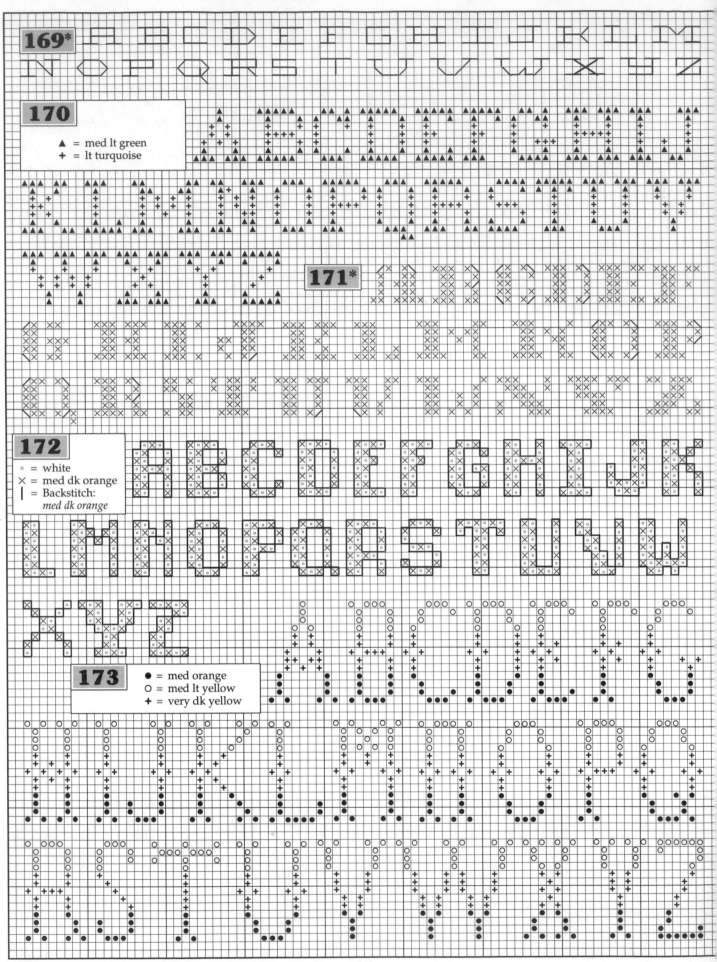

169* ABCDEFGHIJKLM
NOPQRSTUVWXYZ

170

▲ = med lt green
+ = lt turquoise

171*

172

□ = white
× = med dk orange
| = Backstitch:
  med dk orange

173

● = med orange
○ = med lt yellow
+ = very dk yellow

* Use desired color.

78

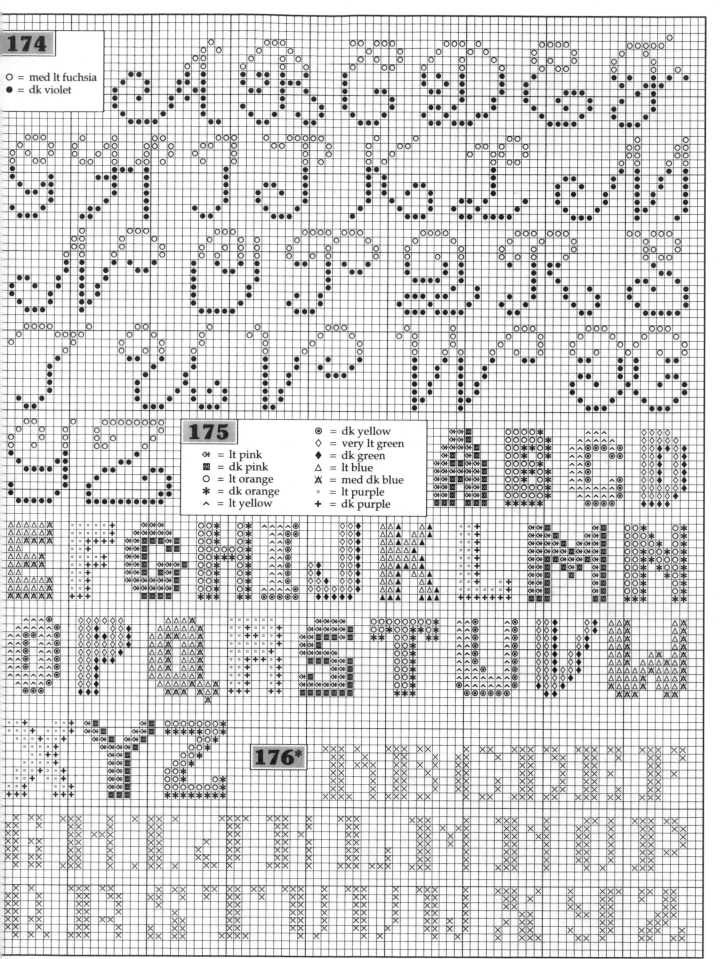

Use desired color.

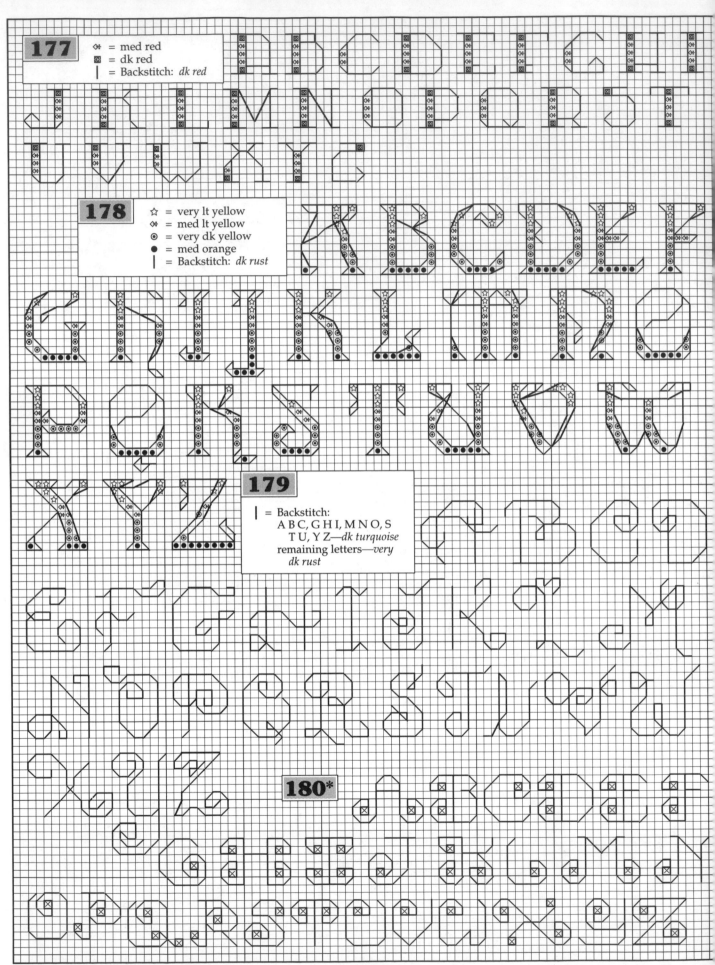

177
◈ = med red
▨ = dk red
| = Backstitch: *dk red*

178
☆ = very lt yellow
✳ = med lt yellow
◉ = very dk yellow
● = med orange
| = Backstitch: *dk rust*

179
| = Backstitch:
 A B C, G H I, M N O, S
 T U, Y Z—*dk turquoise*
remaining letters—*very
 dk rust*

180*

*Use desired color.

ABCDEFGHIJKLMNO
PQRSTUVWXYZ

ABCD EFBH

abcdefghijklmnopqrstuvwxyz
abcdefghijklmnopqrstuvwxyz

IJKLMNOPQR
STUVWXYZ

GAME
SET
MATCH

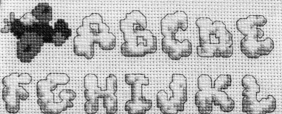

ABCDE
FGHIJKL

abcdefghijklmnopqrstuvwxyz

MNOPQRSTUV

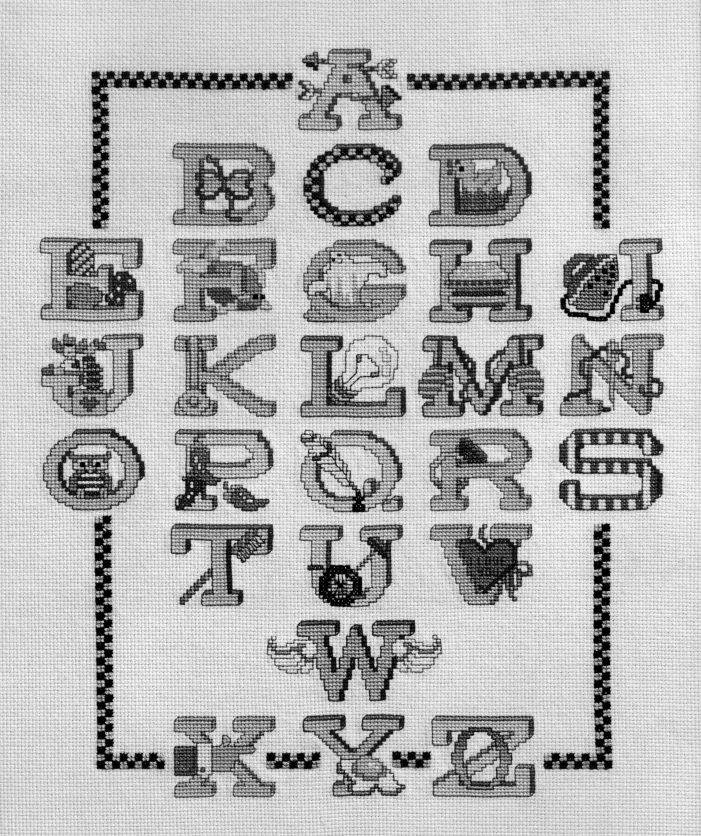

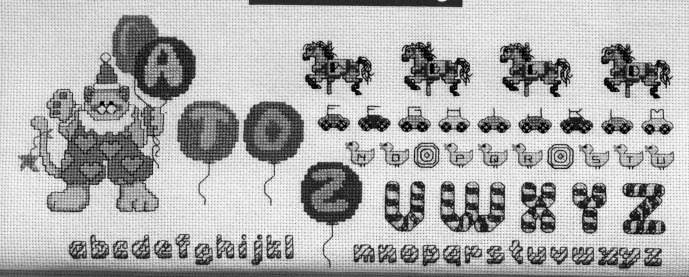

Our Favorite Things Design Directory

The charts are in numerical order beginning on page 86.

page 81

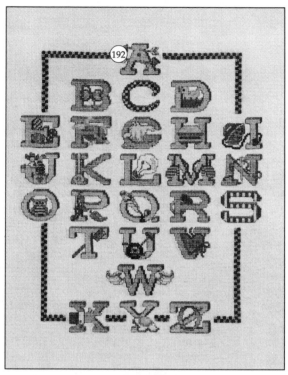

page 82

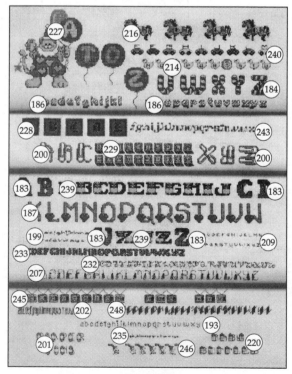

page 83

page 84

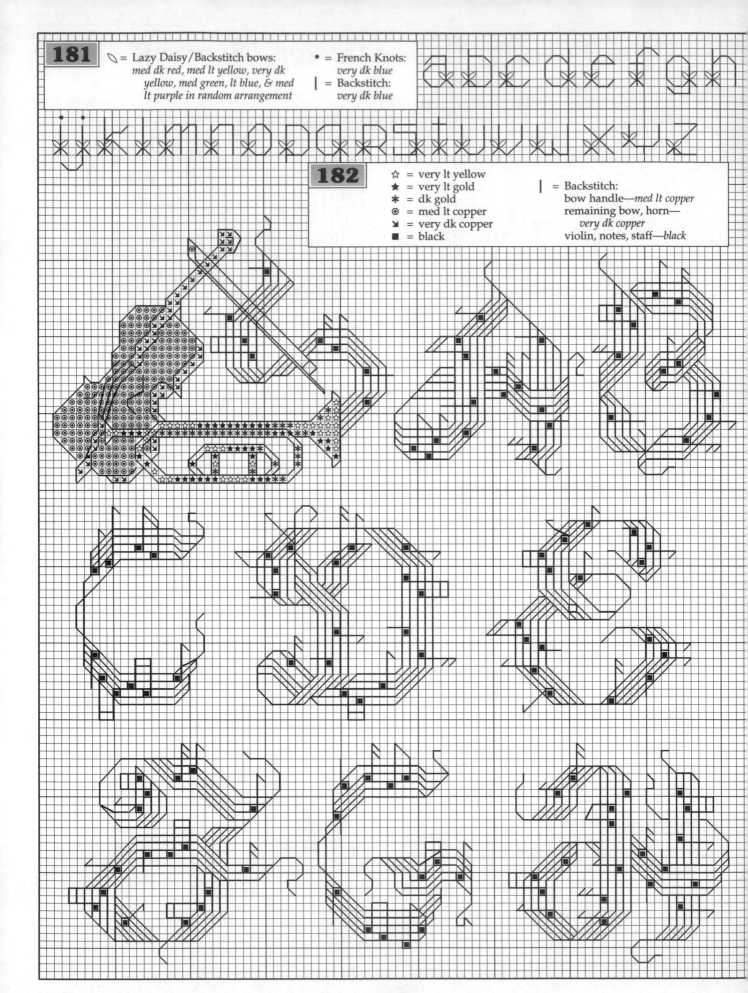

181

✎ = Lazy Daisy/Backstitch bows:
med dk red, med lt yellow, very dk yellow, med green, lt blue, & med lt purple in random arrangement

• = French Knots:
very dk blue

| = Backstitch:
very dk blue

182

☆ = very lt yellow
★ = very lt gold
✳ = dk gold
◉ = med lt copper
⋈ = very dk copper
■ = black

| = Backstitch:
bow handle—*med lt copper*
remaining bow, horn—
very dk copper
violin, notes, staff—*black*

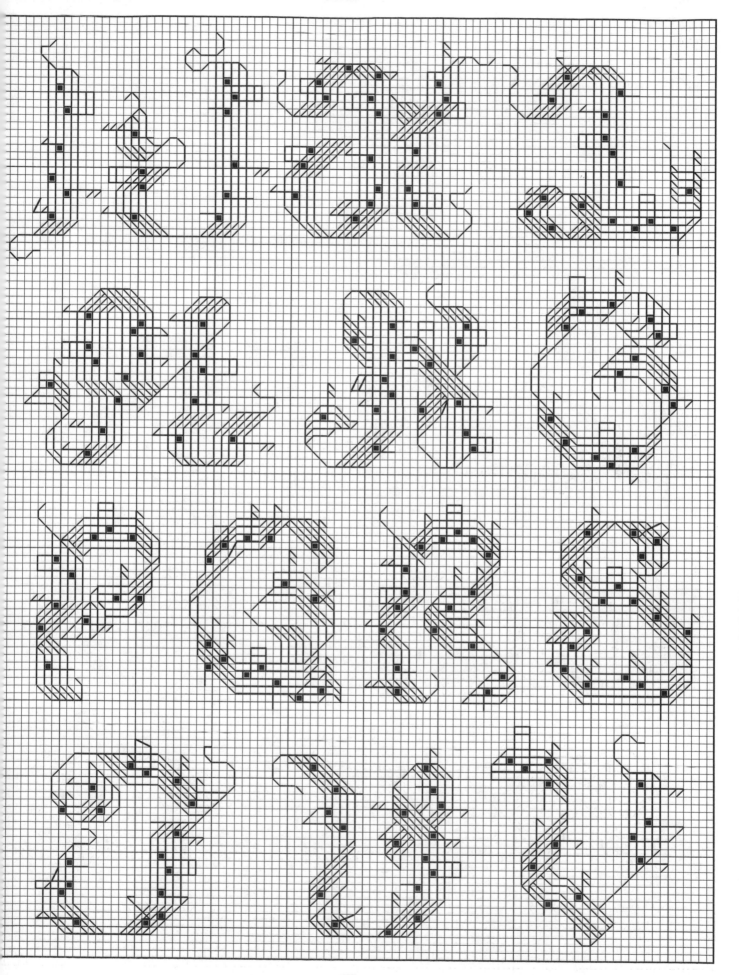

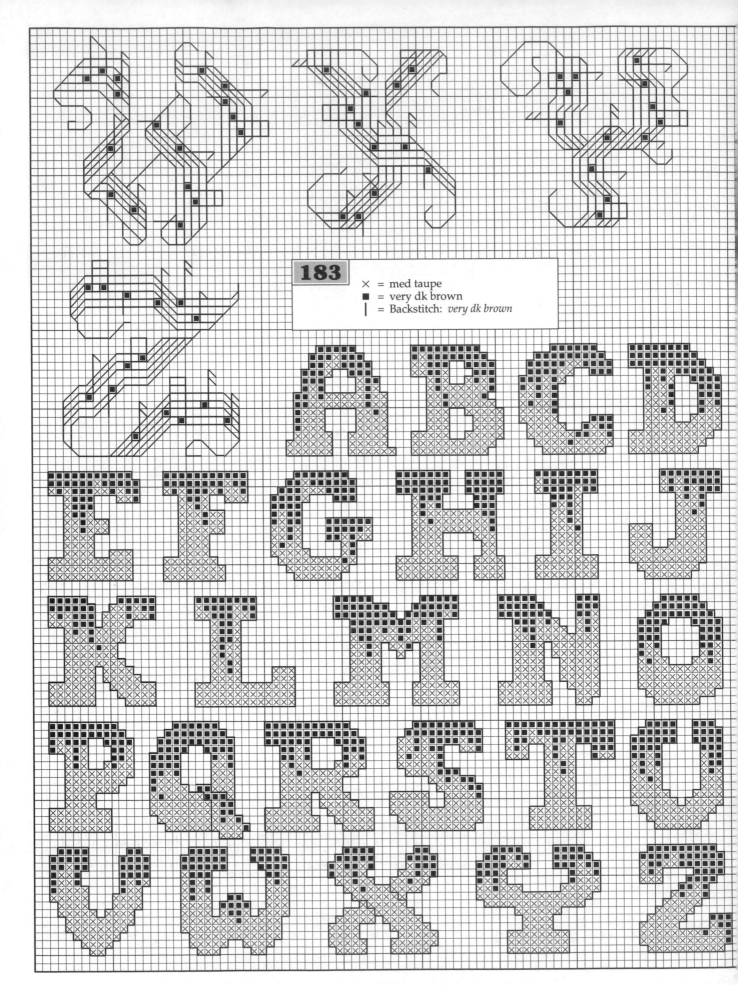

183

× = med taupe
■ = very dk brown
| = Backstitch: *very dk brown*

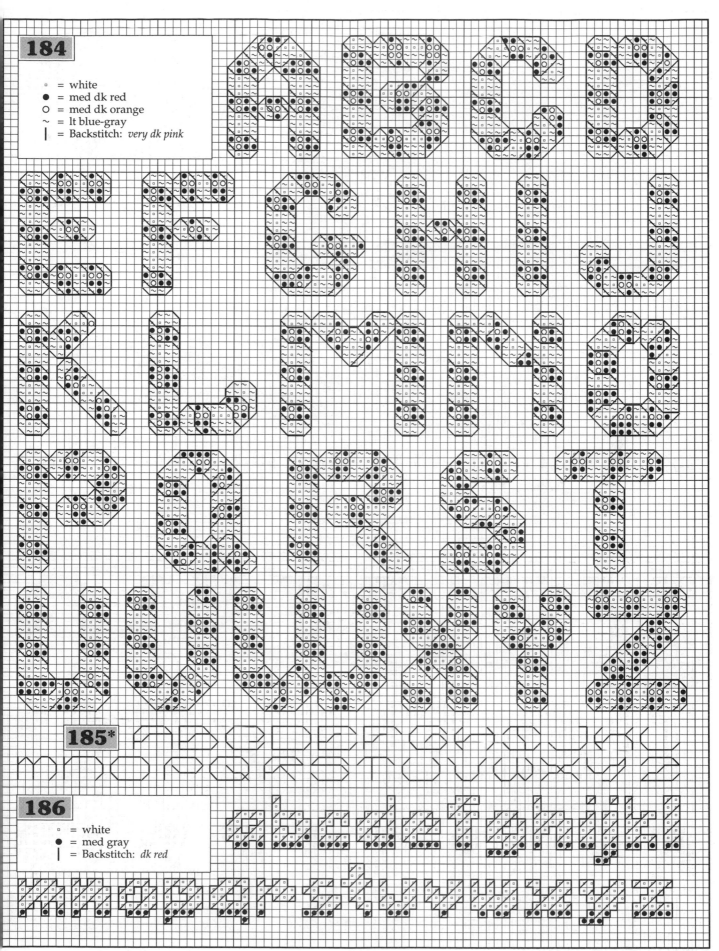

184

□ = white
● = med dk red
○ = med dk orange
~ = lt blue-gray
| = Backstitch: *very dk pink*

185*

186

□ = white
● = med gray
| = Backstitch: *dk red*

*Use desired color.

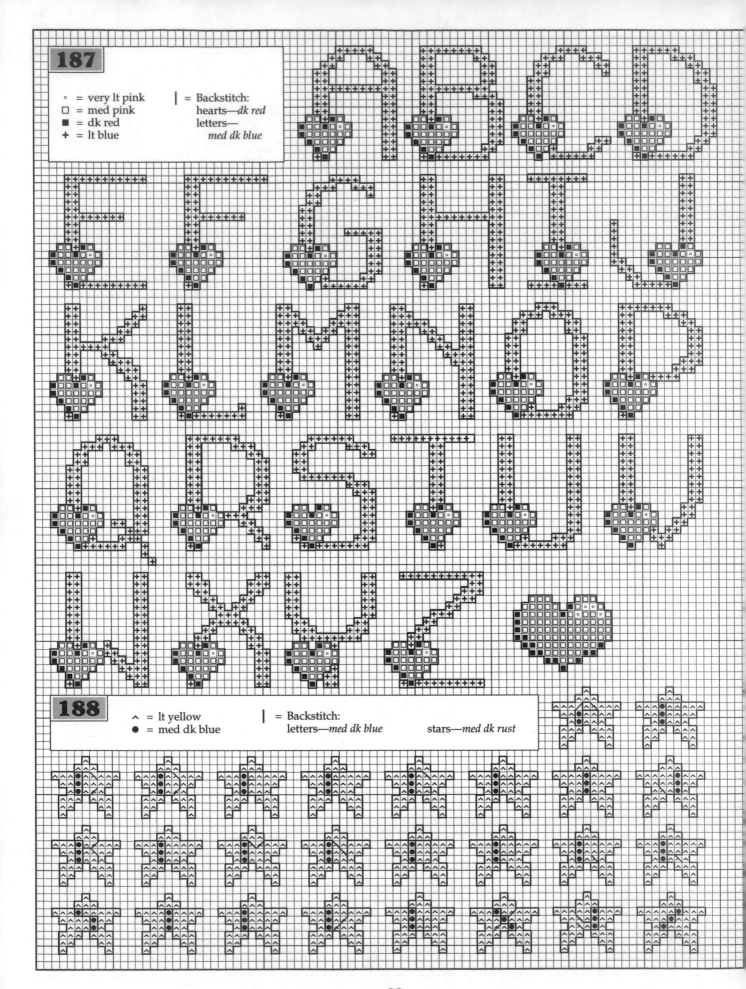

187

- □ = very lt pink
- ☐ = med pink
- ■ = dk red
- ✛ = lt blue

| = Backstitch:
hearts—*dk red*
letters—
  med dk blue

188

- ⌃ = lt yellow
- ● = med dk blue

| = Backstitch:
letters—*med dk blue*   stars—*med dk rust*

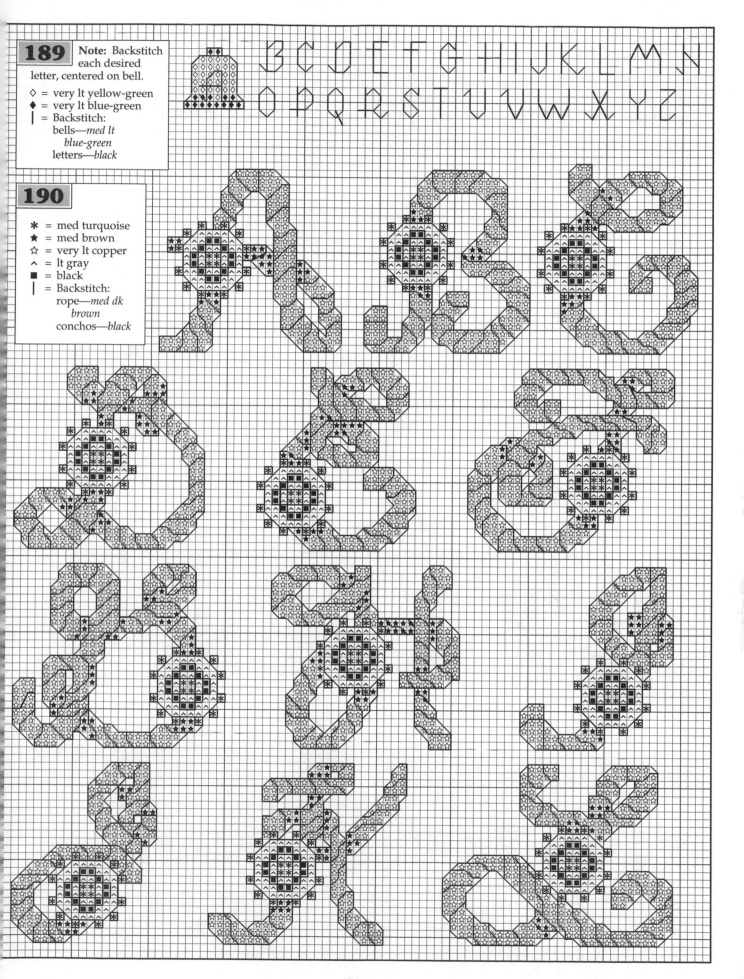

92

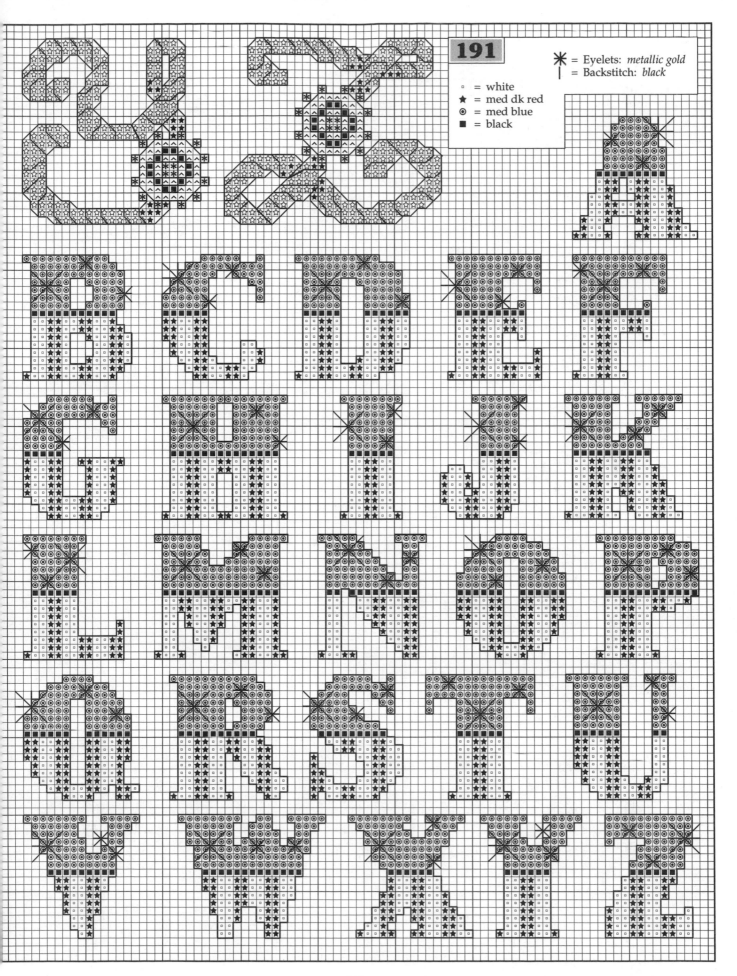

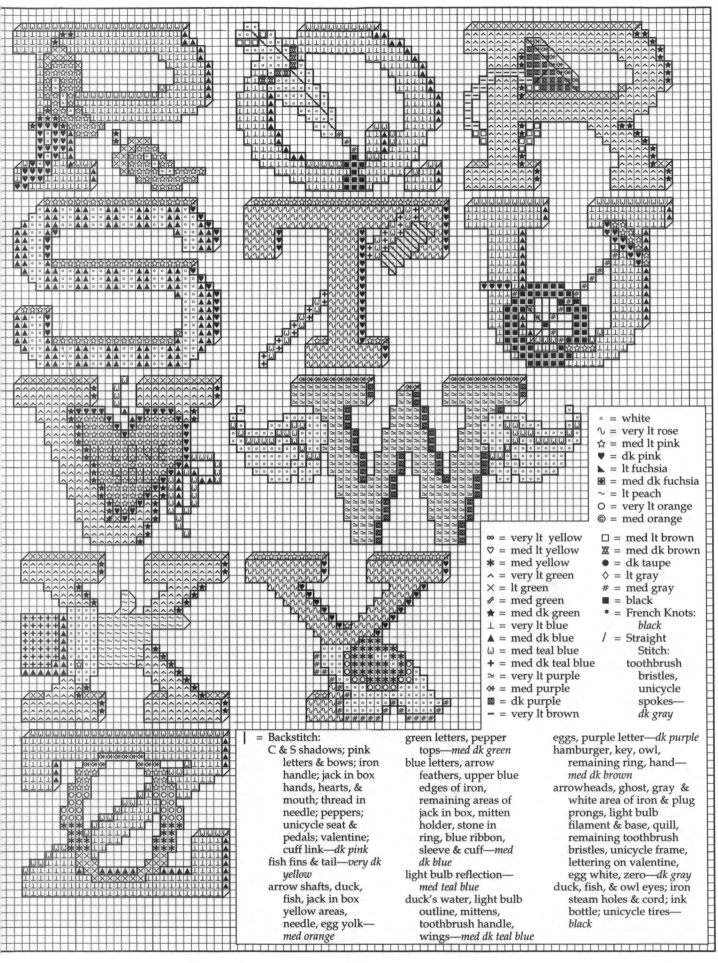

□ = white
∿ = very lt rose
☆ = med lt pink
♥ = dk pink
◣ = lt fuchsia
▣ = med dk fuchsia
~ = lt peach
O = very lt orange
© = med orange

∞ = very lt yellow
♡ = med lt yellow
✳ = med yellow
∧ = very lt green
✕ = lt green
✺ = med green
★ = med dk green
⊥ = very lt blue
▲ = med dk blue
ω = med teal blue
+ = med dk teal blue
≃ = very lt purple
✤ = med purple
▦ = dk purple
— = very lt brown

□ = med lt brown
▨ = med dk brown
● = dk taupe
◇ = lt gray
= med gray
■ = black
• = French Knots:
     black
/ = Straight
     Stitch:
     toothbrush
     bristles,
     unicycle
     spokes—
     dk gray

❘ = Backstitch:
C & S shadows; pink letters & bows; iron handle; jack in box hands, hearts, & mouth; thread in needle; peppers; unicycle seat & pedals; valentine; cuff link—*dk pink*
fish fins & tail—*very dk yellow*
arrow shafts, duck, fish, jack in box yellow areas, needle, egg yolk—*med orange*

green letters, pepper tops—*med dk green*
blue letters, arrow feathers, upper blue edges of iron, remaining areas of jack in box, mitten holder, stone in ring, blue ribbon, sleeve & cuff—*med dk blue*
light bulb reflection—*med teal blue*
duck's water, light bulb outline, mittens, toothbrush handle, wings—*med dk teal blue*

eggs, purple letter—*dk purple*
hamburger, key, owl, remaining ring, hand—*med dk brown*
arrowheads, ghost, gray & white area of iron & plug prongs, light bulb filament & base, quill, remaining toothbrush bristles, unicycle frame, lettering on valentine, egg white, zero—*dk gray*
duck, fish, & owl eyes; iron steam holes & cord; ink bottle; unicycle tires—*black*

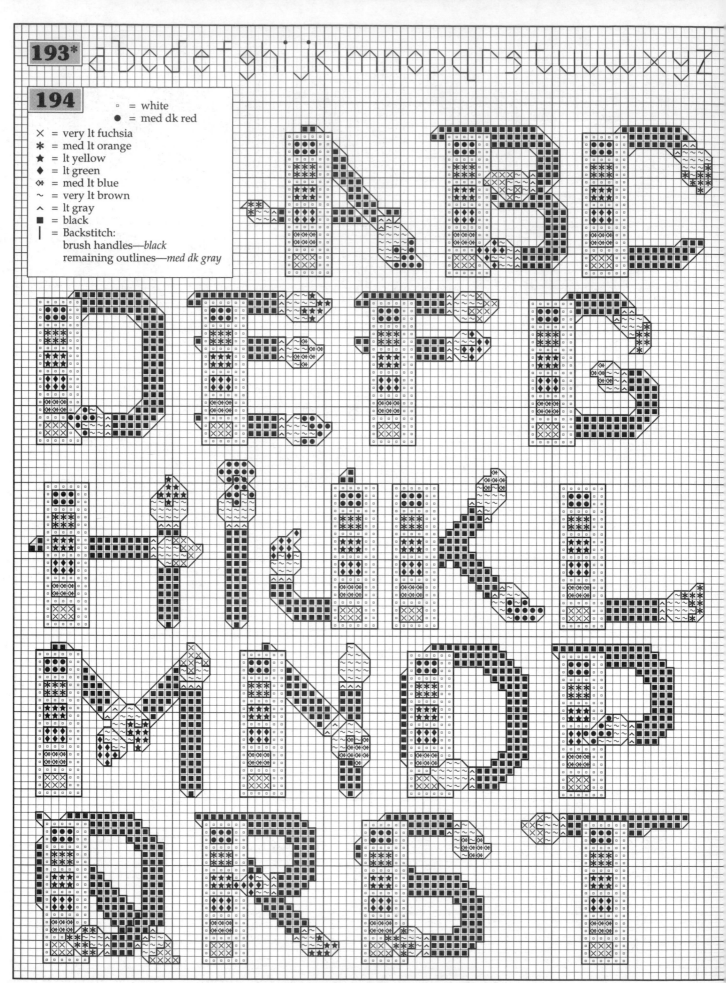

193* abcdefghijklmnopqrstuvwxyz

194
□ = white
● = med dk red
✕ = very lt fuchsia
✳ = med lt orange
★ = lt yellow
◆ = lt green
❁ = med lt blue
~ = very lt brown
∧ = lt gray
■ = black
| = Backstitch:
    brush handles—*black*
    remaining outlines—*med dk gray*

*Use desired color.

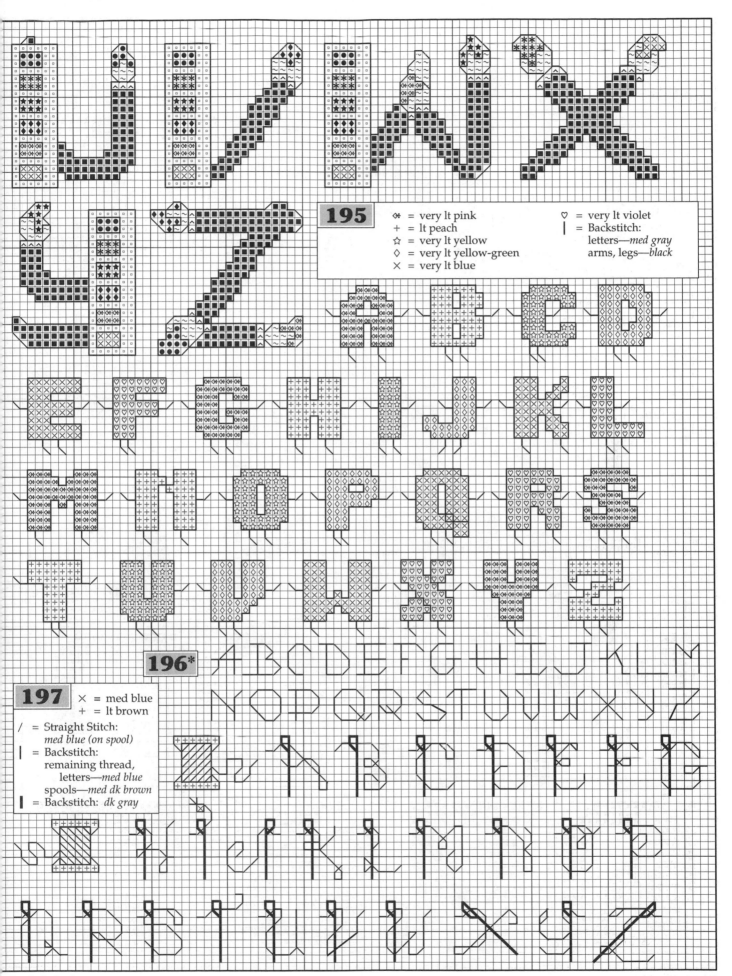

195

❀ = very lt pink
+ = lt peach
☆ = very lt yellow
◇ = very lt yellow-green
✕ = very lt blue

♡ = very lt violet
| = Backstitch:
letters—*med gray*
arms, legs—*black*

196*

197   ✕ = med blue
+ = lt brown

/ = Straight Stitch:
med blue (on spool)
| = Backstitch:
remaining thread,
letters—*med blue*
spools—*med dk brown*
| = Backstitch: *dk gray*

Use desired color.

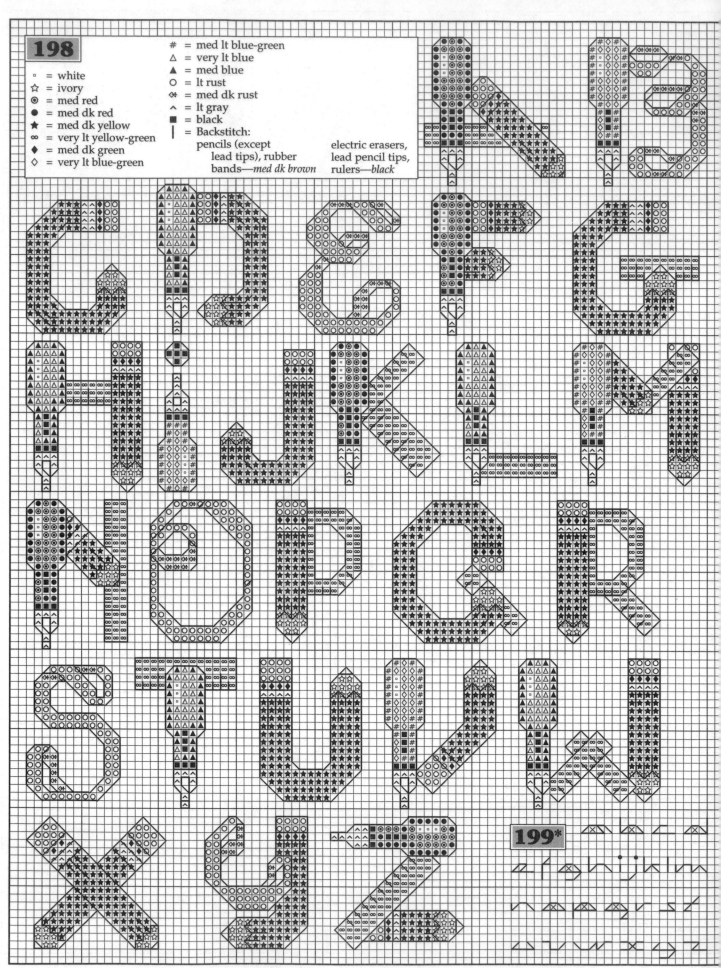

198

- □ = white
- ☆ = ivory
- ⊙ = med red
- ● = med dk red
- ★ = med dk yellow
- ∞ = very lt yellow-green
- ◆ = med dk green
- ◇ = very lt blue-green
- # = med lt blue-green
- △ = very lt blue
- ▲ = med blue
- ○ = lt rust
- ⧓ = med dk rust
- ∧ = lt gray
- ■ = black
- | = Backstitch:
  pencils (except lead tips), rubber bands—*med dk brown*   electric erasers, lead pencil tips, rulers—*black*

199*

*Use desired color.

98

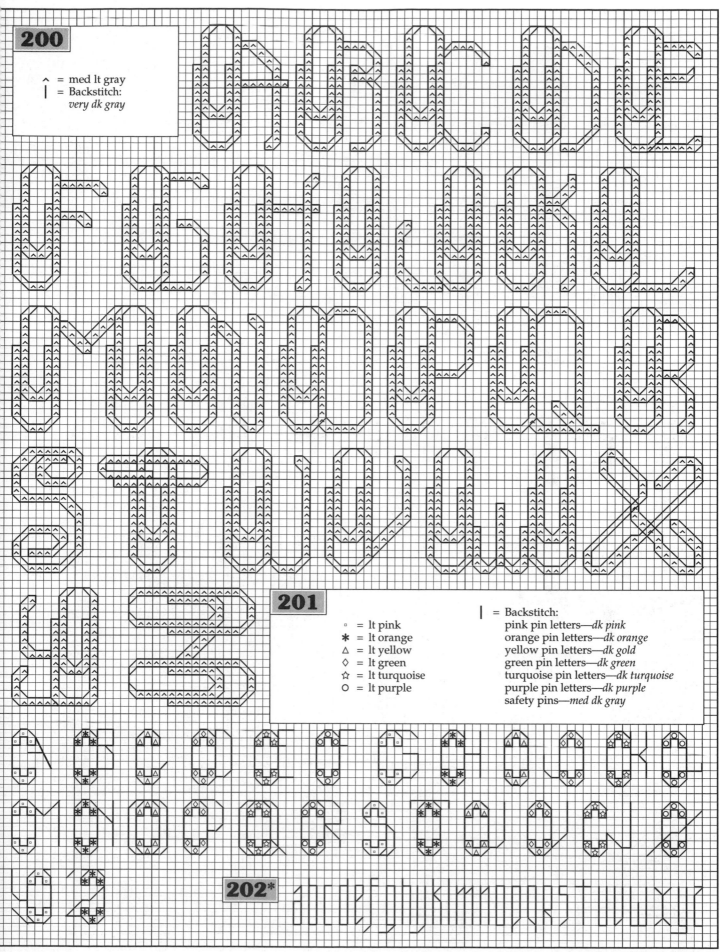

*Use desired color.

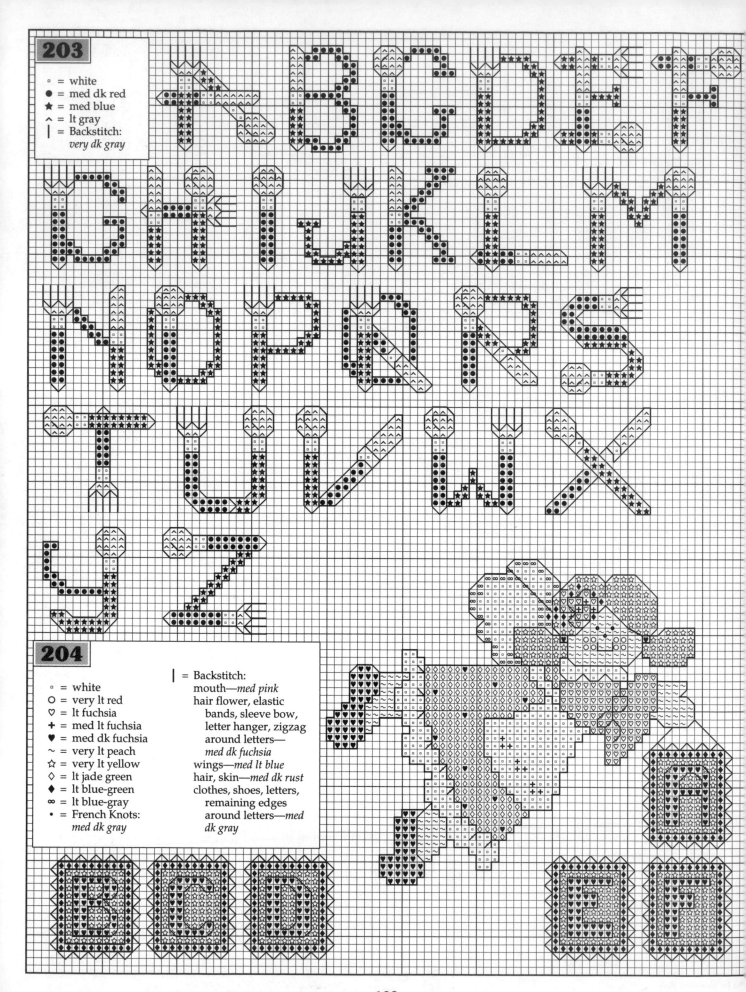

203

- ▫ = white
- ● = med dk red
- ★ = med blue
- ^ = lt gray
- | = Backstitch:
  very dk gray

204

- ▫ = white
- ○ = very lt red
- ♡ = lt fuchsia
- ✛ = med lt fuchsia
- ♥ = med dk fuchsia
- ~ = very lt peach
- ☆ = very lt yellow
- ◇ = lt jade green
- ◆ = lt blue-green
- ∞ = lt blue-gray
- • = French Knots:
  med dk gray

| = Backstitch:
  mouth—*med pink*
  hair flower, elastic
    bands, sleeve bow,
    letter hanger, zigzag
    around letters—
    med dk fuchsia
  wings—*med lt blue*
  hair, skin—*med dk rust*
  clothes, shoes, letters,
    remaining edges
    around letters—*med
    dk gray*

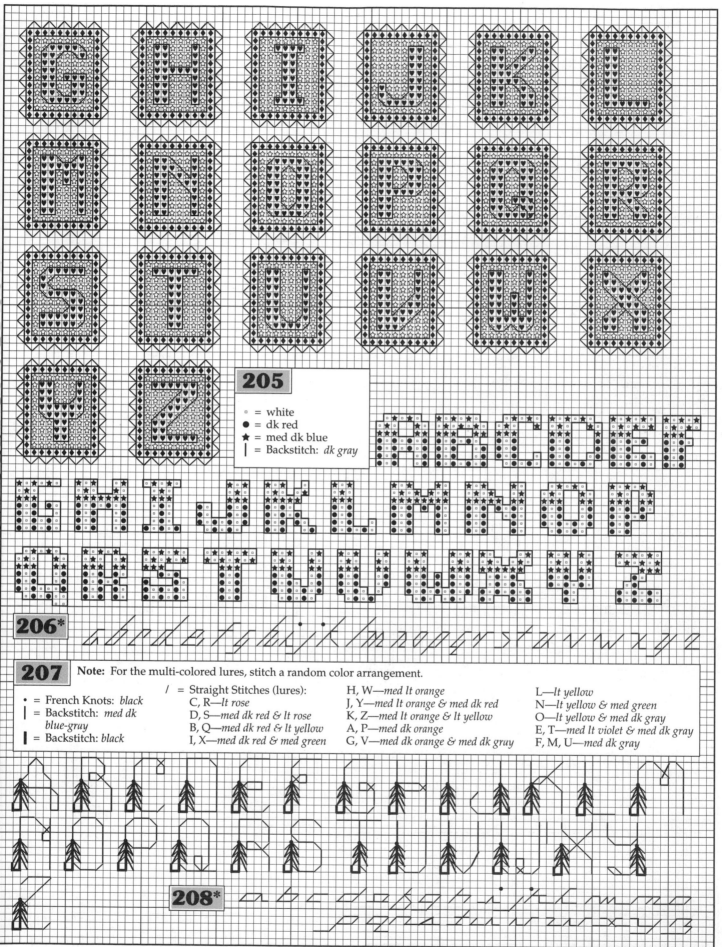

205

- ◻ = white
- ● = dk red
- ★ = med dk blue
- | = Backstitch: *dk gray*

206*

207

Note: For the multi-colored lures, stitch a random color arrangement.

- • = French Knots: *black*
- | = Backstitch: *med dk blue-gray*
- | = Backstitch: *black*

/ = Straight Stitches (lures):
- C, R—*lt rose*
- D, S—*med dk red & lt rose*
- B, Q—*med dk red & lt yellow*
- I, X—*med dk red & med green*

- H, W—*med lt orange*
- J, Y—*med lt orange & med dk red*
- K, Z—*med lt orange & lt yellow*
- A, P—*med dk orange*
- G, V—*med dk orange & med dk gray*

- L—*lt yellow*
- N—*lt yellow & med green*
- O—*lt yellow & med dk gray*
- E, T—*med lt violet & med dk gray*
- F, M, U—*med dk gray*

208*

* *Use desired color.*

101

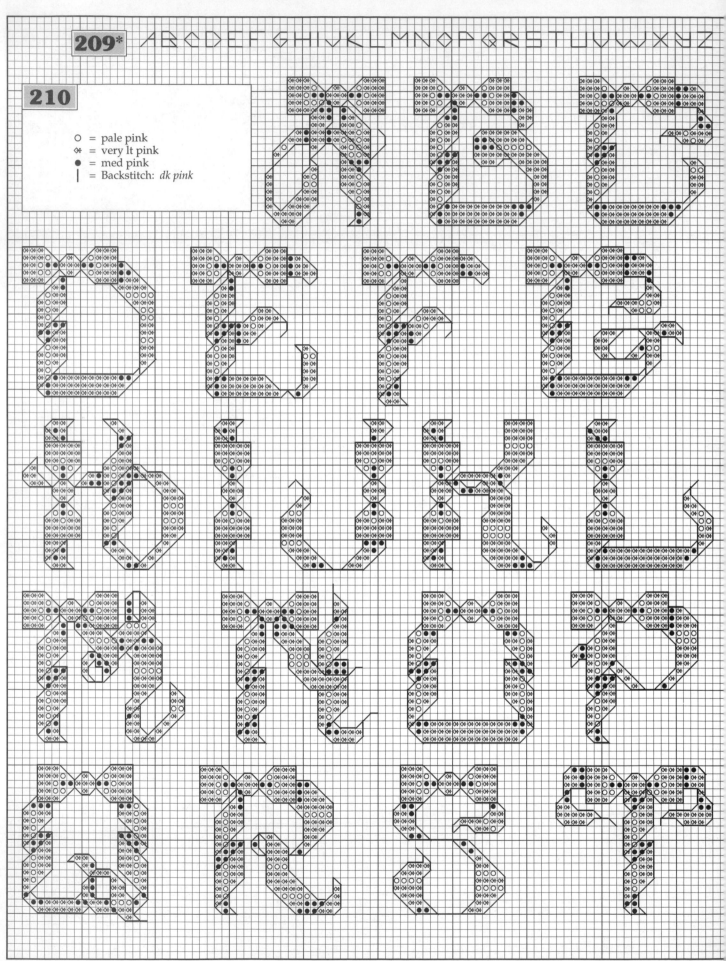

210

○ = pale pink
✤ = very lt pink
● = med pink
| = Backstitch: *dk pink*

Use desired color.

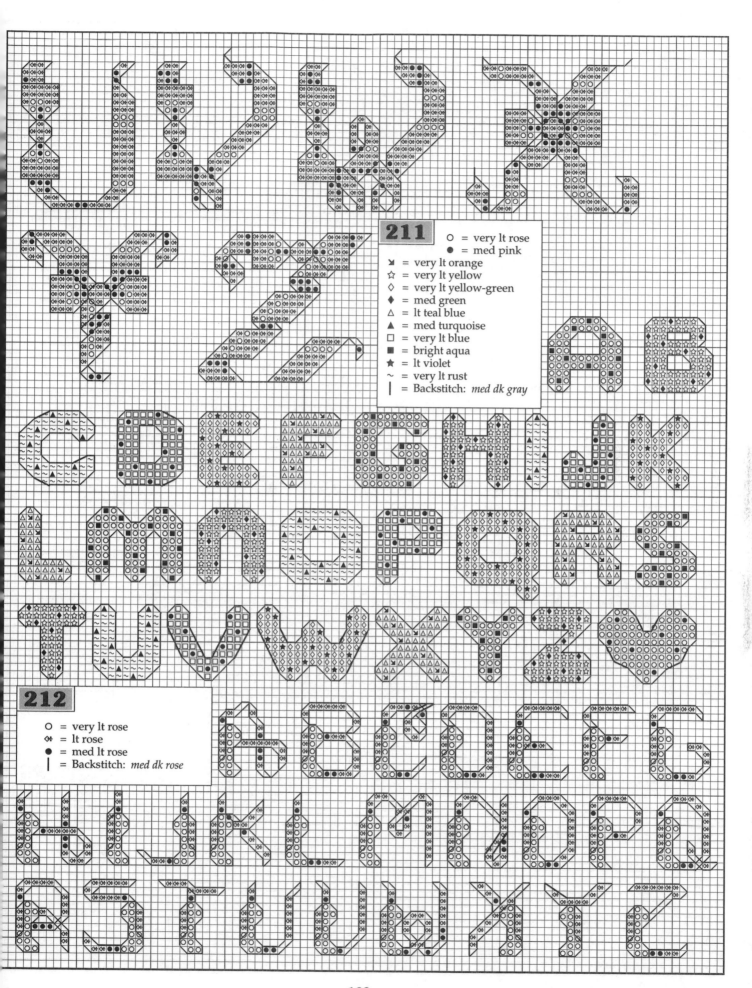

211

O = very lt rose
● = med pink
⋈ = very lt orange
☆ = very lt yellow
◇ = very lt yellow-green
◆ = med green
△ = lt teal blue
▲ = med turquoise
□ = very lt blue
■ = bright aqua
★ = lt violet
~ = very lt rust
| = Backstitch: *med dk gray*

212

O = very lt rose
✿ = lt rose
● = med lt rose
| = Backstitch: *med dk rose*

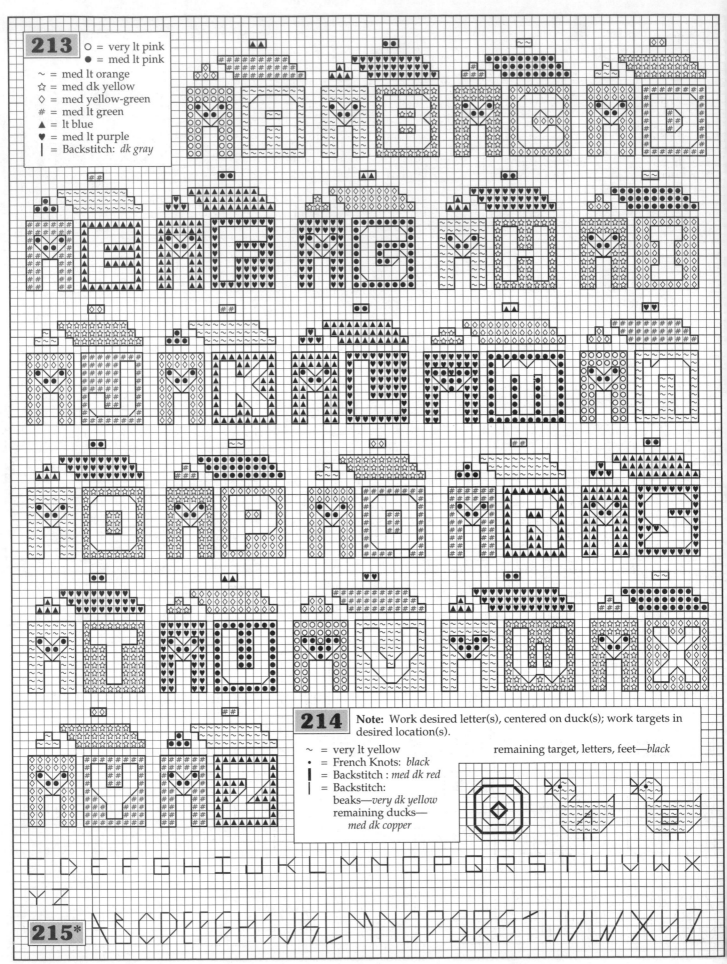

213
- ○ = very lt pink
- ● = med lt pink
- ~ = med lt orange
- ☆ = med dk yellow
- ◇ = med yellow-green
- # = med lt green
- ▲ = lt blue
- ♥ = med lt purple
- | = Backstitch: *dk gray*

214 **Note:** Work desired letter(s), centered on duck(s); work targets in desired location(s).

- ~ = very lt yellow
- • = French Knots: *black*
- | = Backstitch : *med dk red*
- | = Backstitch: beaks—*very dk yellow* remaining ducks— *med dk copper*

remaining target, letters, feet—*black*

215*

*Use desired color.

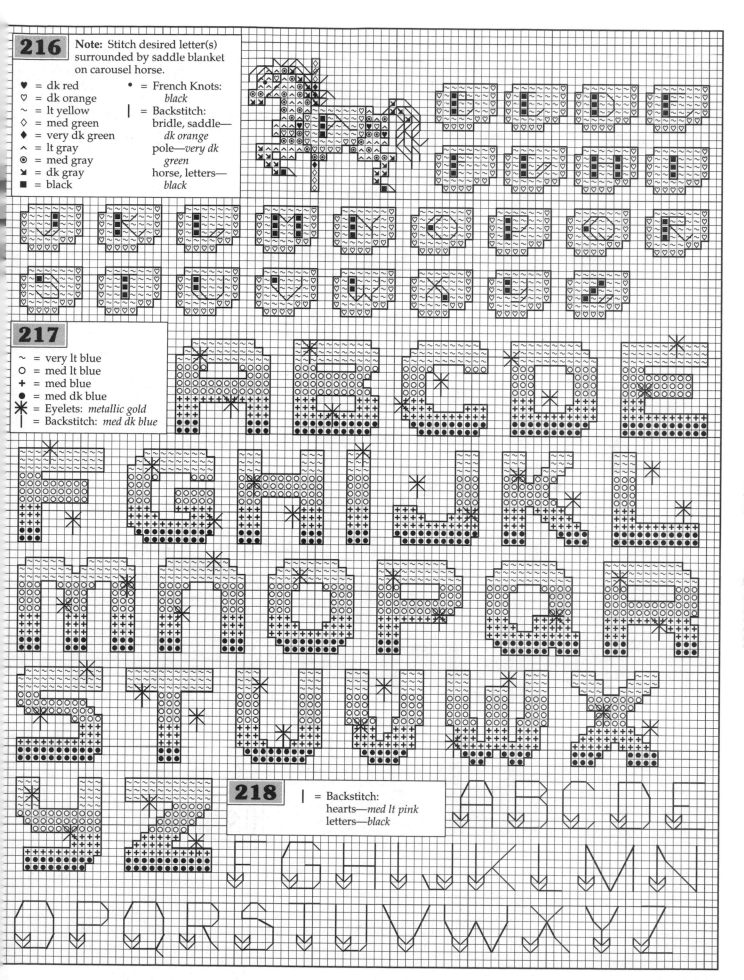

216

Note: Stitch desired letter(s) surrounded by saddle blanket on carousel horse.

♥ = dk red
♡ = dk orange
~ = lt yellow
◇ = med green
◆ = very dk green
∧ = lt gray
⊙ = med gray
⋈ = dk gray
■ = black

• = French Knots: *black*
| = Backstitch:
   bridle, saddle— *dk orange*
   pole— *very dk green*
   horse, letters— *black*

217

~ = very lt blue
○ = med lt blue
+ = med blue
● = med dk blue
✳ = Eyelets: *metallic gold*
| = Backstitch: *med dk blue*

218

| = Backstitch:
   hearts— *med lt pink*
   letters— *black*

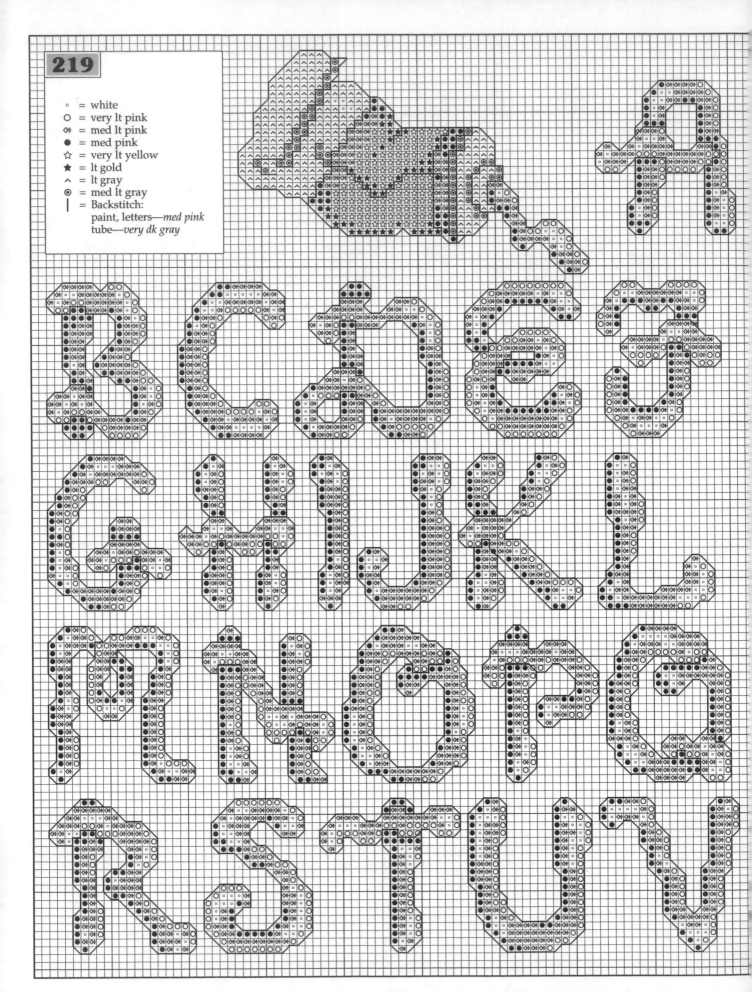

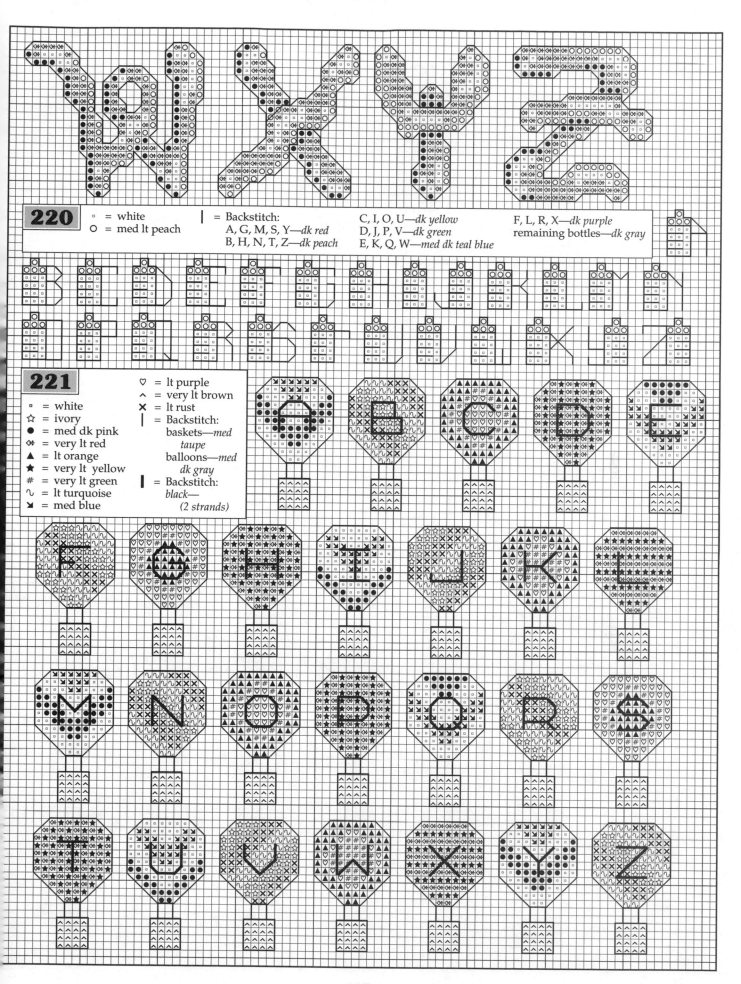

220
□ = white
o = med lt peach
| = Backstitch:
A, G, M, S, Y—dk red
B, H, N, T, Z—dk peach

C, I, O, U—dk yellow
D, J, P, V—dk green
E, K, Q, W—med dk teal blue

F, L, R, X—dk purple
remaining bottles—dk gray

221
□ = white
☆ = ivory
● = med dk pink
✿ = very lt red
▲ = lt orange
★ = very lt yellow
= very lt green
∿ = lt turquoise
⋈ = med blue

♡ = lt purple
^ = very lt brown
✗ = lt rust
| = Backstitch:
baskets—med taupe
balloons—med dk gray
| = Backstitch:
black— (2 strands)

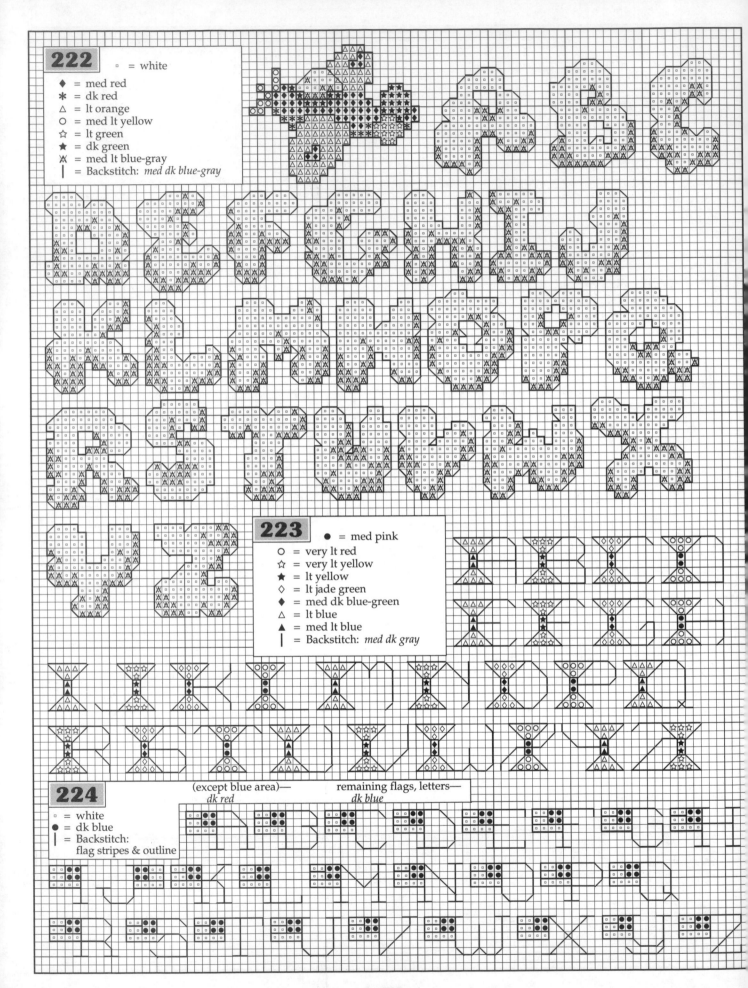

222 □ = white

♦ = med red
✳ = dk red
△ = lt orange
○ = med lt yellow
☆ = lt green
★ = dk green
✕ = med lt blue-gray
| = Backstitch: *med dk blue-gray*

223 ● = med pink

○ = very lt red
☆ = very lt yellow
★ = lt yellow
◇ = lt jade green
♦ = med dk blue-green
△ = lt blue
▲ = med lt blue
| = Backstitch: *med dk gray*

(except blue area)—
dk red

remaining flags, letters—
dk blue

224

□ = white
● = dk blue
| = Backstitch:
    flag stripes & outline

108

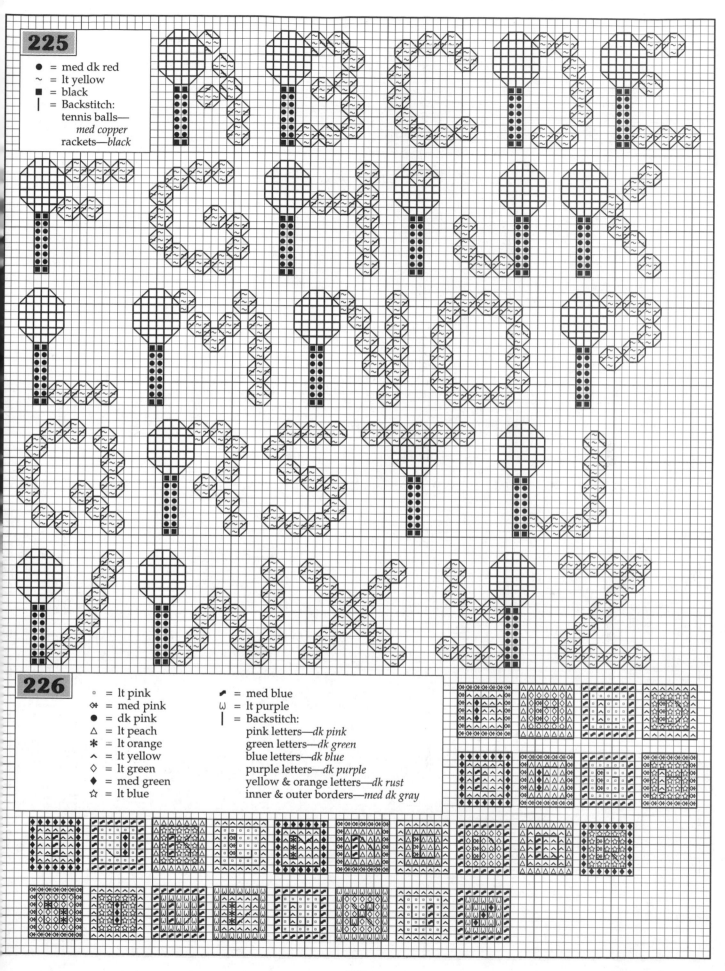

225

- ● = med dk red
- ~ = lt yellow
- ■ = black
- | = Backstitch:
  tennis balls—
    med copper
  rackets—*black*

226

- □ = lt pink
- ✺ = med pink
- ● = dk pink
- △ = lt peach
- ✳ = lt orange
- ʌ = lt yellow
- ◇ = lt green
- ◆ = med green
- ☆ = lt blue
- ✐ = med blue
- ω = lt purple
- | = Backstitch:
  pink letters—*dk pink*
  green letters—*dk green*
  blue letters—*dk blue*
  purple letters—*dk purple*
  yellow & orange letters—*dk rust*
  inner & outer borders—*med dk gray*

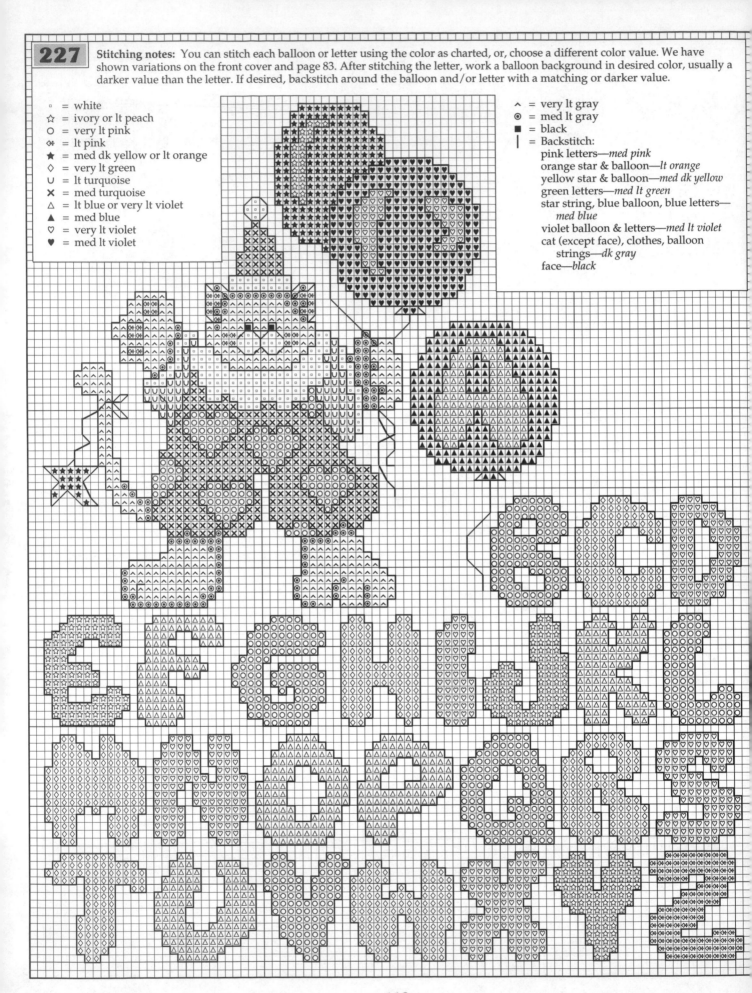

227 **Stitching notes:** You can stitch each balloon or letter using the color as charted, or, choose a different color value. We have shown variations on the front cover and page 83. After stitching the letter, work a balloon background in desired color, usually a darker value than the letter. If desired, backstitch around the balloon and/or letter with a matching or darker value.

□ = white
☆ = ivory or lt peach
○ = very lt pink
❋ = lt pink
★ = med dk yellow or lt orange
◇ = very lt green
∪ = lt turquoise
✕ = med turquoise
△ = lt blue or very lt violet
▲ = med blue
♡ = very lt violet
♥ = med lt violet

∧ = very lt gray
◉ = med lt gray
■ = black
| = Backstitch:
   pink letters—*med pink*
   orange star & balloon—*lt orange*
   yellow star & balloon—*med dk yellow*
   green letters—*med lt green*
   star string, blue balloon, blue letters—
     med blue
   violet balloon & letters—*med lt violet*
   cat (except face), clothes, balloon
     strings—*dk gray*
   face—*black*

228

^ = med red
● = dk red
♦ = black
| = Backstitch:
   border—*black*
   letters—*black*
   (*2 strands*)

229

▫ = lt blue-gray
○ = med lt gray
◉ = med gray
| = Backstitch: *black*

231

○ = lt taupe
● = med taupe
| = Backstitch:
    very dk brown

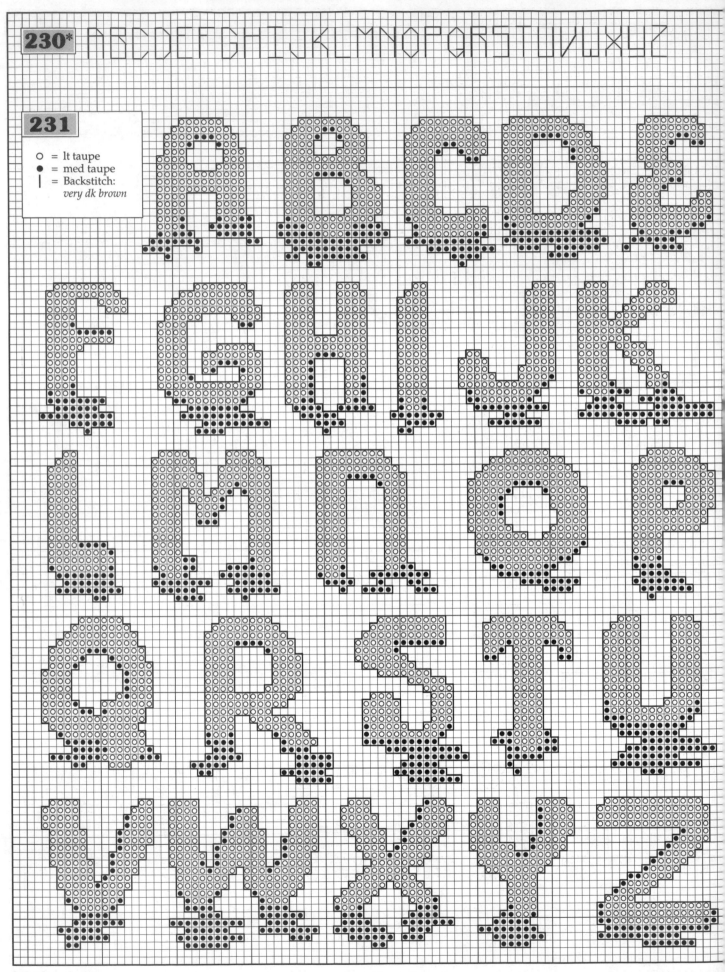

*Use desired color.

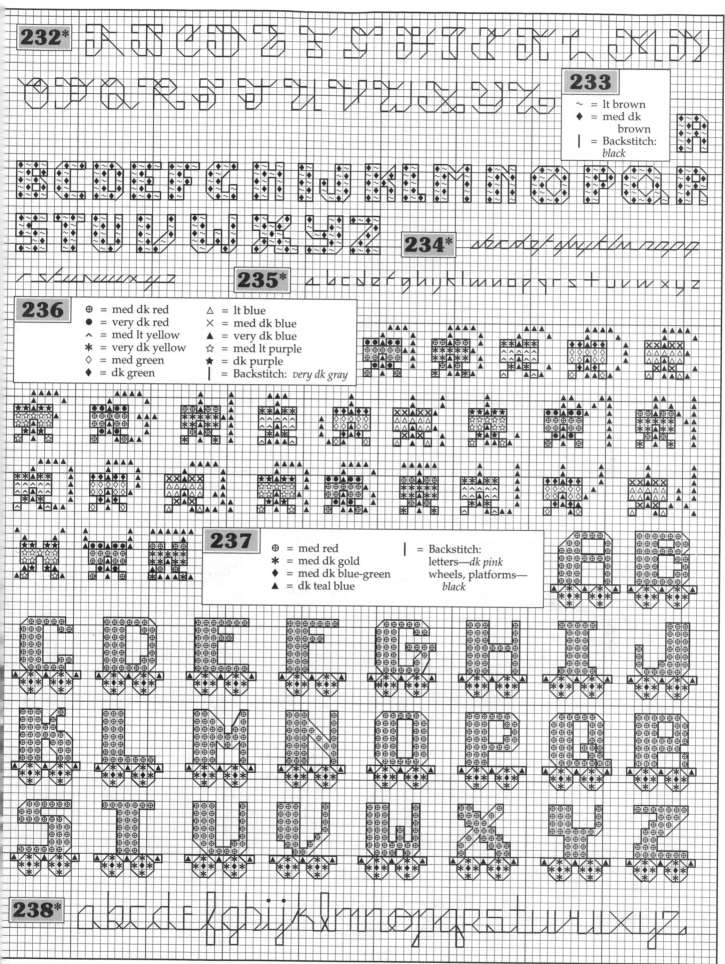

232*

233
- ~ = lt brown
- ♦ = med dk brown
- | = Backstitch: *black*

234*

235*

236
- ⊕ = med dk red
- ● = very dk red
- ∧ = med lt yellow
- ✳ = very dk yellow
- ◇ = med green
- ♦ = dk green
- △ = lt blue
- ✕ = med dk blue
- ▲ = very dk blue
- ☆ = med lt purple
- ★ = dk purple
- | = Backstitch: *very dk gray*

237
- ⊕ = med red
- ✳ = med dk gold
- ♦ = med dk blue-green
- ▲ = dk teal blue
- | = Backstitch:
  letters—*dk pink*
  wheels, platforms—*black*

238*

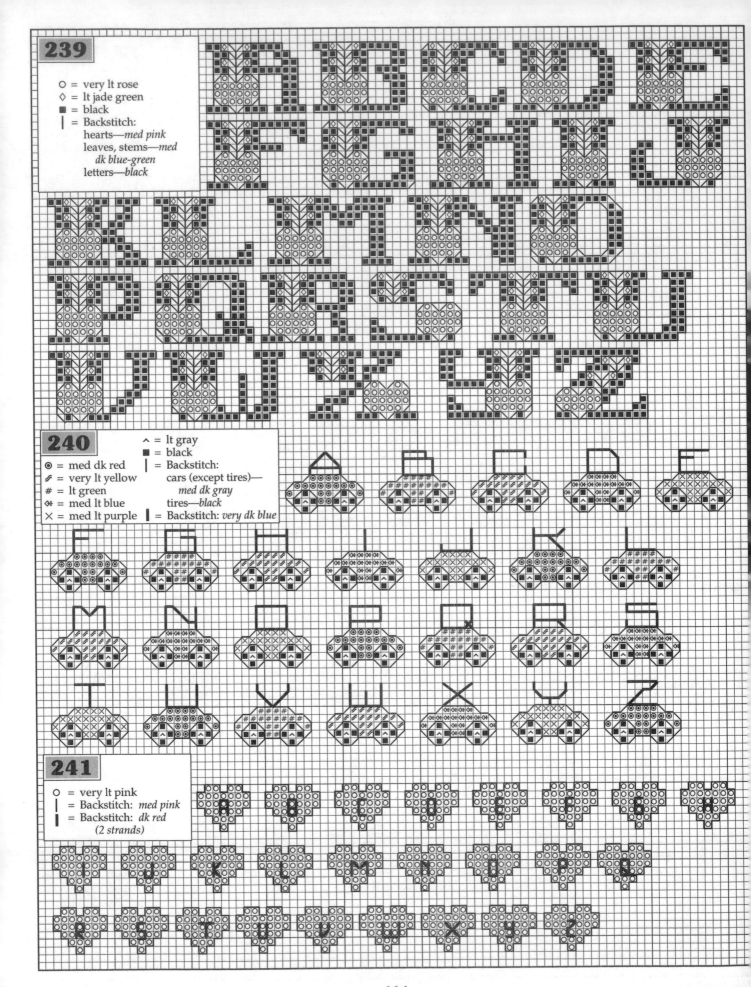

239

O = very lt rose
◇ = lt jade green
■ = black
| = Backstitch:
   hearts—*med pink*
   leaves, stems—*med*
     dk blue-green
   letters—*black*

240

⊙ = med dk red
𝄪 = very lt yellow
= lt green
❂ = med lt blue
× = med lt purple

^ = lt gray
■ = black
| = Backstitch:
   cars (except tires)—
     med dk gray
   tires—*black*
| = Backstitch: *very dk blue*

241

O = very lt pink
| = Backstitch: *med pink*
| = Backstitch: *dk red*
   (*2 strands*)

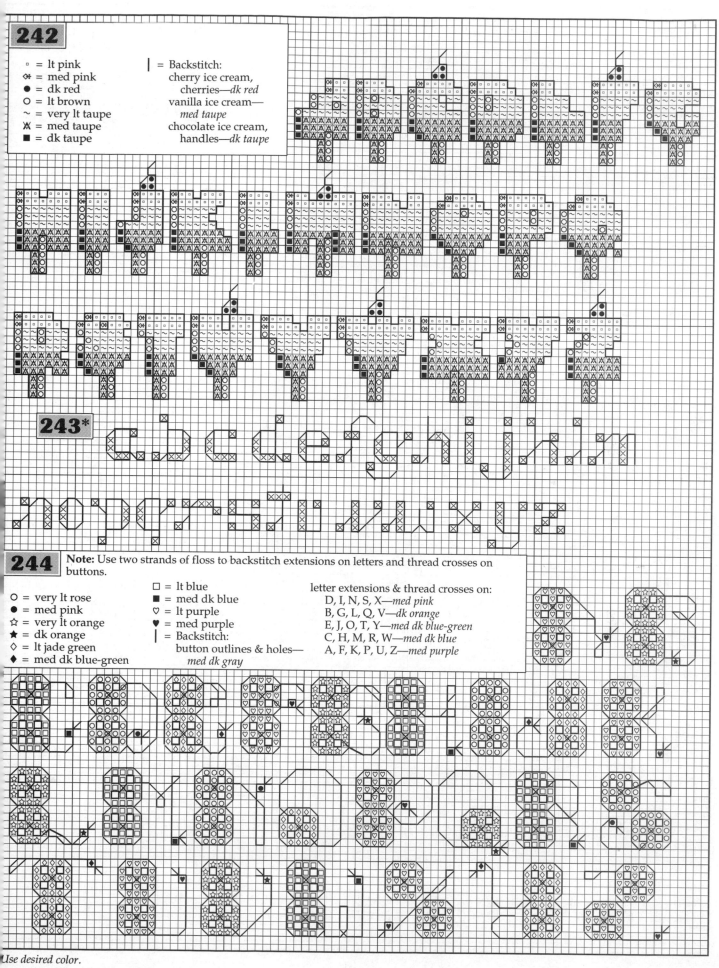

242

- ▫ = lt pink
- ✿ = med pink
- ● = dk red
- ○ = lt brown
- ~ = very lt taupe
- ✖ = med taupe
- ■ = dk taupe

| = Backstitch:
cherry ice cream,
    cherries—*dk red*
vanilla ice cream—
    med taupe
chocolate ice cream,
    handles—*dk taupe*

243*

244

Note: Use two strands of floss to backstitch extensions on letters and thread crosses on buttons.

- ○ = very lt rose
- ● = med pink
- ☆ = very lt orange
- ★ = dk orange
- ◇ = lt jade green
- ◆ = med dk blue-green

- ▢ = lt blue
- ■ = med dk blue
- ♡ = lt purple
- ♥ = med purple
- | = Backstitch:
  button outlines & holes—
      med dk gray

letter extensions & thread crosses on:
D, I, N, S, X—*med pink*
B, G, L, Q, V—*dk orange*
E, J, O, T, Y—*med dk blue-green*
C, H, M, R, W—*med dk blue*
A, F, K, P, U, Z—*med purple*

*Use desired color.

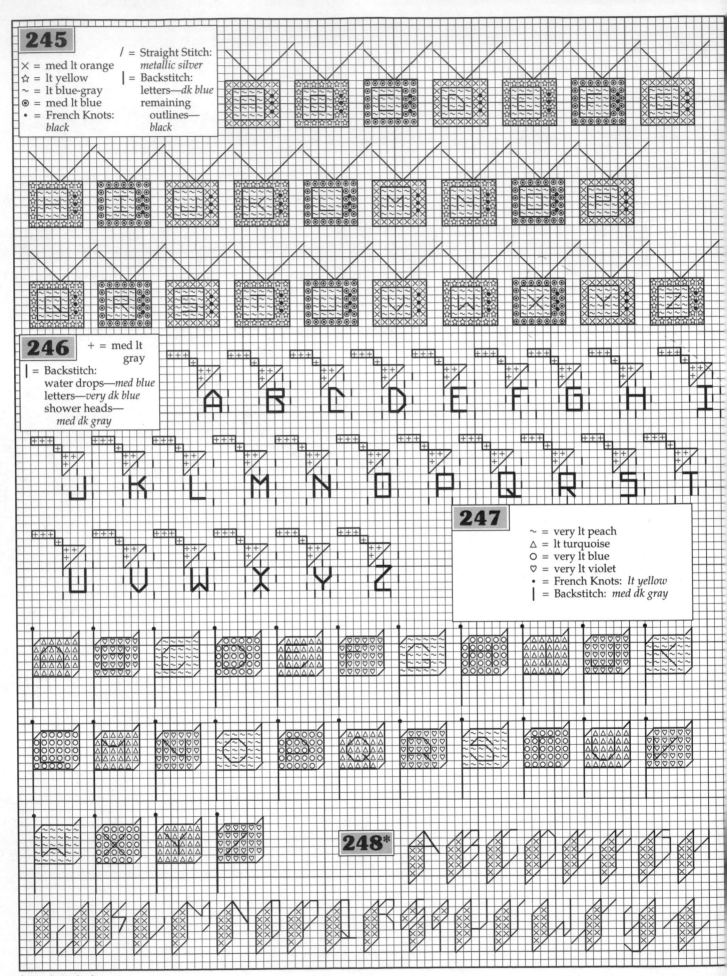

245

× = med lt orange
☆ = lt yellow
~ = lt blue-gray
⊙ = med lt blue
• = French Knots: black

/ = Straight Stitch: metallic silver

| = Backstitch: letters—dk blue remaining outlines—black

246

+ = med lt gray

| = Backstitch:
water drops—med blue
letters—very dk blue
shower heads—med dk gray

247

~ = very lt peach
△ = lt turquoise
○ = very lt blue
♡ = very lt violet
• = French Knots: lt yellow
| = Backstitch: med dk gray

248*

*Use desired color.

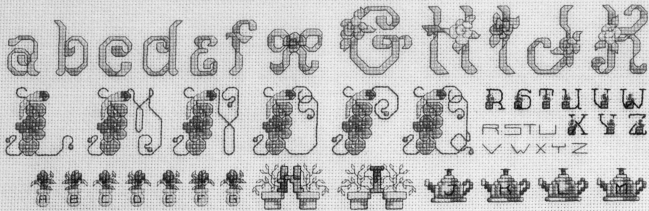

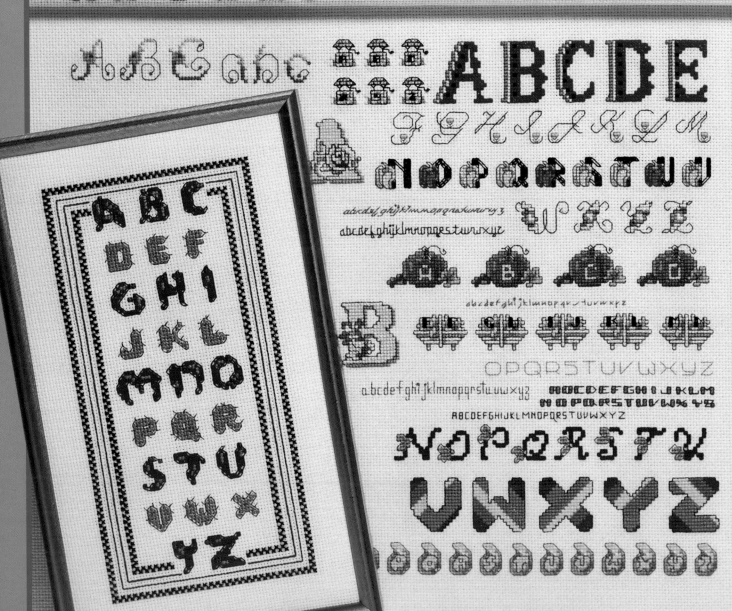

From The Garden Design Directory

The charts are in numerical order beginning on page 122.

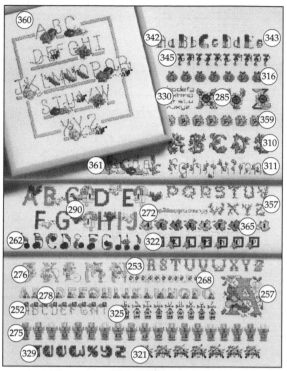

page 117

page 118

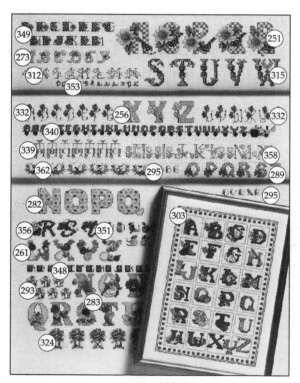

page 119

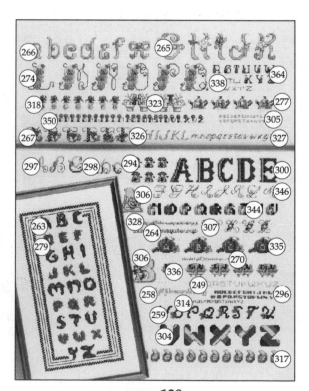

page 120

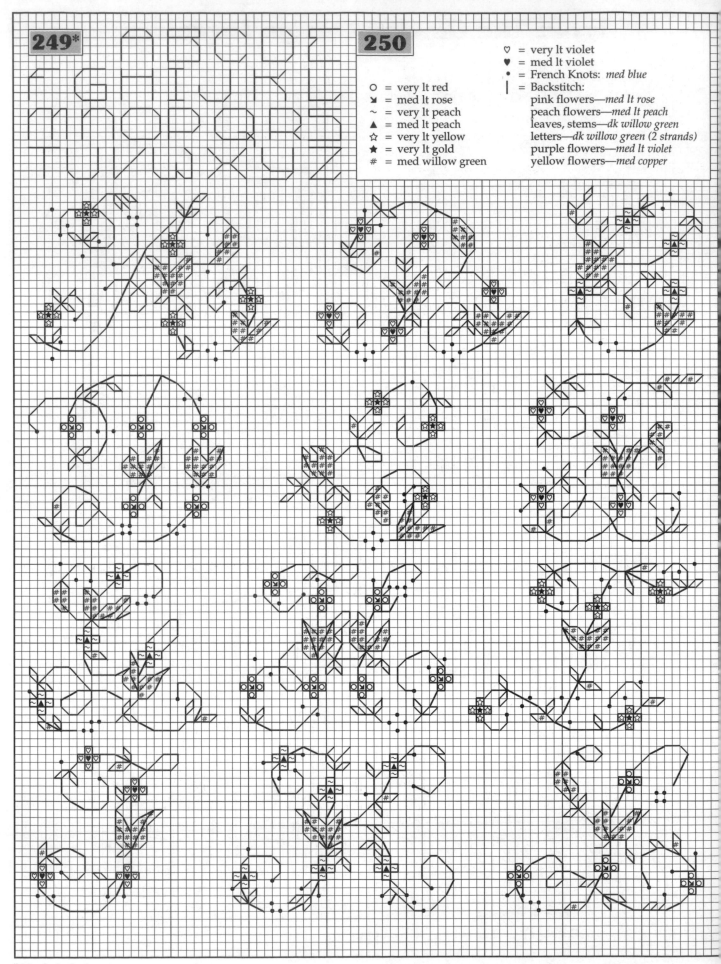

249*

250

♡ = very lt violet
♥ = med lt violet
• = French Knots: *med blue*
| = Backstitch:

○ = very lt red
⋈ = med lt rose
~ = very lt peach
▲ = med lt peach
☆ = very lt yellow
★ = very lt gold
= med willow green

pink flowers—*med lt rose*
peach flowers—*med lt peach*
leaves, stems—*dk willow green*
letters—*dk willow green (2 strands)*
purple flowers—*med lt violet*
yellow flowers—*med copper*

*** *Use desired color.*

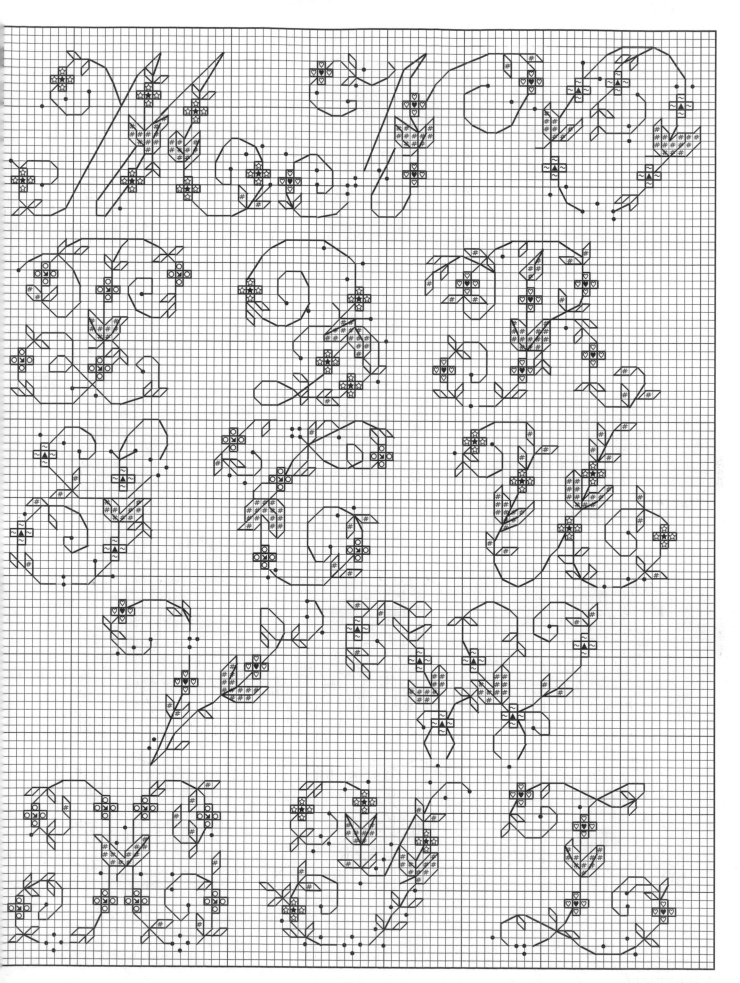

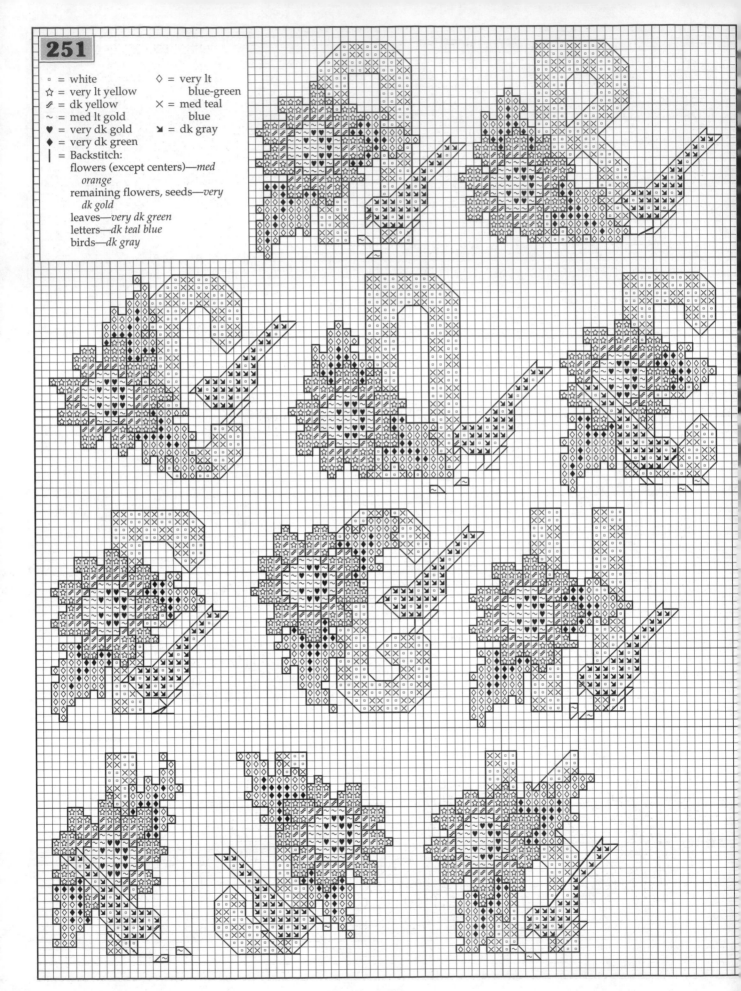

251

□ = white
☆ = very lt yellow
✱ = dk yellow
~ = med lt gold
♥ = very dk gold
♦ = very dk green
| = Backstitch:
    flowers (except centers)—*med orange*
    remaining flowers, seeds—*very dk gold*
    leaves—*very dk green*
    letters—*dk teal blue*
    birds—*dk gray*

◇ = very lt blue-green
✕ = med teal blue
◢ = dk gray

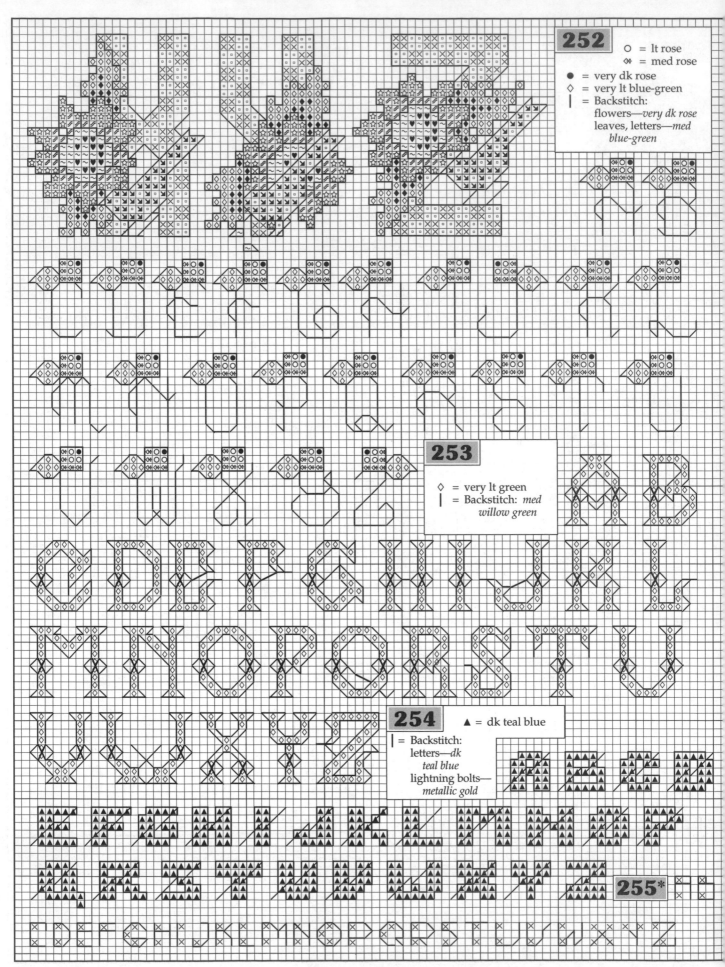

252

○ = lt rose
❋ = med rose
● = very dk rose
◇ = very lt blue-green
| = Backstitch:
flowers—*very dk rose*
leaves, letters—*med blue-green*

253

◇ = very lt green
| = Backstitch: *med willow green*

254

▲ = dk teal blue
| = Backstitch:
letters—*dk teal blue*
lightning bolts—*metallic gold*

255*

*Use desired color.

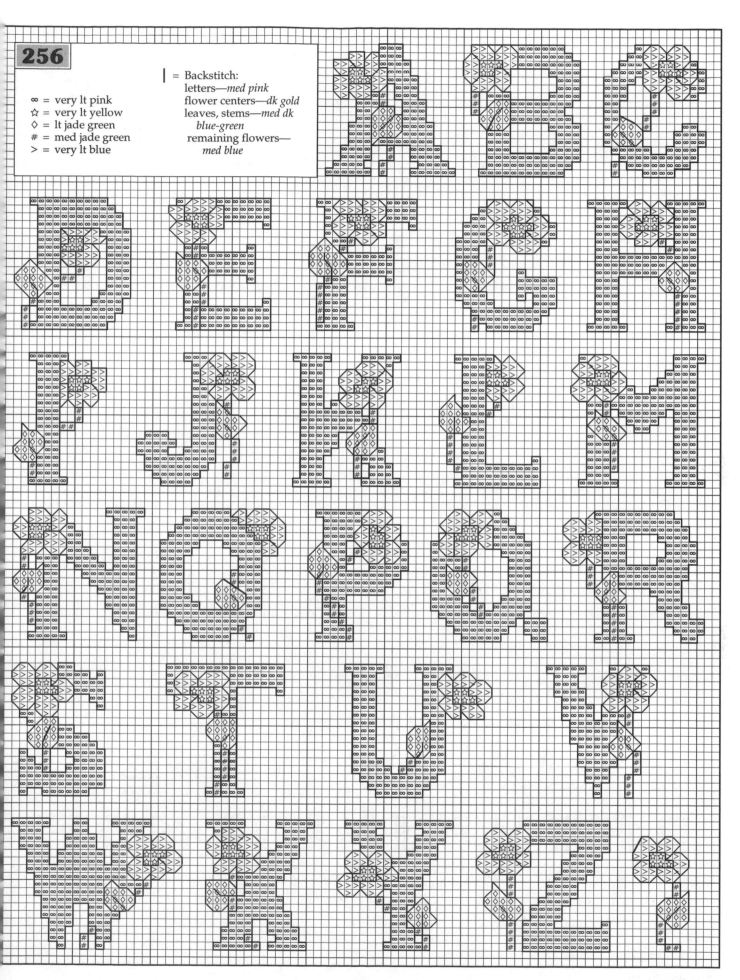

256

| = Backstitch:
letters—*med pink*
flower centers—*dk gold*
leaves, stems—*med dk blue-green*
remaining flowers—*med blue*

∞ = very lt pink
☆ = very lt yellow
◇ = lt jade green
= med jade green
> = very lt blue

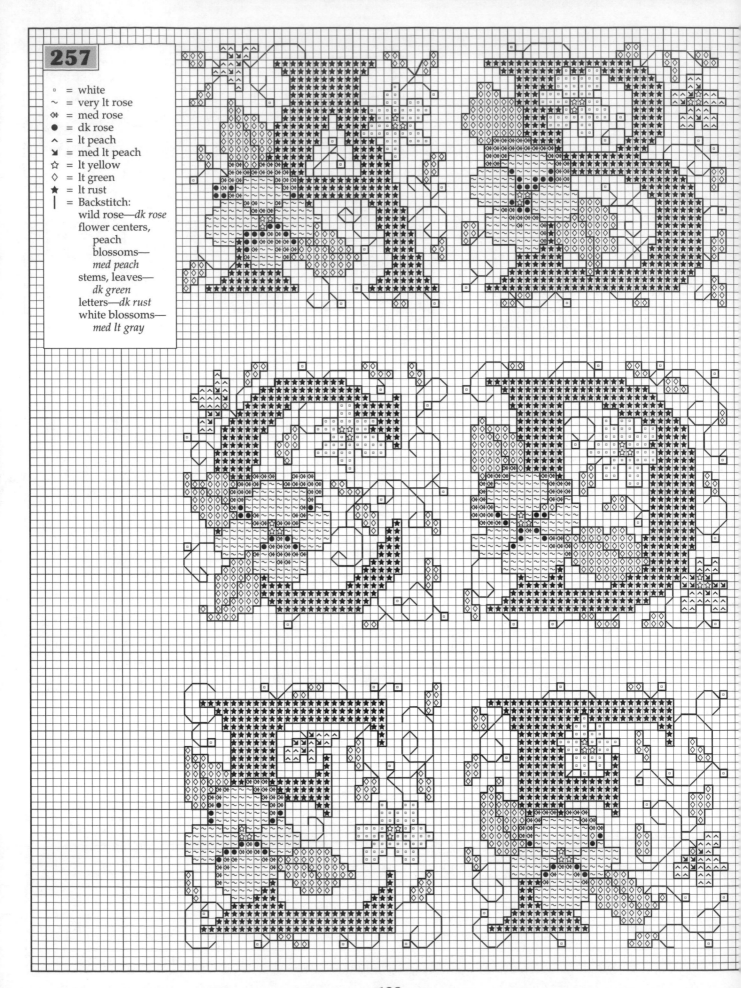

257

□	= white
~	= very lt rose
✿	= med rose
●	= dk rose
∧	= lt peach
⋈	= med lt peach
☆	= lt yellow
◇	= lt green
★	= lt rust
│	= Backstitch:

wild rose—*dk rose*
flower centers,
peach
blossoms—
med peach
stems, leaves—
dk green
letters—*dk rust*
white blossoms—
med lt gray

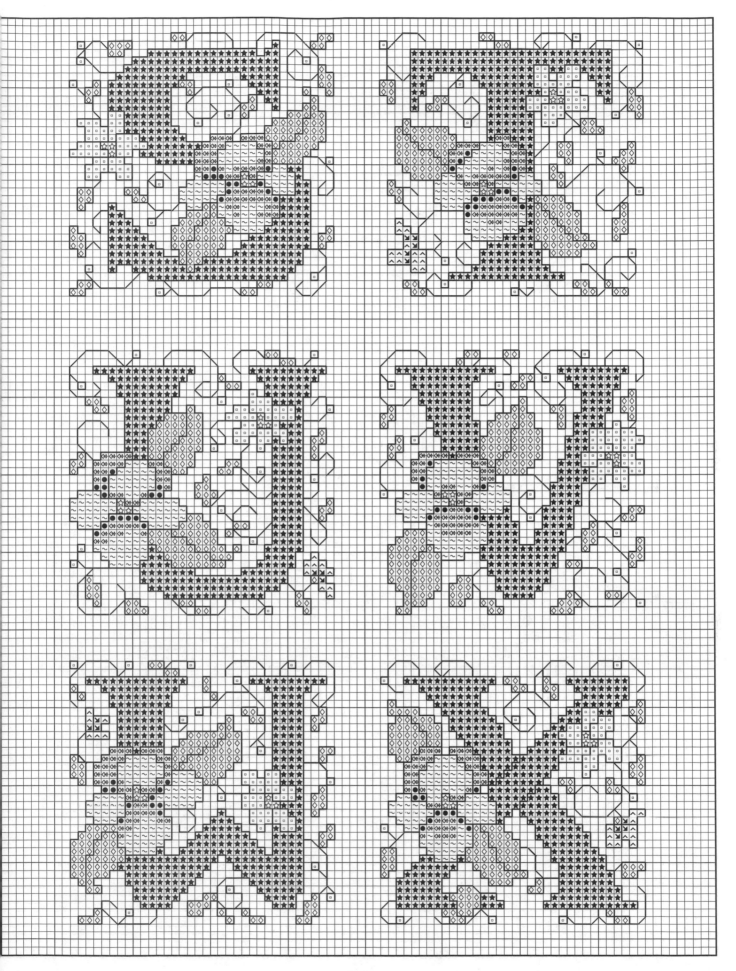

131

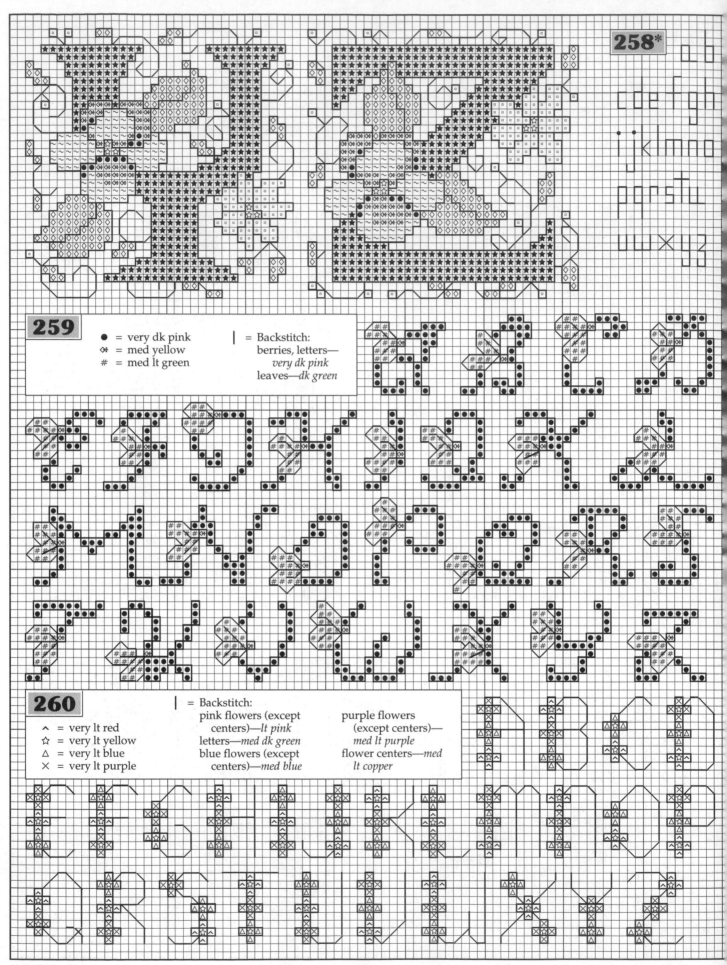

258*

259
- ● = very dk pink
- ✧ = med yellow
- # = med lt green

| = Backstitch:
berries, letters—
very dk pink
leaves—*dk green*

260
- ＾ = very lt red
- ☆ = very lt yellow
- △ = very lt blue
- × = very lt purple

| = Backstitch:
pink flowers (except centers)—*lt pink*
letters—*med dk green*
blue flowers (except centers)—*med blue*
purple flowers (except centers)—*med lt purple*
flower centers—*med lt copper*

*Use desired color.

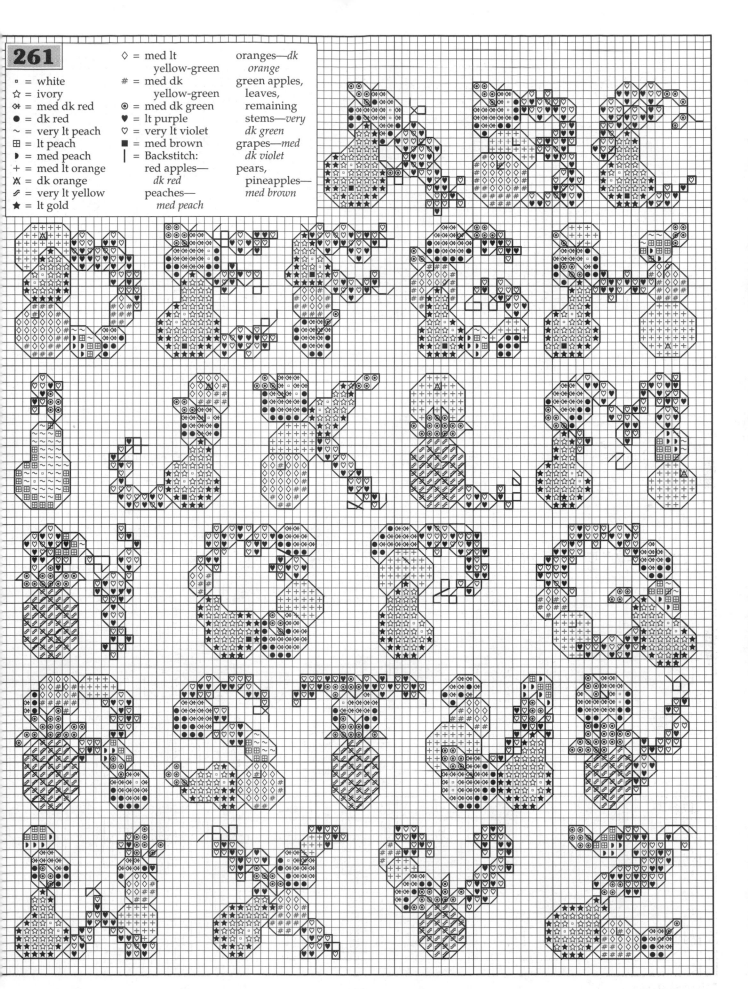

261

- □ = white
- ☆ = ivory
- ✾ = med dk red
- ● = dk red
- ~ = very lt peach
- ⊞ = lt peach
- ◗ = med peach
- + = med lt orange
- ⋈ = dk orange
- ✐ = very lt yellow
- ★ = lt gold

- ◇ = med lt yellow-green
- # = med dk yellow-green
- ◉ = med dk green
- ♥ = lt purple
- ♡ = very lt violet
- ■ = med brown
- | = Backstitch: red apples— *dk red* peaches— *med peach*

oranges—*dk orange*
green apples, leaves, remaining stems—*very dk green* grapes—*med dk violet* pears, pineapples— *med brown*

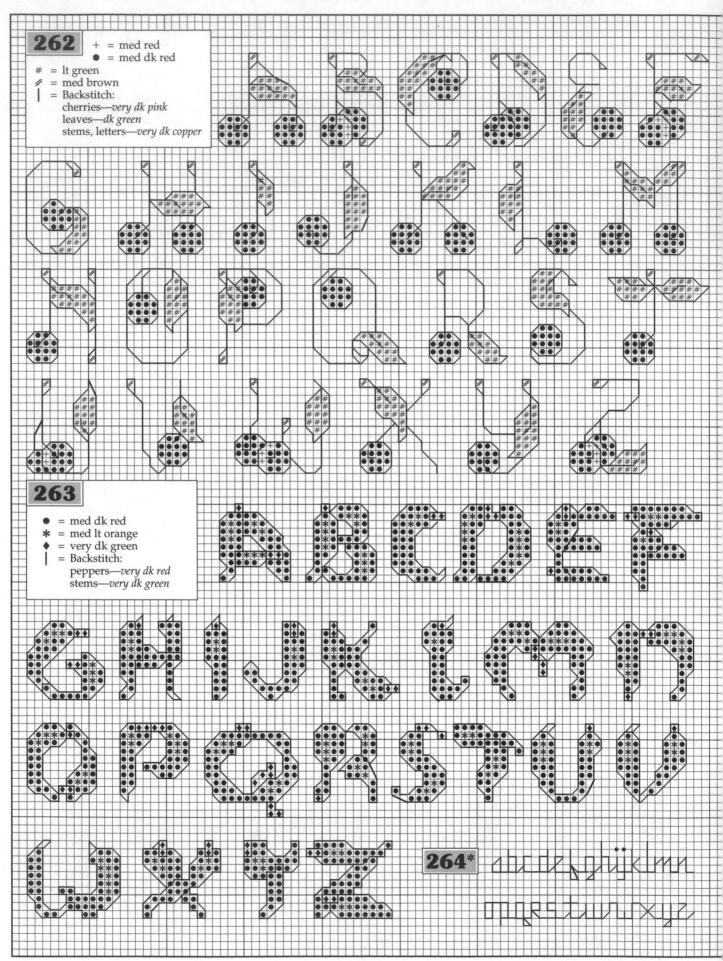

262

+ = med red
● = med dk red
= lt green
✎ = med brown
| = Backstitch:
   cherries—*very dk pink*
   leaves—*dk green*
   stems, letters—*very dk copper*

263

● = med dk red
✳ = med lt orange
◆ = very dk green
| = Backstitch:
   peppers—*very dk red*
   stems—*very dk green*

264*

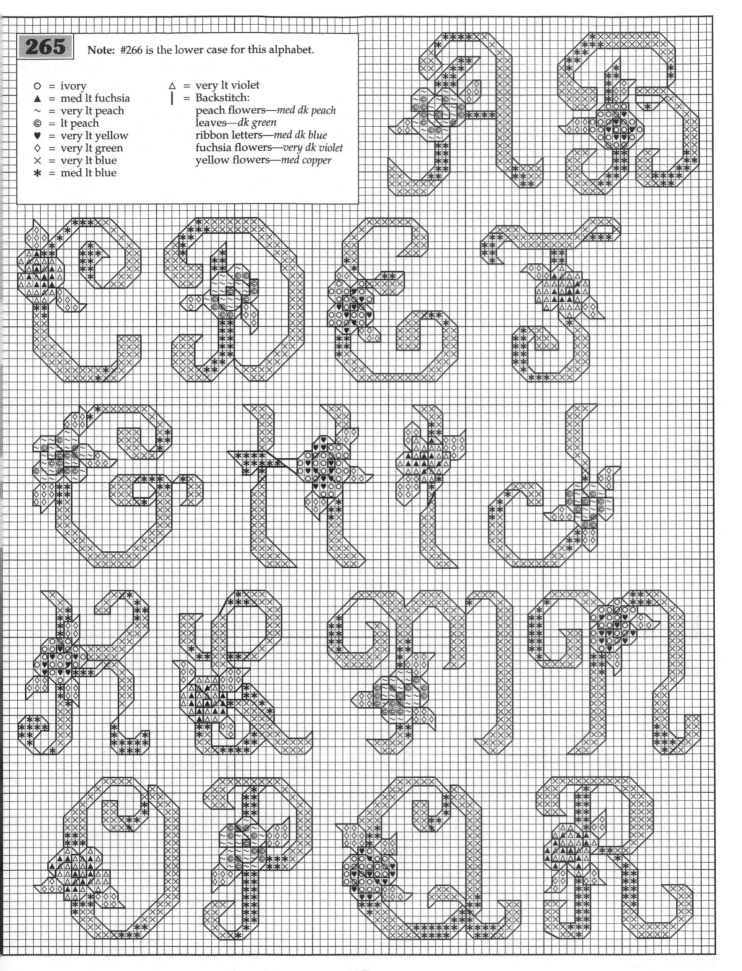

265 Note: #266 is the lower case for this alphabet.

○ = ivory
▲ = med lt fuchsia
~ = very lt peach
© = lt peach
♥ = very lt yellow
◇ = very lt green
✕ = very lt blue
✳ = med lt blue

△ = very lt violet
| = Backstitch:
    peach flowers—*med dk peach*
    leaves—*dk green*
    ribbon letters—*med dk blue*
    fuchsia flowers—*very dk violet*
    yellow flowers—*med copper*

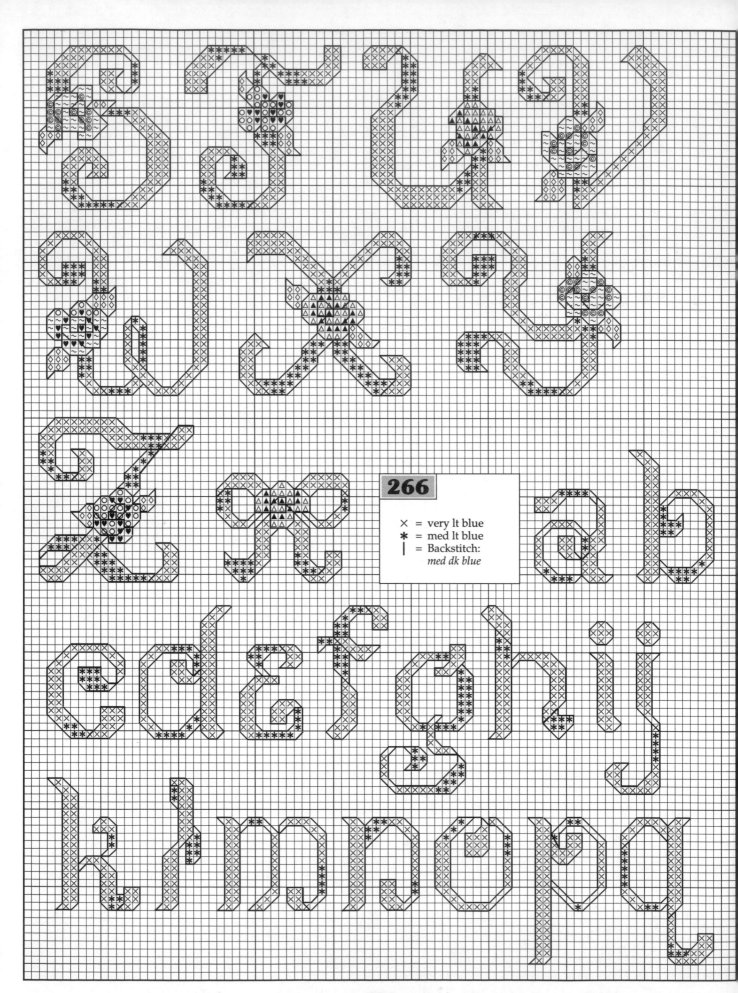

266

× = very lt blue
∗ = med lt blue
| = Backstitch:
   med dk blue

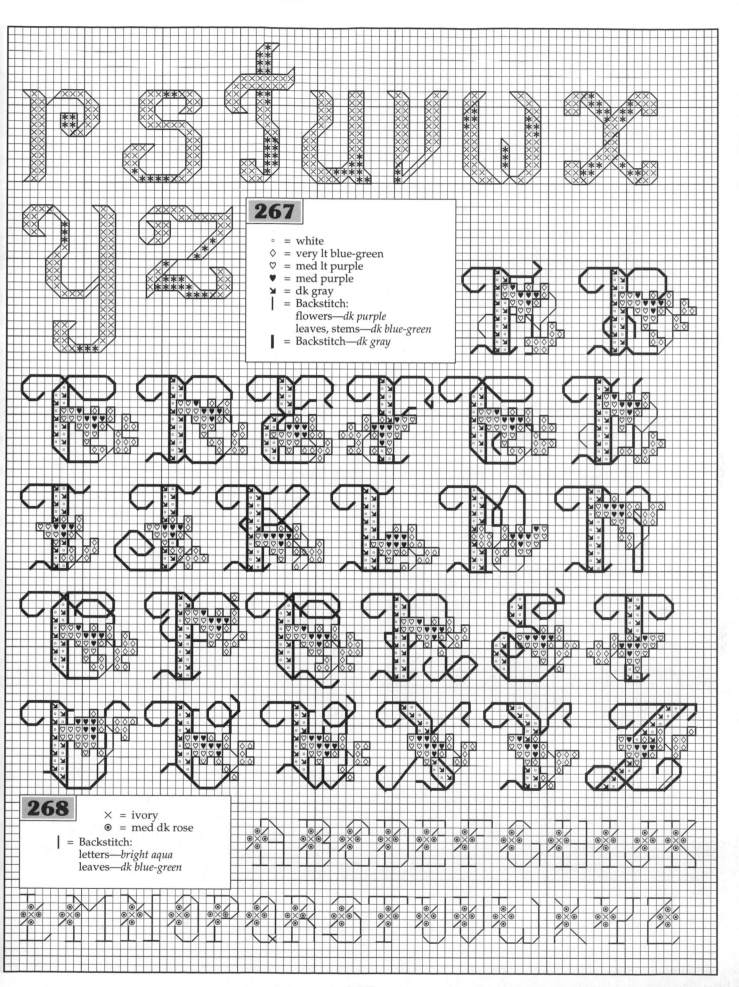

267

- □ = white
- ◇ = very lt blue-green
- ♡ = med lt purple
- ♥ = med purple
- ⋈ = dk gray
- | = Backstitch:
  flowers—*dk purple*
  leaves, stems—*dk blue-green*
- | = Backstitch—*dk gray*

268

- × = ivory
- ⊙ = med dk rose
- | = Backstitch:
  letters—*bright aqua*
  leaves—*dk blue-green*

137

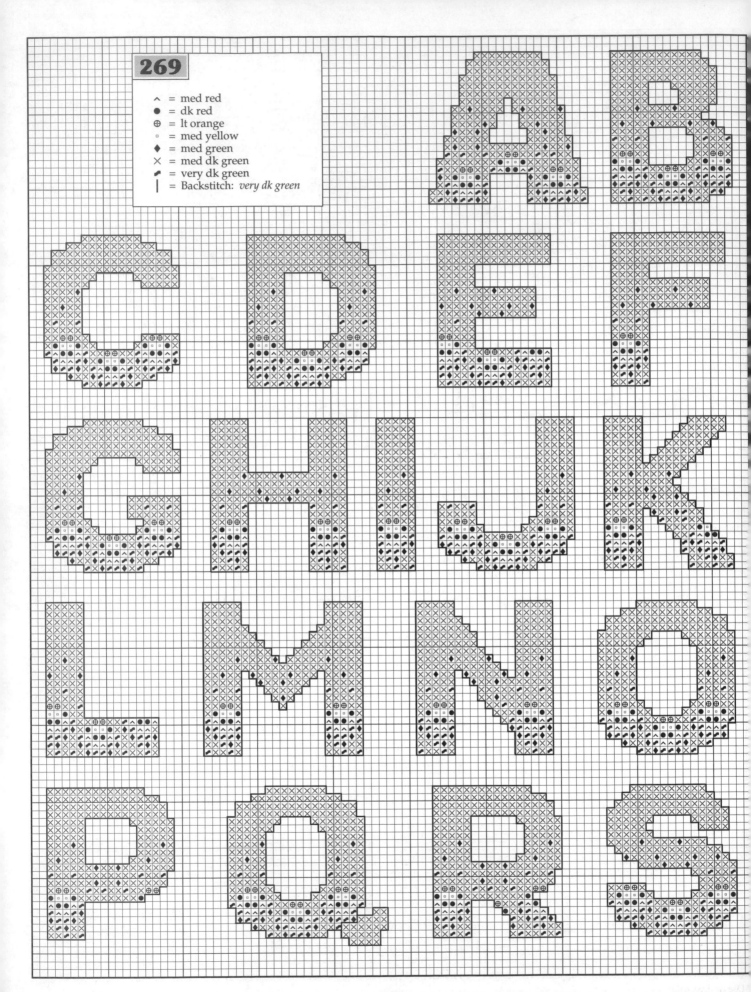

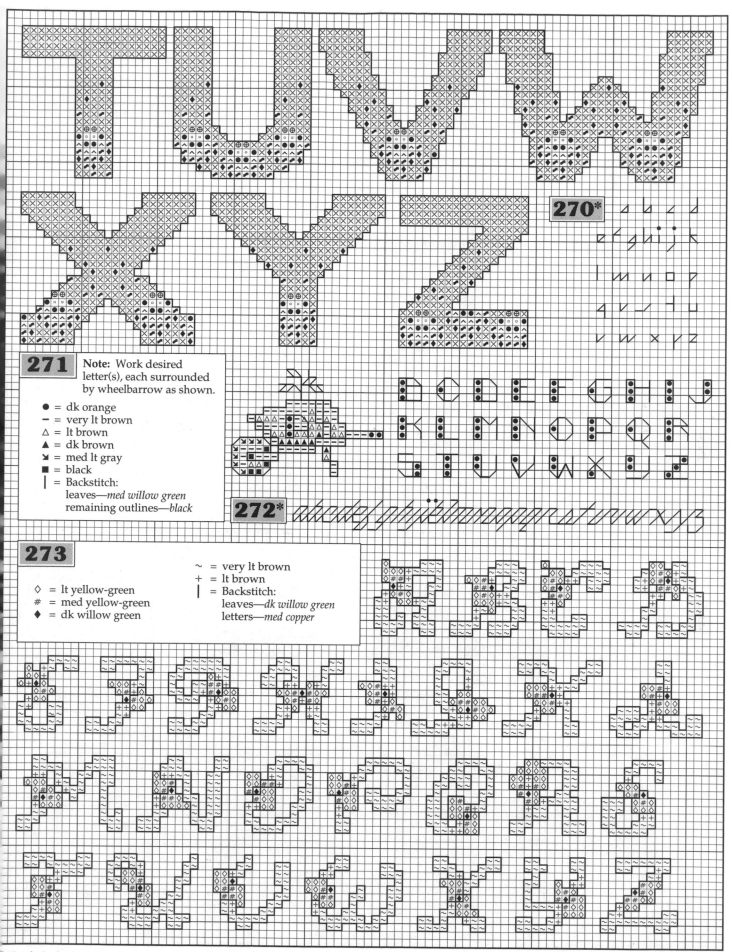

270*

271 Note: Work desired letter(s), each surrounded by wheelbarrow as shown.

● = dk orange
− = very lt brown
△ = lt brown
▲ = dk brown
⋈ = med lt gray
■ = black
| = Backstitch:
   leaves—*med willow green*
   remaining outlines—*black*

272*

273

◇ = lt yellow-green
= med yellow-green
◆ = dk willow green

~ = very lt brown
+ = lt brown
| = Backstitch:
   leaves—*dk willow green*
   letters—*med copper*

Use desired color.

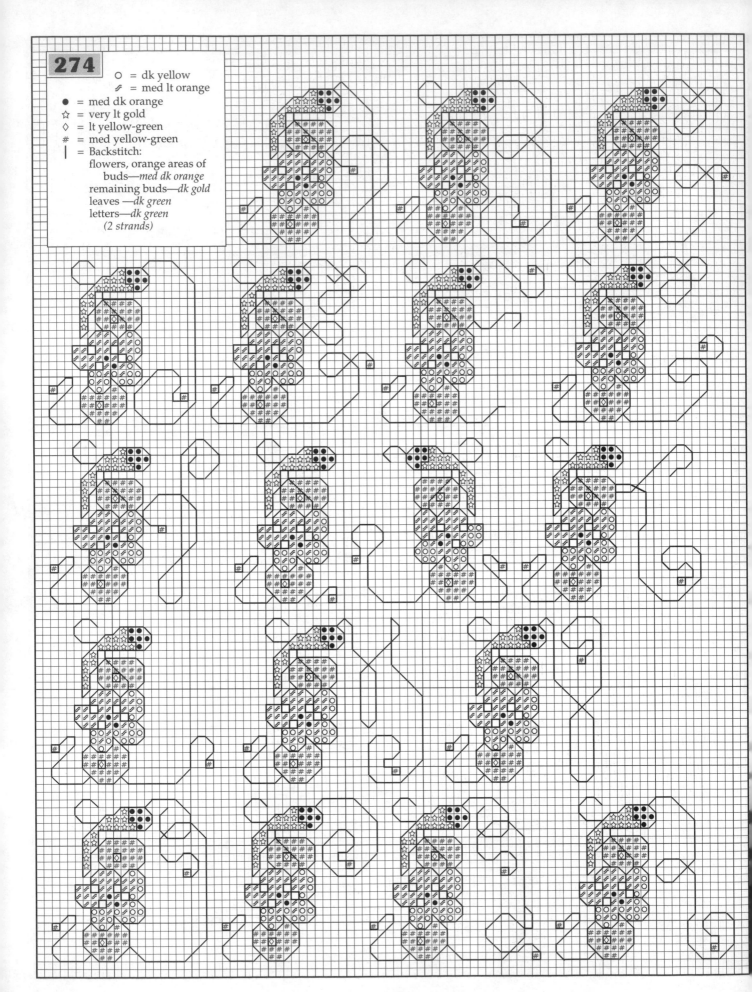

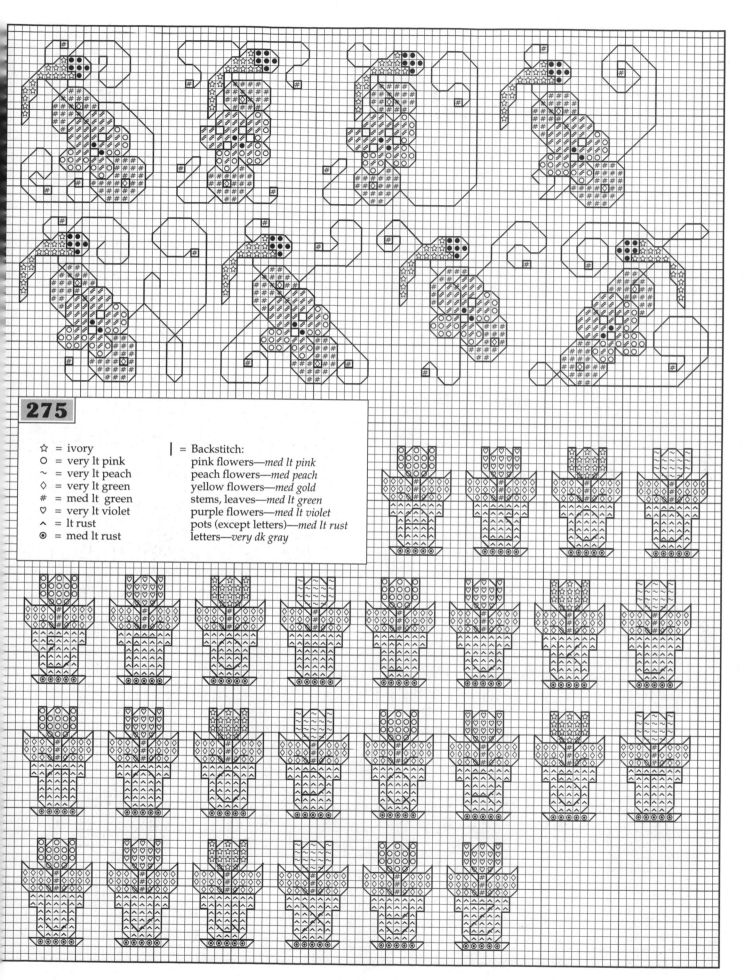

275

☆ = ivory
○ = very lt pink
~ = very lt peach
◇ = very lt green
= med lt green
♡ = very lt violet
^ = lt rust
◉ = med lt rust

| = Backstitch:
   pink flowers—*med lt pink*
   peach flowers—*med peach*
   yellow flowers—*med gold*
   stems, leaves—*med lt green*
   purple flowers—*med lt violet*
   pots (except letters)—*med lt rust*
   letters—*very dk gray*

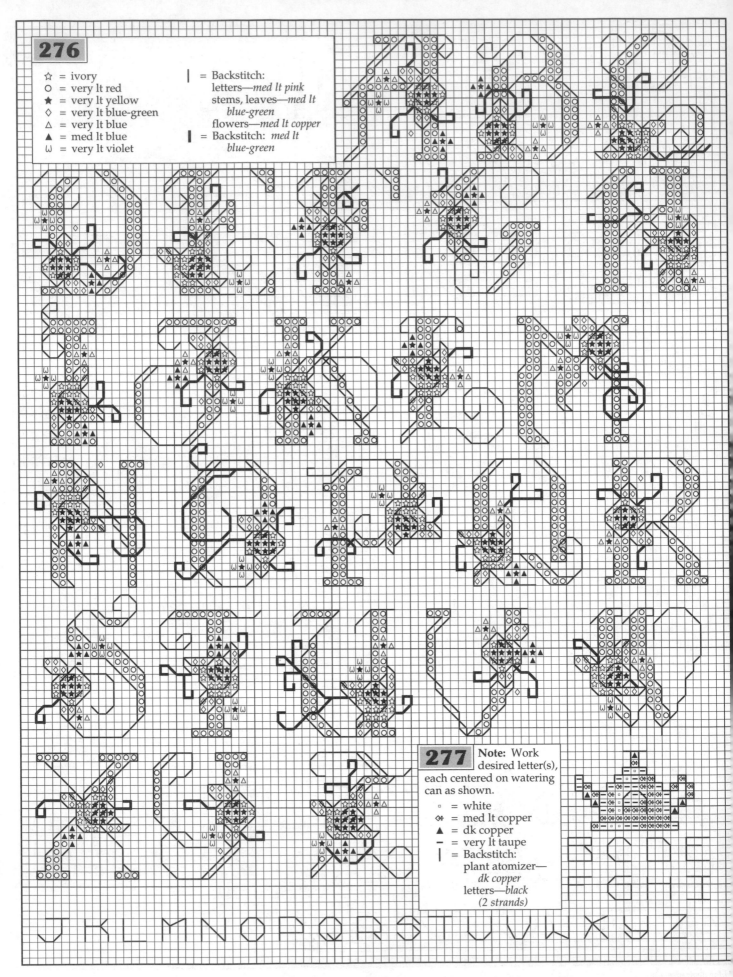

276

☆ = ivory
○ = very lt red
★ = very lt yellow
◇ = very lt blue-green
△ = very lt blue
▲ = med lt blue
ω = very lt violet

| = Backstitch:
letters—*med lt pink*
stems, leaves—*med lt blue-green*
flowers—*med lt copper*
| = Backstitch: *med lt blue-green*

277 **Note:** Work desired letter(s), each centered on watering can as shown.

▫ = white
⬧ = med lt copper
▲ = dk copper
− = very lt taupe
| = Backstitch:
plant atomizer—*dk copper*
letters—*black (2 strands)*

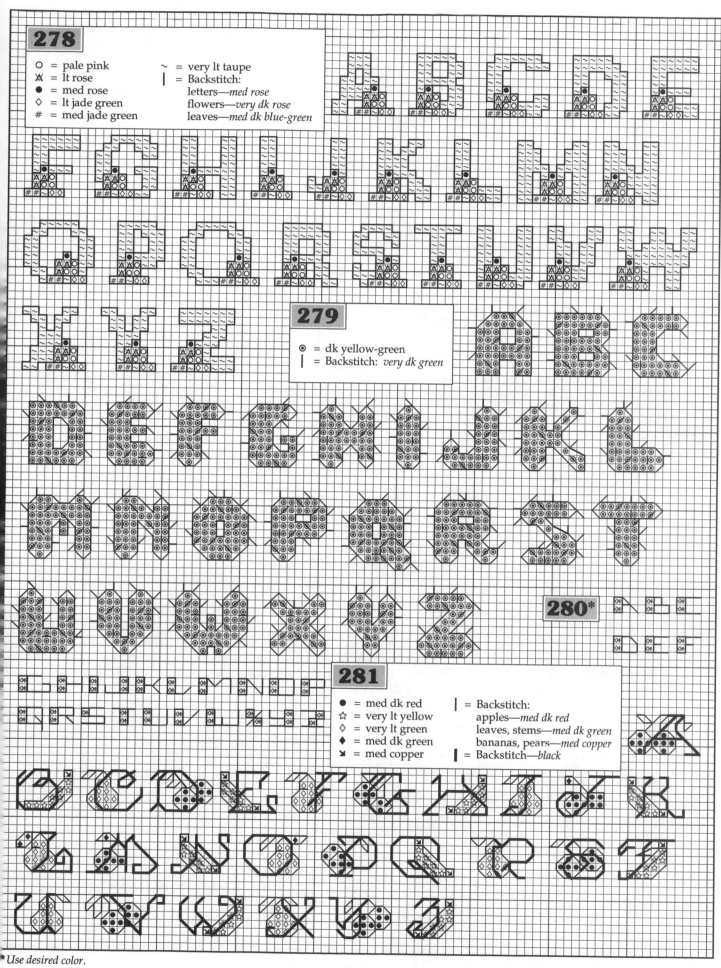

278

○ = pale pink
✗ = lt rose
● = med rose
◇ = lt jade green
= med jade green

~ = very lt taupe
| = Backstitch:
   letters—*med rose*
   flowers—*very dk rose*
   leaves—*med dk blue-green*

279

⊙ = dk yellow-green
| = Backstitch: *very dk green*

280*

281

● = med dk red
☆ = very lt yellow
◇ = very lt green
◆ = med dk green
⅄ = med copper

| = Backstitch:
   apples—*med dk red*
   leaves, stems—*med dk green*
   bananas, pears—*med copper*
| = Backstitch—*black*

* *Use desired color.*

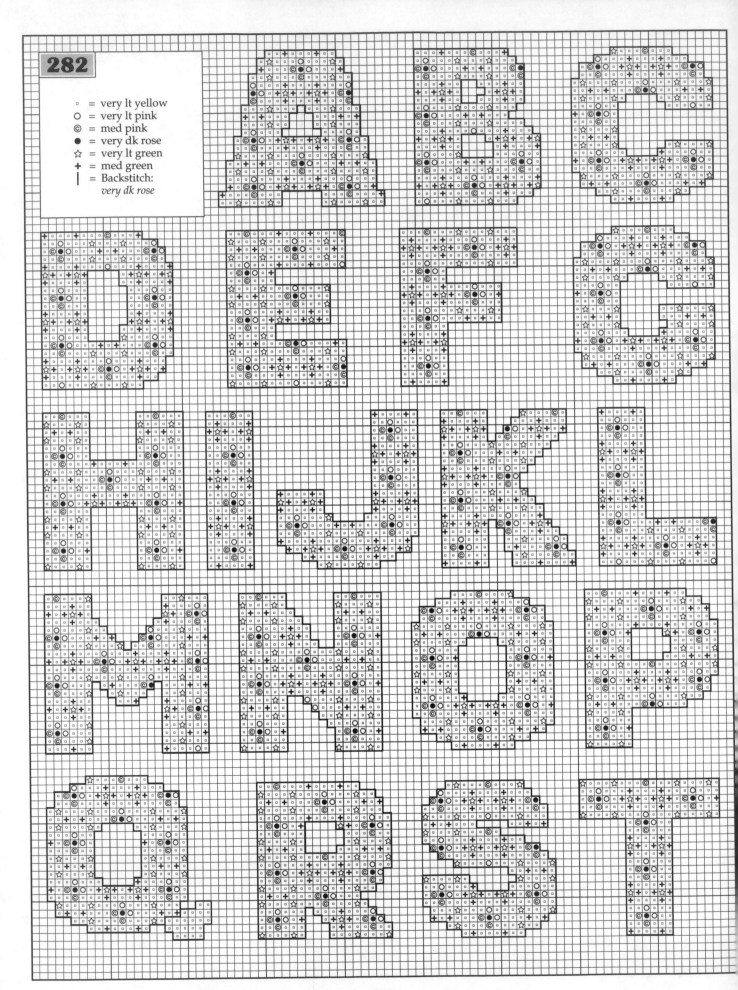

282

= very lt yellow
= very lt pink
= med pink
= very dk rose
= very lt green
= med green
= Backstitch:
very dk rose

144

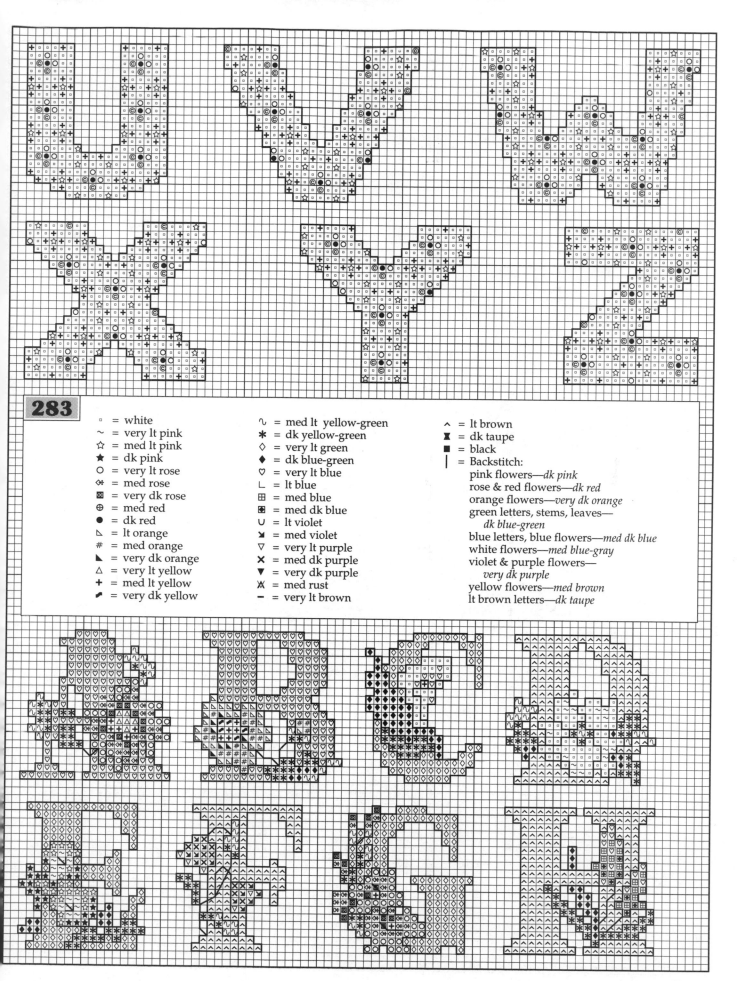

283

▫ = white	∿ = med lt yellow-green	∧ = lt brown
~ = very lt pink	✳ = dk yellow-green	⊠ = dk taupe
☆ = med lt pink	◇ = very lt green	■ = black
★ = dk pink	◆ = dk blue-green	∣ = Backstitch:
○ = very lt rose	♡ = very lt blue	pink flowers—*dk pink*
✿ = med rose	∟ = lt blue	rose & red flowers—*dk red*
▩ = very dk rose	⊞ = med blue	orange flowers—*very dk orange*
⊕ = med red	▣ = med dk blue	green letters, stems, leaves—
● = dk red	∪ = lt violet	*dk blue-green*
◹ = lt orange	⋈ = med violet	blue letters, blue flowers—*med dk blue*
# = med orange	▽ = very lt purple	white flowers—*med blue-gray*
◣ = very dk orange	✕ = med dk purple	violet & purple flowers—
△ = very lt yellow	▼ = very dk purple	*very dk purple*
+ = med lt yellow	✖ = med rust	yellow flowers—*med brown*
✔ = very dk yellow	— = very lt brown	lt brown letters—*dk taupe*

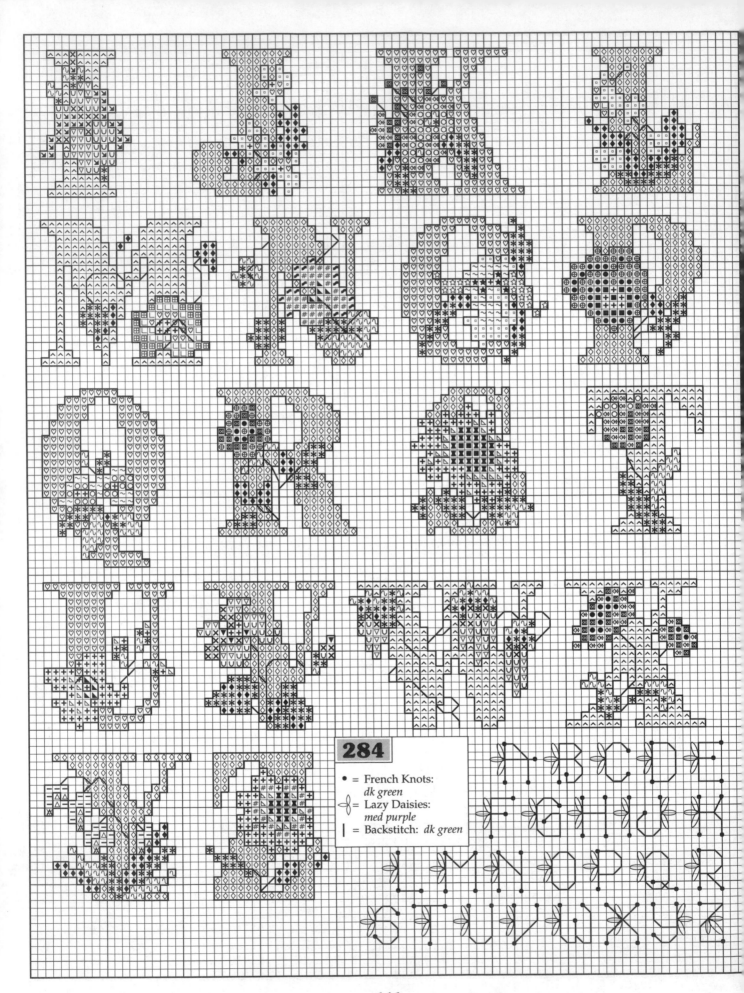

284

• = French Knots: *dk green*
❀ = Lazy Daisies: *med purple*
| = Backstitch: *dk green*

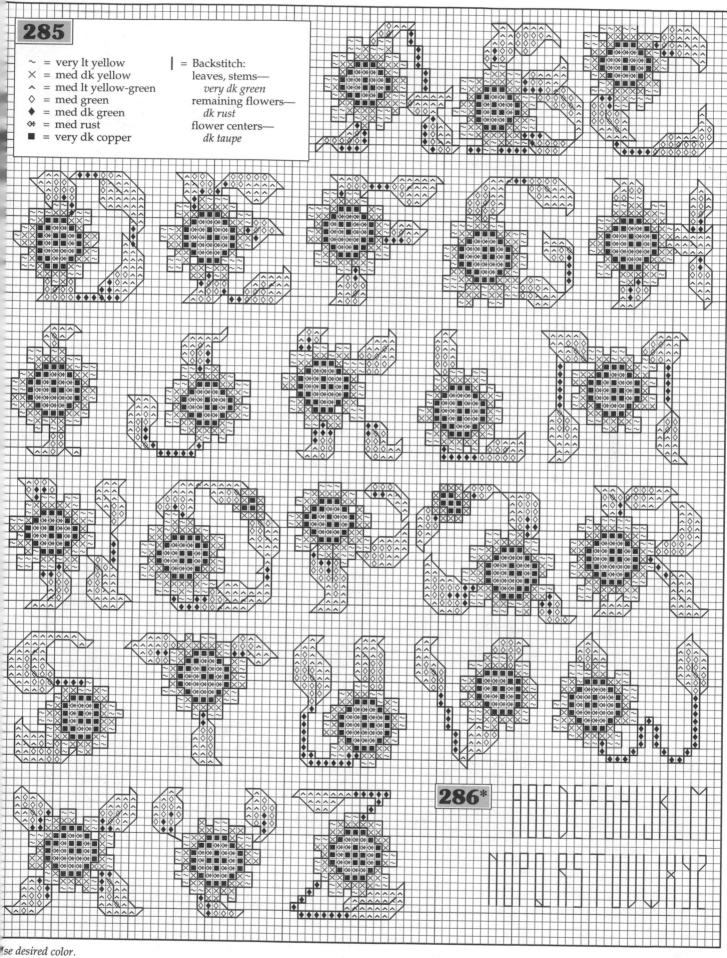

285

~ = very lt yellow	= Backstitch:
✕ = med dk yellow	leaves, stems—
∧ = med lt yellow-green	*very dk green*
◇ = med green	remaining flowers—
◆ = med dk green	*dk rust*
✤ = med rust	flower centers—
■ = very dk copper	*dk taupe*

286*

se desired color.

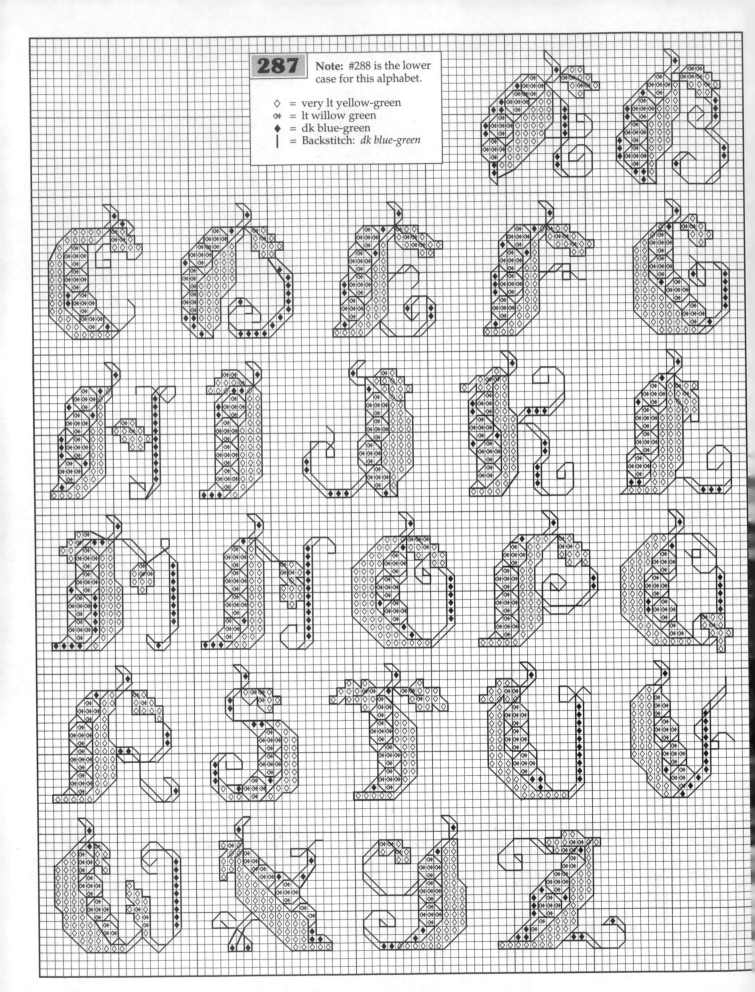

287 **Note:** #288 is the lower case for this alphabet.

◇ = very lt yellow-green
✢ = lt willow green
◆ = dk blue-green
| = Backstitch: *dk blue-green*

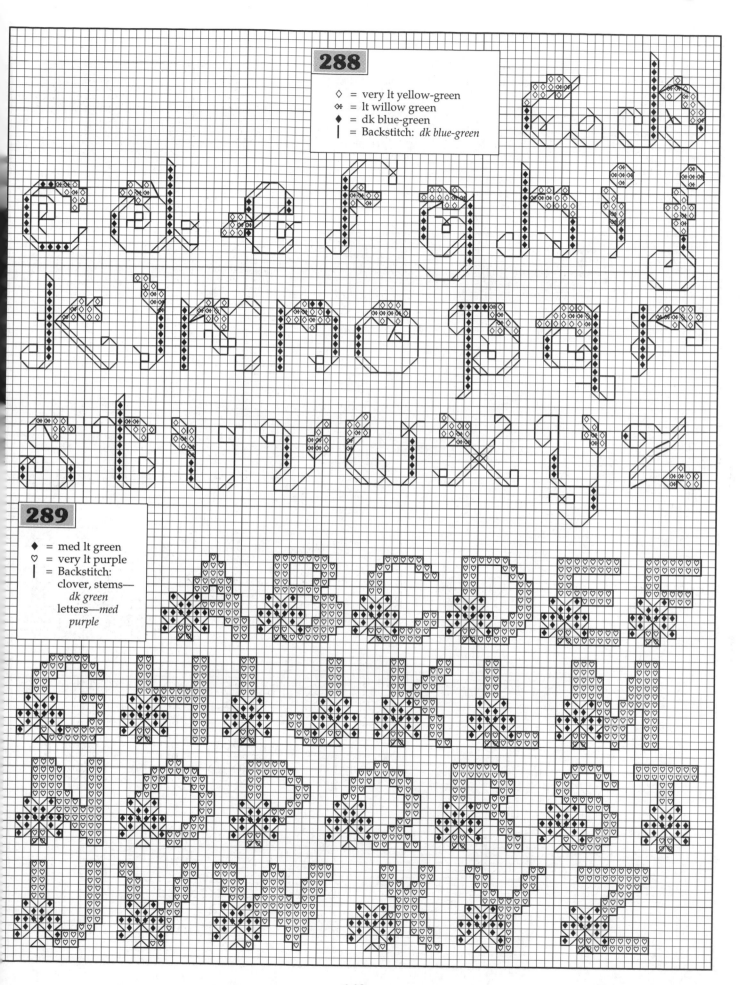

288

◇ = very lt yellow-green
✿ = lt willow green
◆ = dk blue-green
| = Backstitch: *dk blue-green*

289

◆ = med lt green
♡ = very lt purple
| = Backstitch:
 clover, stems—
  dk green
 letters—*med*
  purple

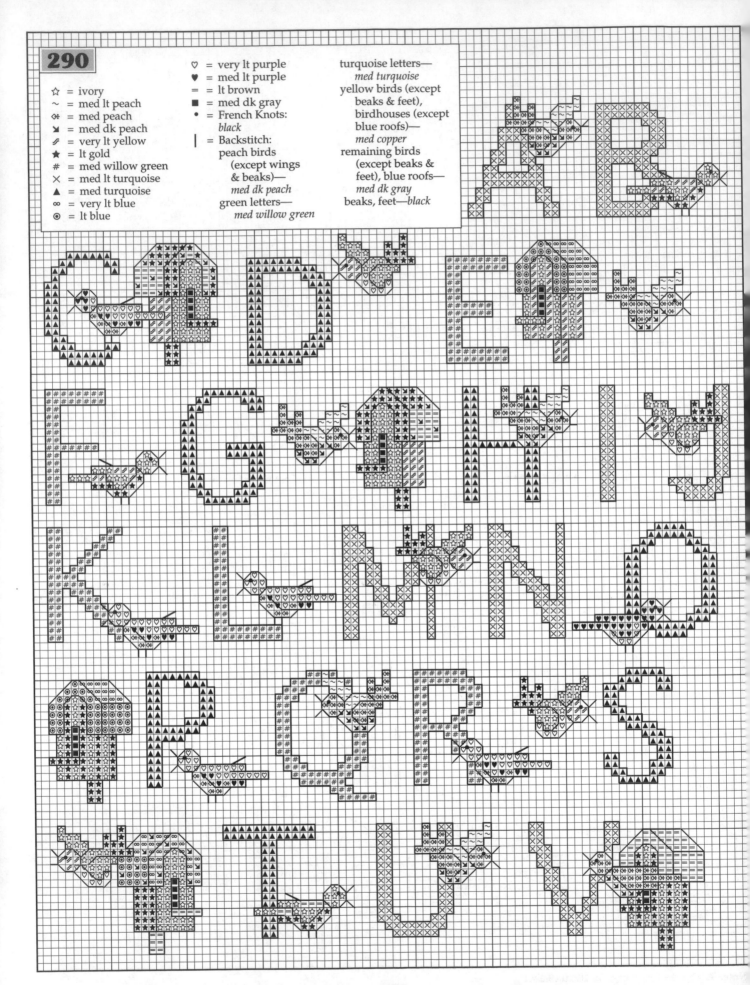

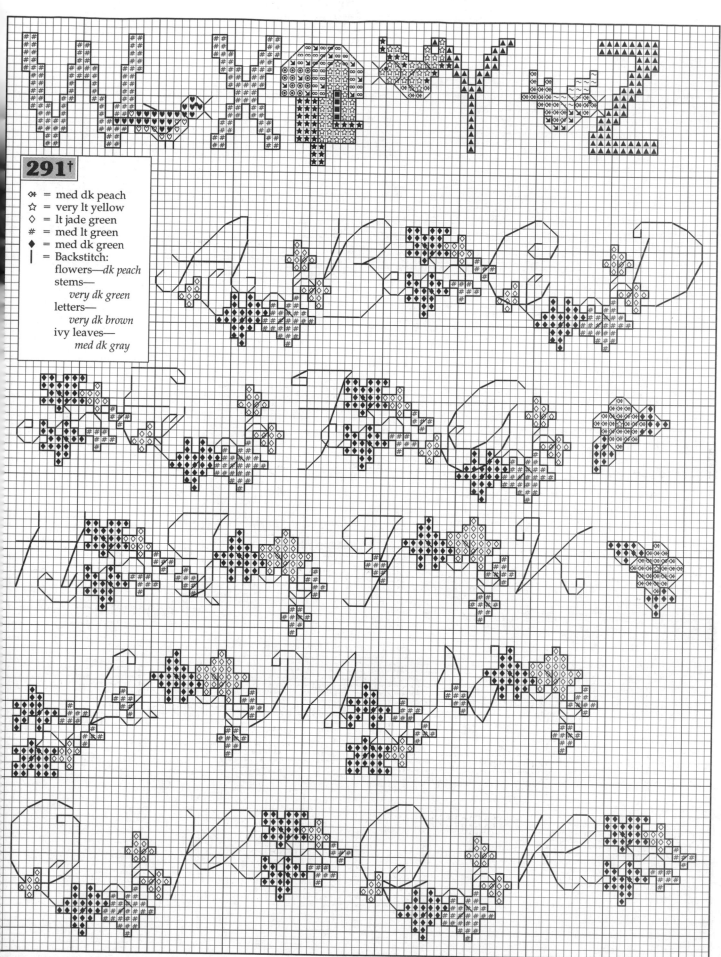

291†

✛ = med dk peach
☆ = very lt yellow
◇ = lt jade green
= med lt green
◆ = med dk green
| = Backstitch:
 flowers—*dk peach*
 stems—
  very dk green
 letters—
  very dk brown
 ivy leaves—
  med dk gray

Note: #292 is the lower case for this alphabet.

151

292

♦ = med dk green
| = Backstitch:
   stems—*very dk green*
   letters—*very dk brown*
   ivy leaves—*med dk gray*

293 **Note:** Work desired letter(s), each surrounded by tree and swing as shown.

◇ = lt willow green
♦ = dk willow green
| = Backstitch:
   grass line—*dk willow green*
   swing—*med lt brown*
   tree, branches—*very dk brown*

| = Backstitch:
   black (2 strands)

294 **Note:** Work desired letter(s), each surrounded by wishing well as shown.

◇ = very lt
      yellow-green
♦ = med willow green
+ = lt brown
∧ = very lt gray
⊙ = med lt gray
■ = black
• = French Knot:
      black

| = Backstitch:
   bricks—
      med dk gray
   letter
   extensions—
      black (2 strands)
   remaining
   outlines—*black*

295*

296

∧ = med lt pink | = Backstitch: *very dk pink*

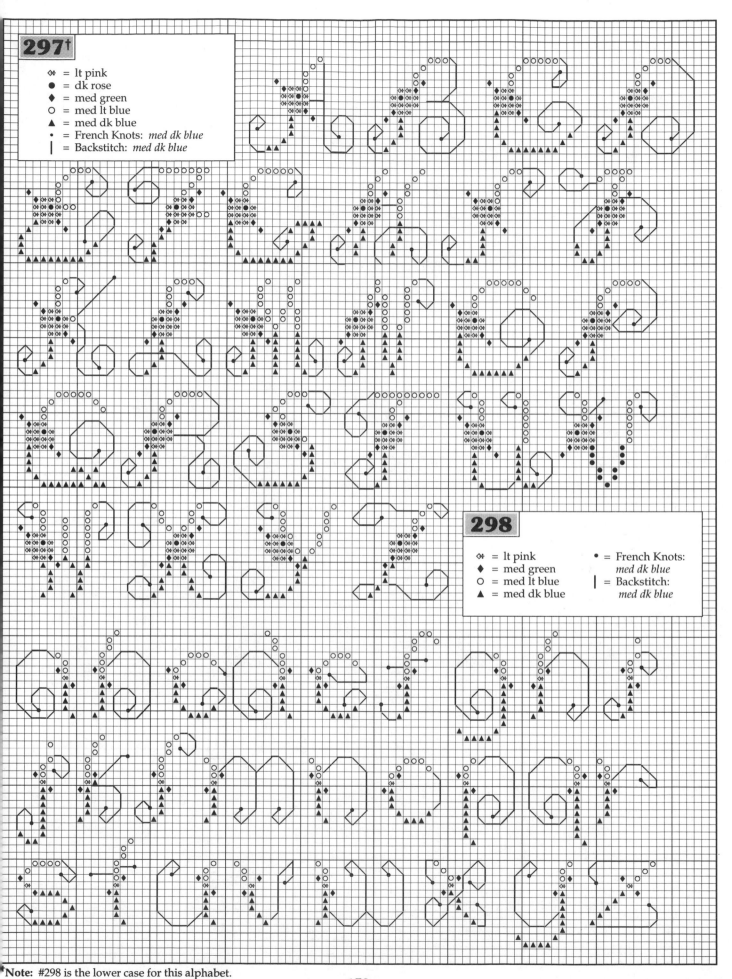

297†

⬧ = lt pink
● = dk rose
♦ = med green
○ = med lt blue
▲ = med dk blue
• = French Knots: *med dk blue*
| = Backstitch: *med dk blue*

298

⬧ = lt pink   • = French Knots:
♦ = med green   *med dk blue*
○ = med lt blue | = Backstitch:
▲ = med dk blue   *med dk blue*

†**Note:** #298 is the lower case for this alphabet.

153

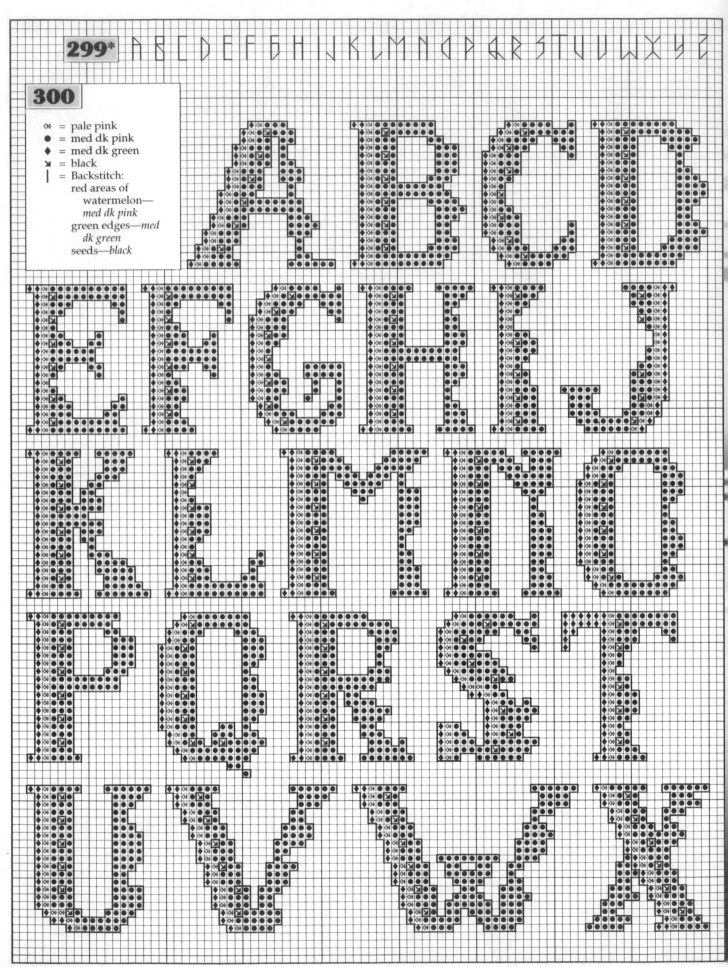

300

⋇ = pale pink
● = med dk pink
♦ = med dk green
⋈ = black
| = Backstitch:
    red areas of
        watermelon—
        med dk pink
    green edges—*med
        dk green*
    seeds—*black*

Use desired color.

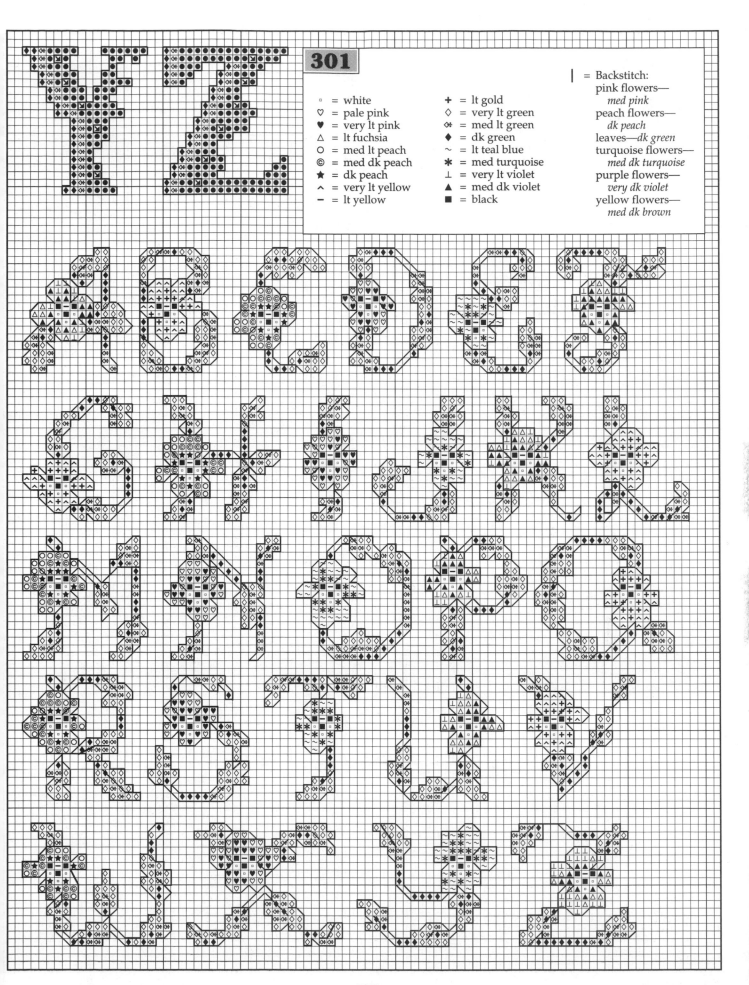

301

□ = white
♡ = pale pink
♥ = very lt pink
△ = lt fuchsia
○ = med lt peach
◎ = med dk peach
★ = dk peach
^ = very lt yellow
– = lt yellow

+ = lt gold
◇ = very lt green
✿ = med lt green
◆ = dk green
~ = lt teal blue
✳ = med turquoise
⊥ = very lt violet
▲ = med dk violet
■ = black

| = Backstitch:
pink flowers—
  med pink
peach flowers—
  dk peach
leaves—*dk green*
turquoise flowers—
  med dk turquoise
purple flowers—
  very dk violet
yellow flowers—
  med dk brown

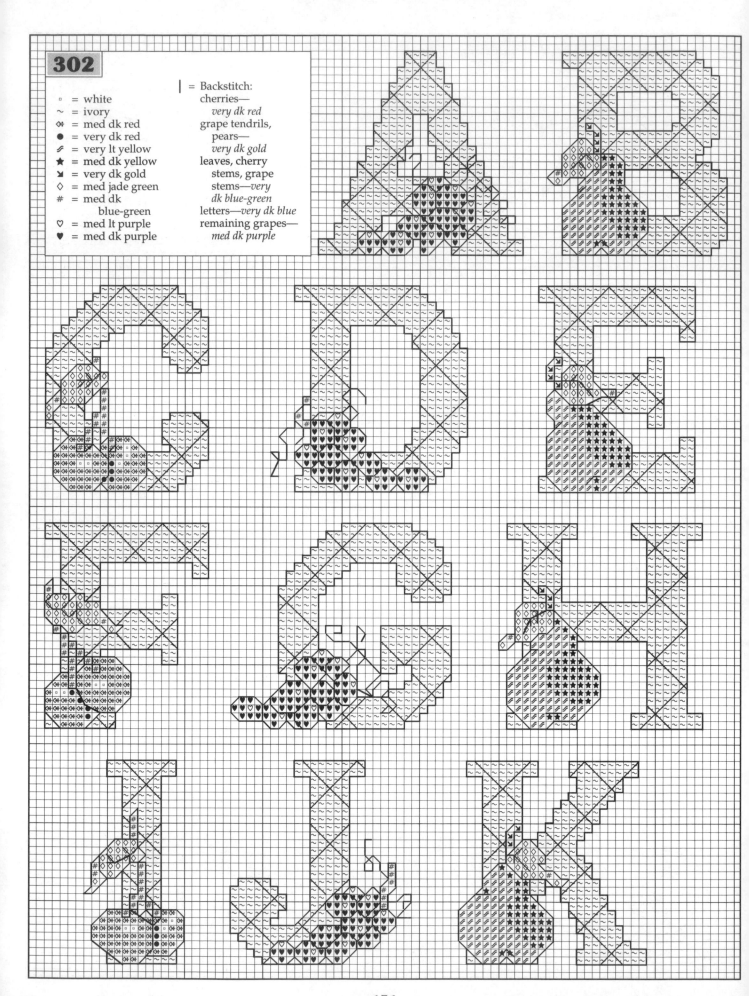

302

□ = white
~ = ivory
✿ = med dk red
● = very dk red
ℱ = very lt yellow
★ = med dk yellow
⛏ = very dk gold
◇ = med jade green
= med dk
    blue-green
♡ = med lt purple
♥ = med dk purple

| = Backstitch:
  cherries—
    very dk red
  grape tendrils,
    pears—
    very dk gold
  leaves, cherry
    stems, grape
    stems—*very*
    dk blue-green
  letters—*very dk blue*
  remaining grapes—
    med dk purple

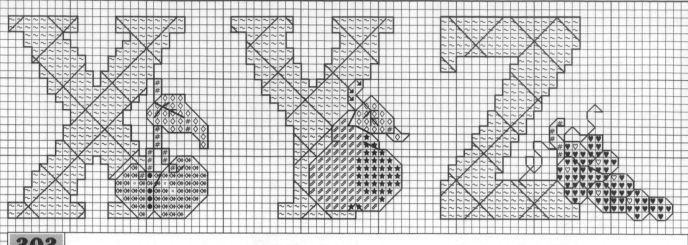

303

- • = white
- ✿ = very lt red
- ▨ = med lt red
- ⊕ = med red
- ● = dk red
- ✐ = very lt peach
- △ = very lt orange
- # = med orange
- ▲ = very dk orange
- ○ = very lt yellow
- ✳ = med gold
- ∧ = lt yellow-green
- ⊞ = med dk yellow-green
- ◇ = very lt green
- ⊙ = lt green
- ◆ = med dk green
- + = med blue

- ♥ = med dk blue
- ჺ = med lt fuchsia
- ✕ = med dk violet
- ~ = lt brown
- ⋇ = med brown
- □ = very lt gray
- ⊠ = med lt gray
- ■ = black
- | = Backstitch:
   red letters, pink flowers,
      nectarines (except stems),
      oranges, tomatoes (except
      stems), pink watermelon
      edge—*very dk red*
   section lines on orange,
      carrots—*very dk orange*
   green letters, leaves, green
      vegetable outlines, nectarine
      & tomato stems—*dk green*

blue letters—*very dk blue*
eggplant—*dk fuchsia*
beet, radishes—*very dk violet*
asparagus tips, remaining oranges, yellow
   vegetables—*med brown*
fig, hoe—*dk brown*
cabbage interior, garlic—*dk gray*
insect—*black*

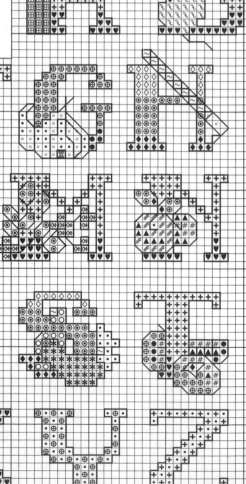

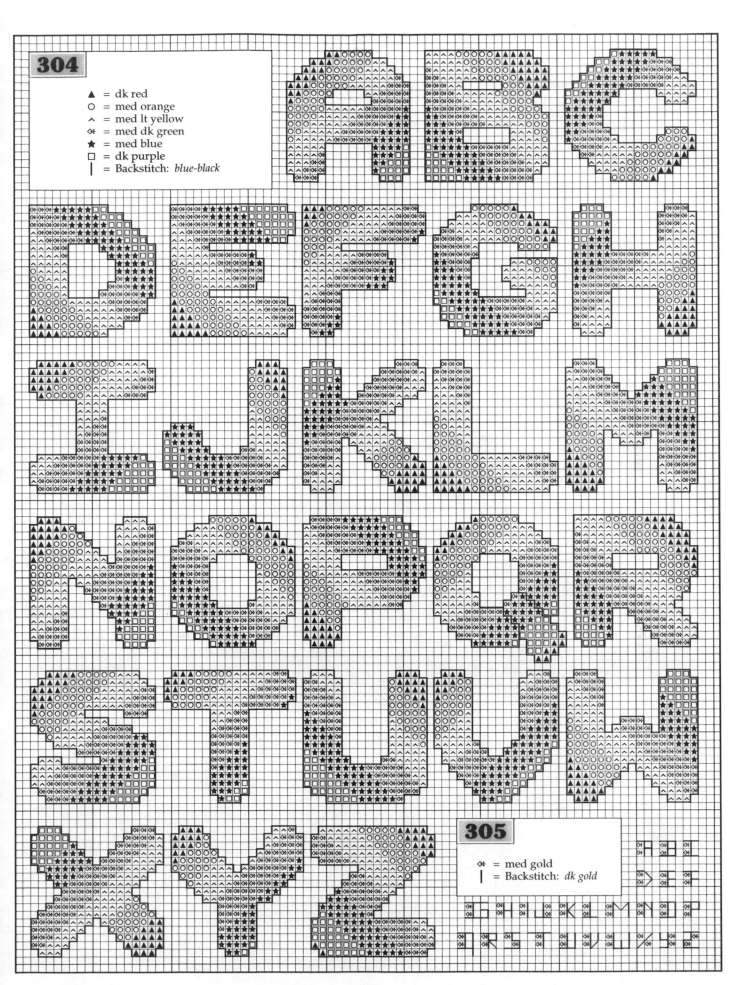

304

- ▲ = dk red
- ○ = med orange
- ∧ = med lt yellow
- ⊕ = med dk green
- ★ = med blue
- □ = dk purple
- | = Backstitch: *blue-black*

305

- ⊕ = med gold
- | = Backstitch: *dk gold*

306

▫	= white
⌃	= pale pink
○	= very lt pink
⬖	= med lt pink
✳	= med pink
▣	= dk pink
●	= very dk pink
◉	= med red
✕	= dk red
⬛	= very dk red
♡	= very lt peach
=	= very lt orange
♥	= lt orange
⊥	= med orange
◣	= med dk orange
⊖	= med yellow

~	= very lt yellow-green
◇	= med lt yellow-green
#	= dk yellow-green
◆	= dk willow green
△	= very lt blue
≃	= med blue
■	= med dk blue
☆	= med lt teal blue
★	= med dk teal blue
−	= very lt purple
⬨	= med lt purple
◢	= dk purple
⍵	= med dk rust
••	= very lt brown
+	= med lt taupe
▼	= black

| = Backstitch letter outlines:
  D, G, K, Q, S, Z—*dk willow green*
  A, H, L, N, P, T, X—*med dk blue*
  C, E, J, O, V, Y—*dk purple*
  B, F, I, M, R, U, W—*med dk taupe*
| = Backstitch flower centers:
  B, D, I, O—*med dk rust*
  L—*black*
| = Backstitch flower outlines:
  K, M, V, Y—*very dk pink*
  L, X—*dk red*
  A, F, N, Q, R, S—*very dk red*
  C—*med dk orange*
  D, J—*med blue*
  B, I—*med dk blue*
  W—*med dk teal blue*
  G, O, U, Z—*dk purple*
  E, H, P, T—*med dk rust*
| = Backstitch leaves & stems—
  dk willow green

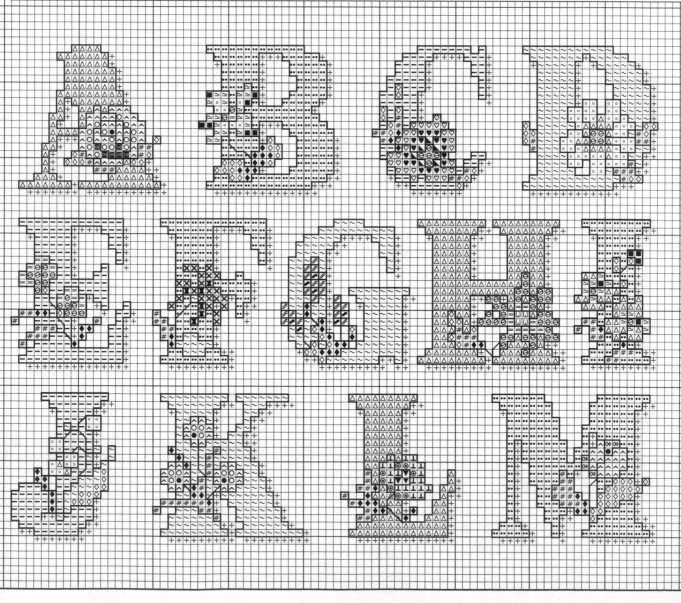

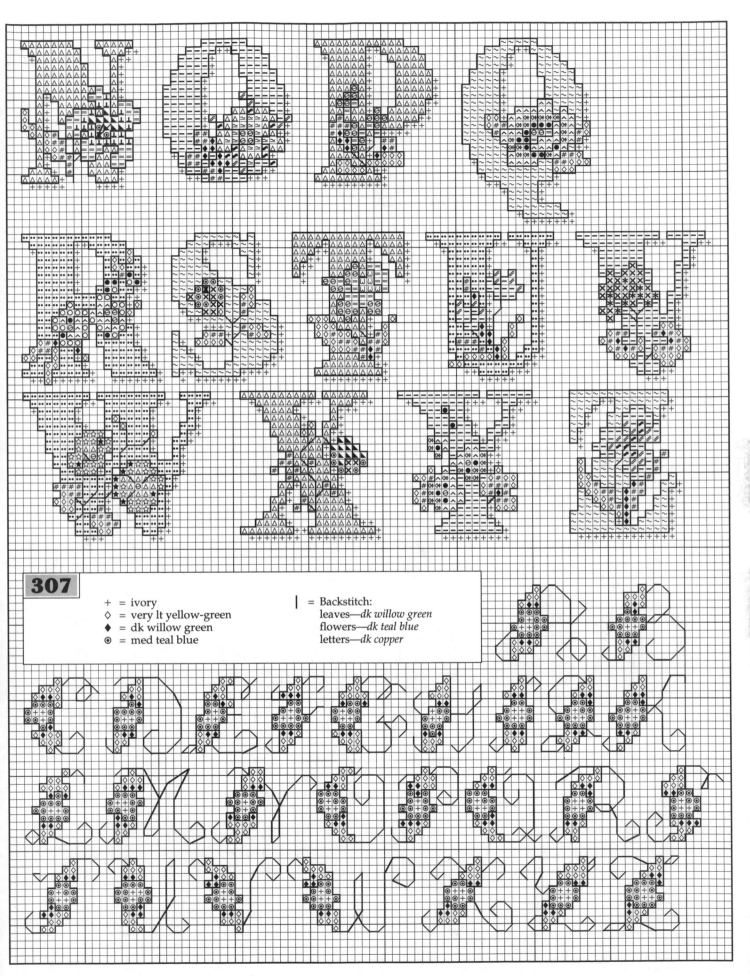

307

+ = ivory

◇ = very lt yellow-green

◆ = dk willow green

⊙ = med teal blue

| = Backstitch:
leaves—*dk willow green*
flowers—*dk teal blue*
letters—*dk copper*

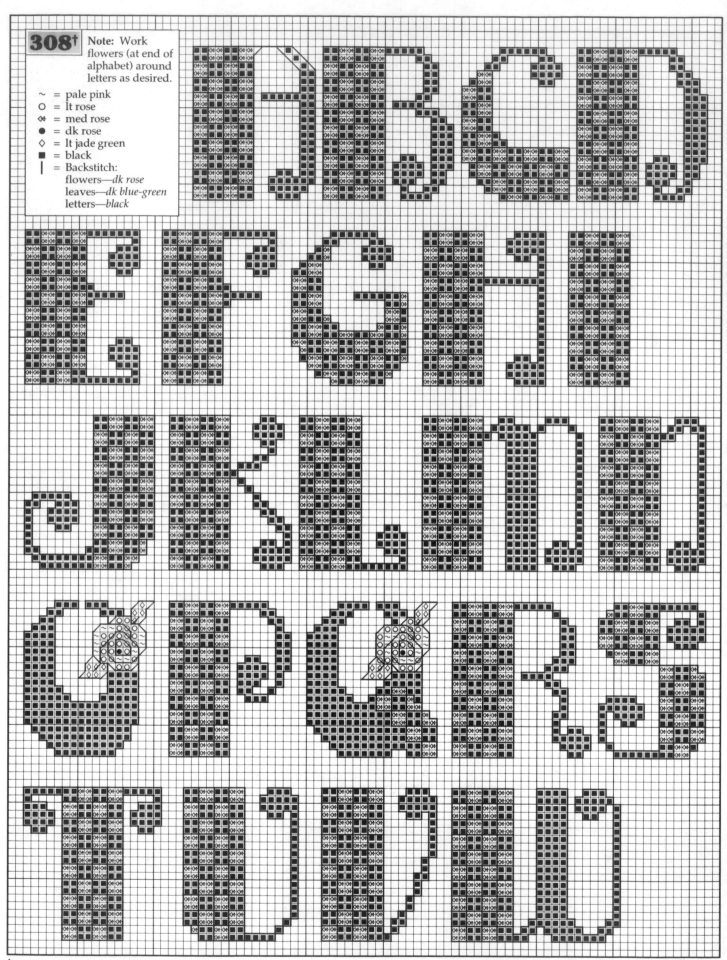

308† **Note:** Work flowers (at end of alphabet) around letters as desired.

~ = pale pink
○ = lt rose
✿ = med rose
● = dk rose
◇ = lt jade green
■ = black
| = Backstitch:
flowers—*dk rose*
leaves—*dk blue-green*
letters—*black*

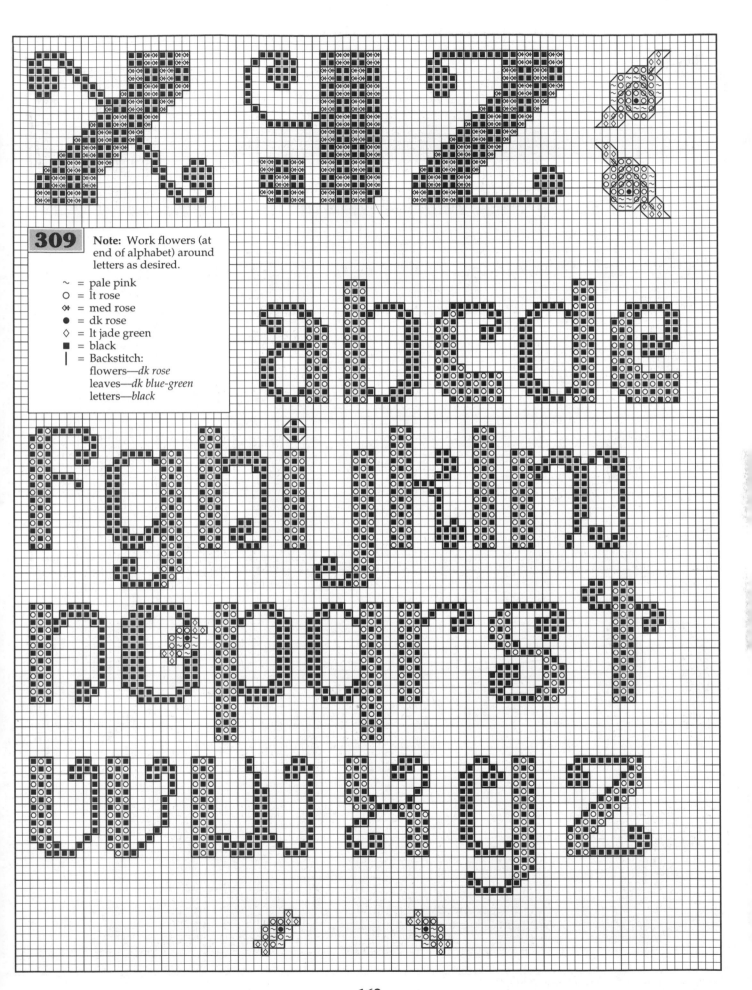

309 **Note:** Work flowers (at end of alphabet) around letters as desired.

~ = pale pink
○ = lt rose
✢ = med rose
● = dk rose
◇ = lt jade green
■ = black
| = Backstitch:
   flowers—*dk rose*
   leaves—*dk blue-green*
   letters—*black*

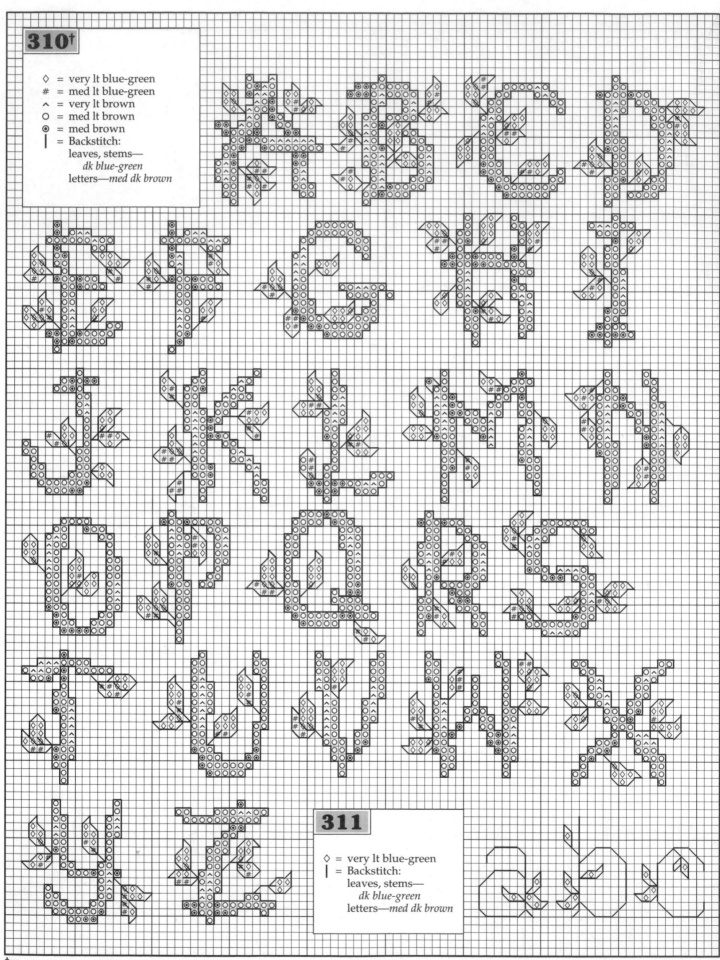

310[†]

◇ = very lt blue-green
= med lt blue-green
∧ = very lt brown
○ = med lt brown
⊙ = med brown
| = Backstitch:
    leaves, stems—
        dk blue-green
    letters—*med dk brown*

311

◇ = very lt blue-green
| = Backstitch:
    leaves, stems—
        dk blue-green
    letters—*med dk brown*

[†]**Note:** #311 is the lower case for this alphabet.

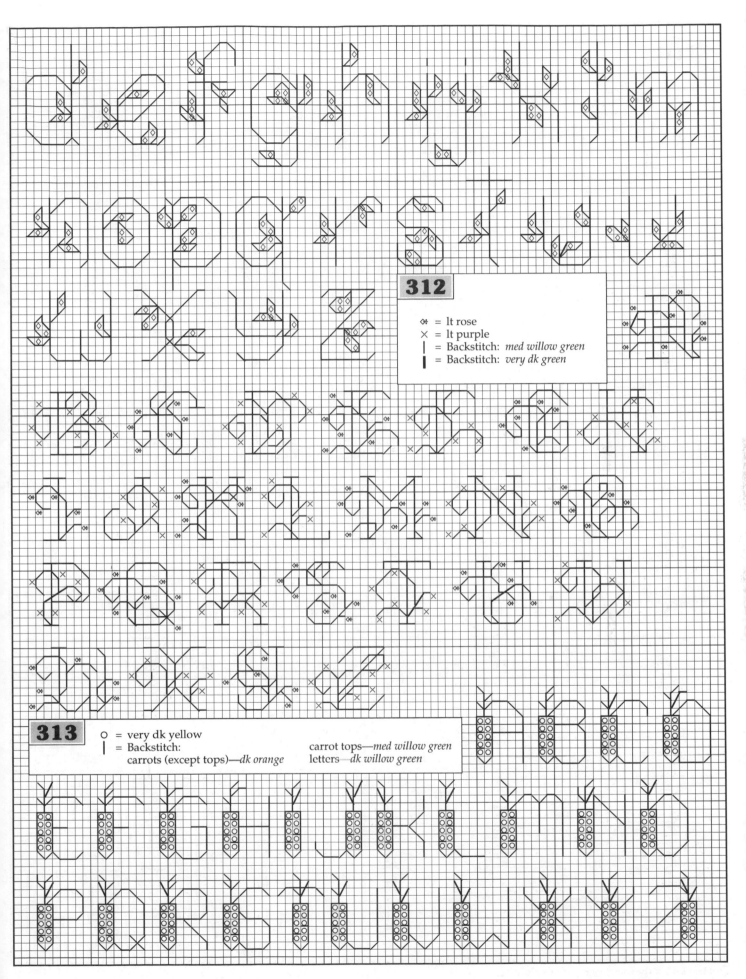

312

◊ = lt rose
× = lt purple
| = Backstitch: *med willow green*
| = Backstitch: *very dk green*

313

○ = very dk yellow
| = Backstitch:
carrots (except tops)—*dk orange*
carrot tops—*med willow green*
letters—*dk willow green*

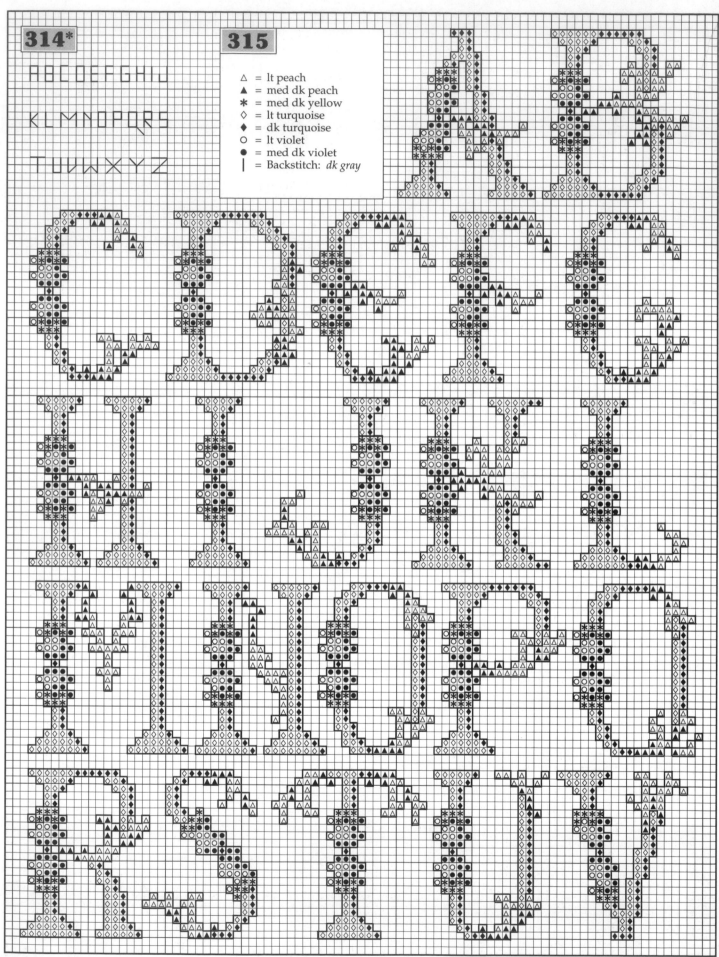

314*

A B C D E F G H I J
K L M N O P Q R S
T U V W X Y Z

315

△ = lt peach
▲ = med dk peach
✳ = med dk yellow
◇ = lt turquoise
◆ = dk turquoise
○ = lt violet
● = med dk violet
| = Backstitch: *dk gray*

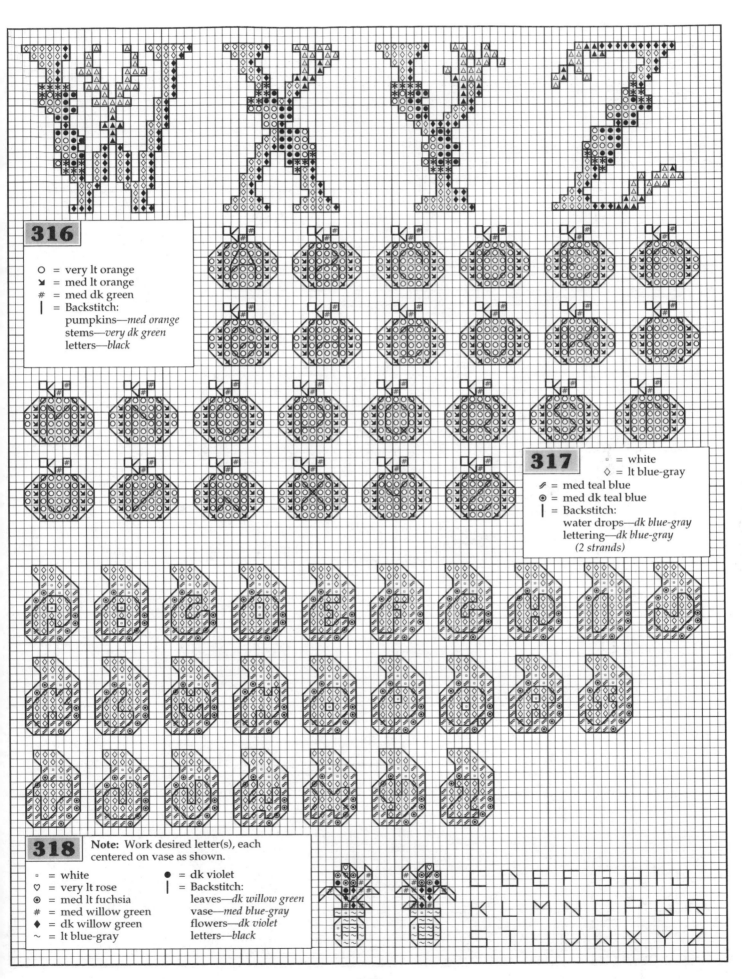

316

O = very lt orange
⚑ = med lt orange
= med dk green
| = Backstitch:
  pumpkins—*med orange*
  stems—*very dk green*
  letters—*black*

317

▫ = white
◇ = lt blue-gray
⚏ = med teal blue
⊙ = med dk teal blue
| = Backstitch:
  water drops—*dk blue-gray*
  lettering—*dk blue-gray*
  (2 strands)

318

Note: Work desired letter(s), each
centered on vase as shown.

▫ = white
♡ = very lt rose
⊙ = med lt fuchsia
= med willow green
♦ = dk willow green
~ = lt blue-gray

● = dk violet
| = Backstitch:
  leaves—*dk willow green*
  vase—*med blue-gray*
  flowers—*dk violet*
  letters—*black*

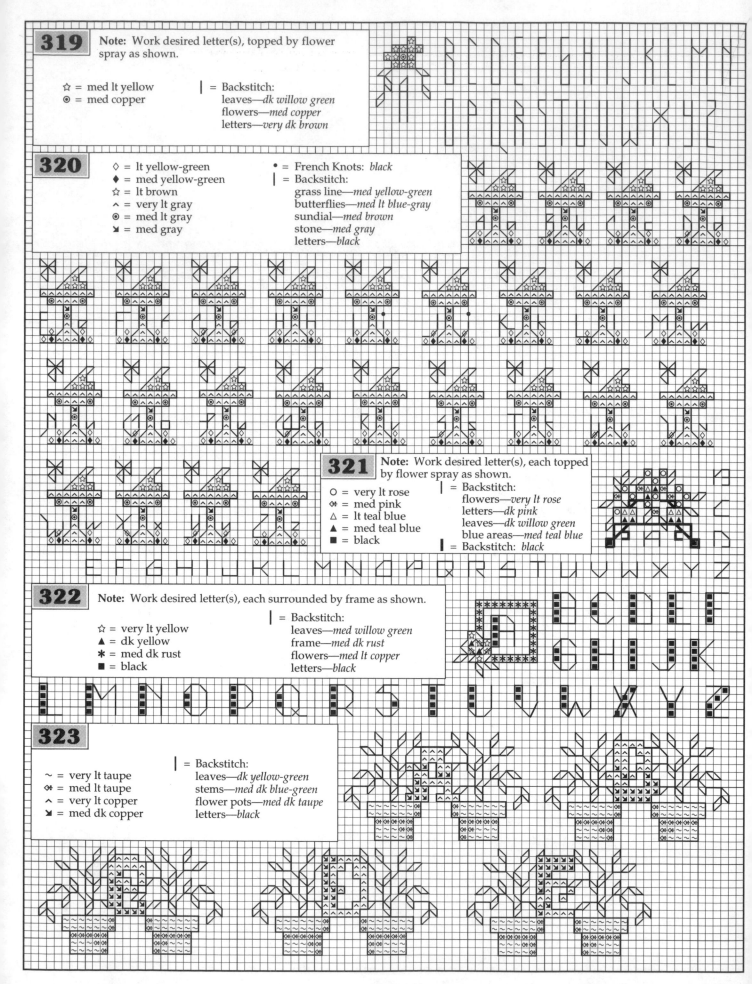

319 Note: Work desired letter(s), topped by flower spray as shown.

☆ = med lt yellow
⊙ = med copper

| = Backstitch:
    leaves—*dk willow green*
    flowers—*med copper*
    letters—*very dk brown*

320

◇ = lt yellow-green
♦ = med yellow-green
☆ = lt brown
∧ = very lt gray
⊙ = med lt gray
⋈ = med gray

• = French Knots: *black*
| = Backstitch:
    grass line—*med yellow-green*
    butterflies—*med lt blue-gray*
    sundial—*med brown*
    stone—*med gray*
    letters—*black*

321 Note: Work desired letter(s), each topped by flower spray as shown.

○ = very lt rose
⊛ = med pink
△ = lt teal blue
▲ = med teal blue
■ = black

| = Backstitch:
    flowers—*very lt rose*
    letters—*dk pink*
    leaves—*dk willow green*
    blue areas—*med teal blue*
| = Backstitch: *black*

322 Note: Work desired letter(s), each surrounded by frame as shown.

☆ = very lt yellow
▲ = dk yellow
✻ = med dk rust
■ = black

| = Backstitch:
    leaves—*med willow green*
    frame—*med dk rust*
    flowers—*med lt copper*
    letters—*black*

323

~ = very lt taupe
⊛ = med lt taupe
∧ = very lt copper
⋈ = med dk copper

| = Backstitch:
    leaves—*dk yellow-green*
    stems—*med dk blue-green*
    flower pots—*med dk taupe*
    letters—*black*

168

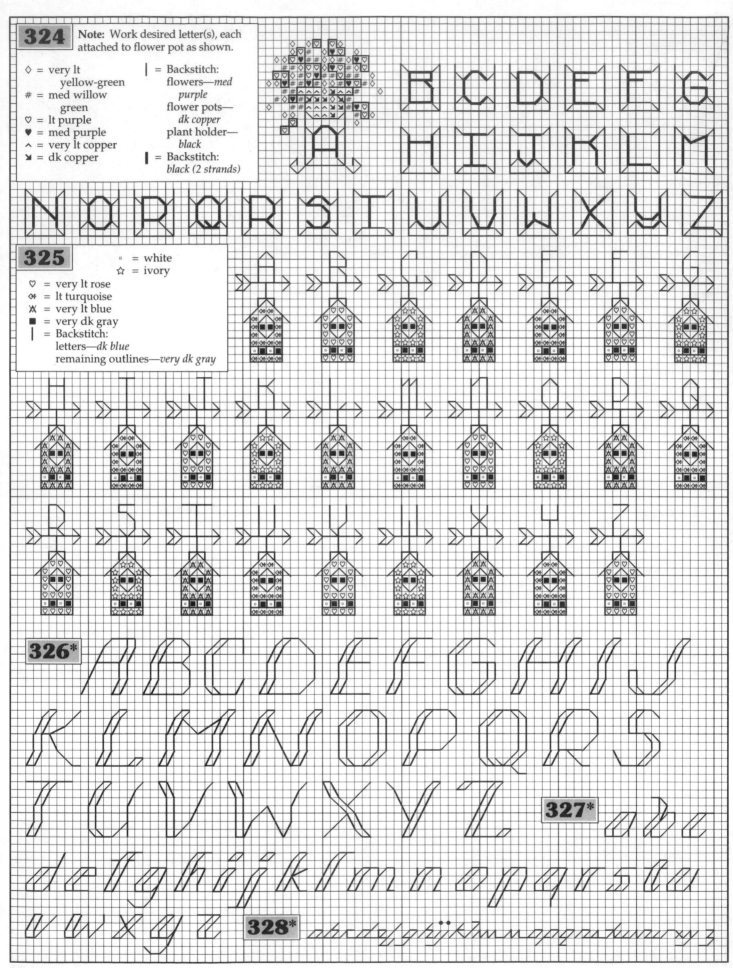

324 Note: Work desired letter(s), each attached to flower pot as shown.

◇ = very lt yellow-green
\# = med willow green
♡ = lt purple
♥ = med purple
^ = very lt copper
✄ = dk copper

| = Backstitch: flowers—*med purple* flower pots—*dk copper* plant holder—*black*
| = Backstitch: *black (2 strands)*

325

▫ = white
☆ = ivory

♡ = very lt rose
✿ = lt turquoise
✖ = very lt blue
■ = very dk gray
| = Backstitch: letters—*dk blue* remaining outlines—*very dk gray*

326*

327*

328*

* *Use desired color.*

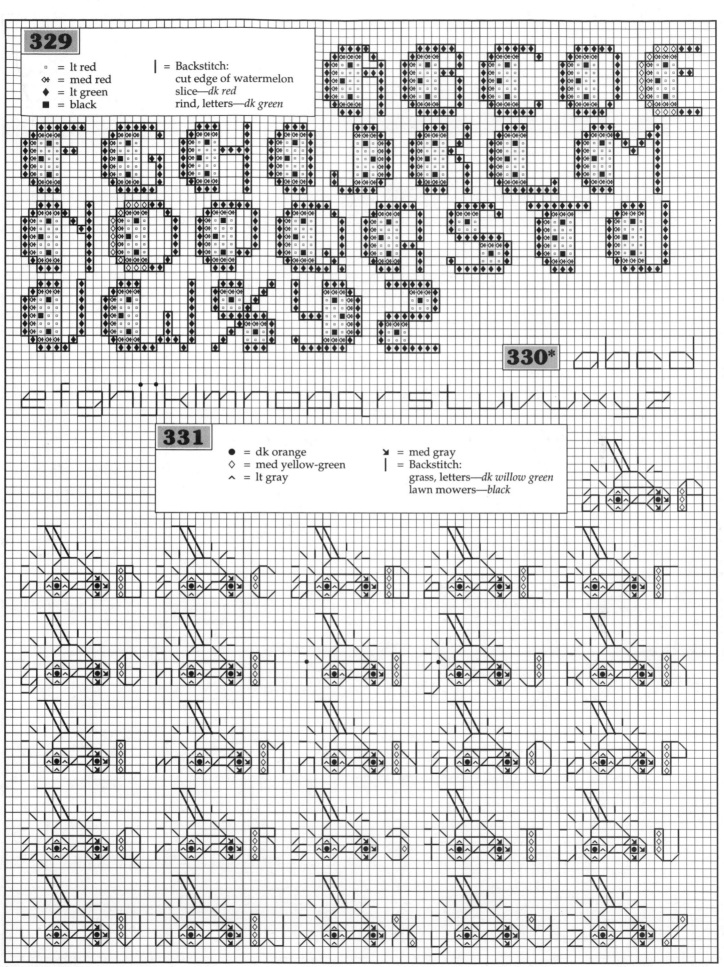

329

- ▫ = lt red
- ✧ = med red
- ◆ = lt green
- ■ = black

| = Backstitch:
cut edge of watermelon
slice—*dk red*
rind, letters—*dk green*

330*

331

- ● = dk orange
- ◇ = med yellow-green
- ⋏ = lt gray
- ↘ = med gray
- | = Backstitch:
grass, letters—*dk willow green*
lawn mowers—*black*

* *Use desired color.*

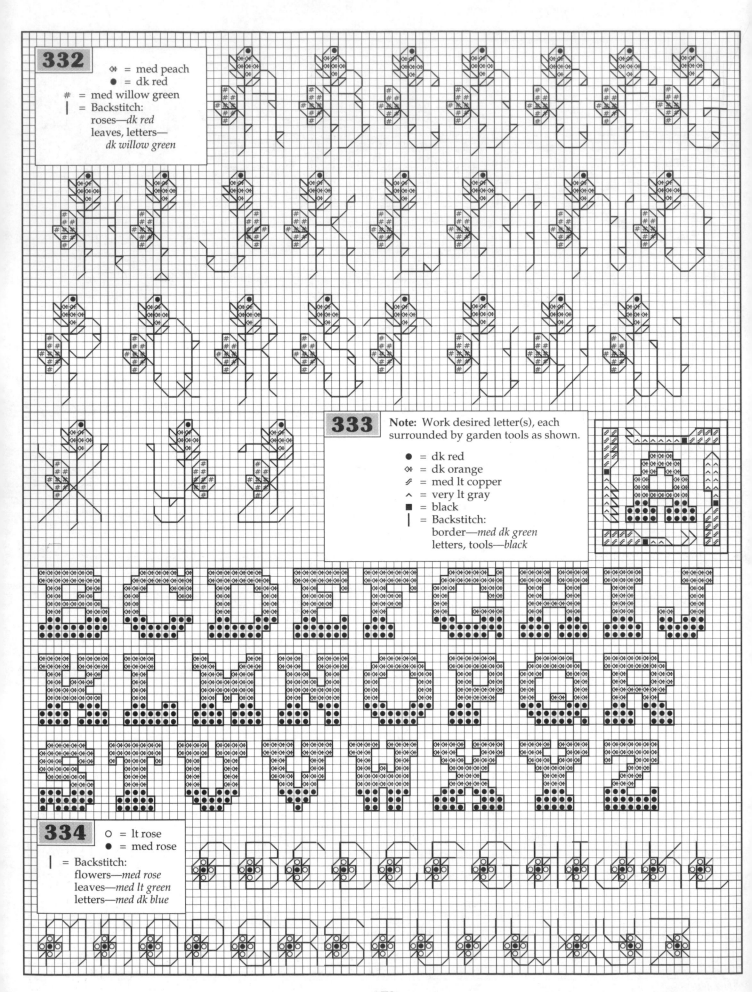

332
✤ = med peach
● = dk red
= med willow green
| = Backstitch:
roses—*dk red*
leaves, letters—
dk willow green

333 **Note:** Work desired letter(s), each surrounded by garden tools as shown.

● = dk red
✤ = dk orange
≈ = med lt copper
∧ = very lt gray
■ = black
| = Backstitch:
border—*med dk green*
letters, tools—*black*

334
○ = lt rose
● = med rose
| = Backstitch:
flowers—*med rose*
leaves—*med lt green*
letters—*med dk blue*

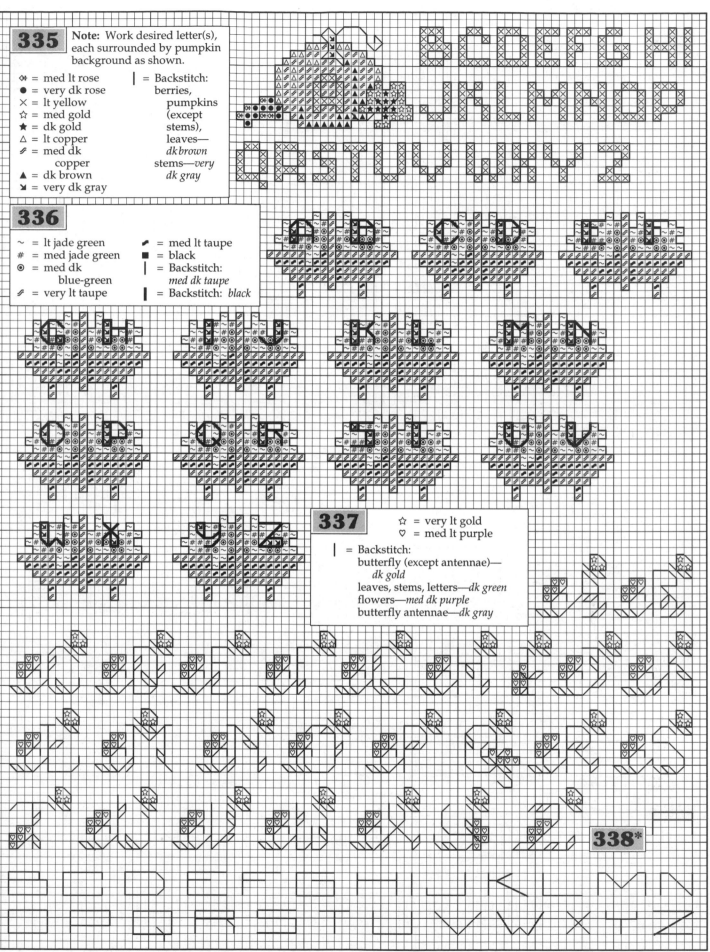

335 Note: Work desired letter(s), each surrounded by pumpkin background as shown.

⌖ = med lt rose
● = very dk rose
✕ = lt yellow
☆ = med gold
★ = dk gold
△ = lt copper
⌿ = med dk copper
▲ = dk brown
⌾ = very dk gray

| = Backstitch: berries, pumpkins (except stems), leaves— *dk brown* stems—*very dk gray*

336

~ = lt jade green
# = med jade green
⊙ = med dk blue-green
⌿ = very lt taupe
⌁ = med lt taupe
■ = black

| = Backstitch: *med dk taupe*
| = Backstitch: *black*

337

☆ = very lt gold
♡ = med lt purple

| = Backstitch:
butterfly (except antennae)— *dk gold*
leaves, stems, letters—*dk green*
flowers—*med dk purple*
butterfly antennae—*dk gray*

338*

*Use desired color.

173

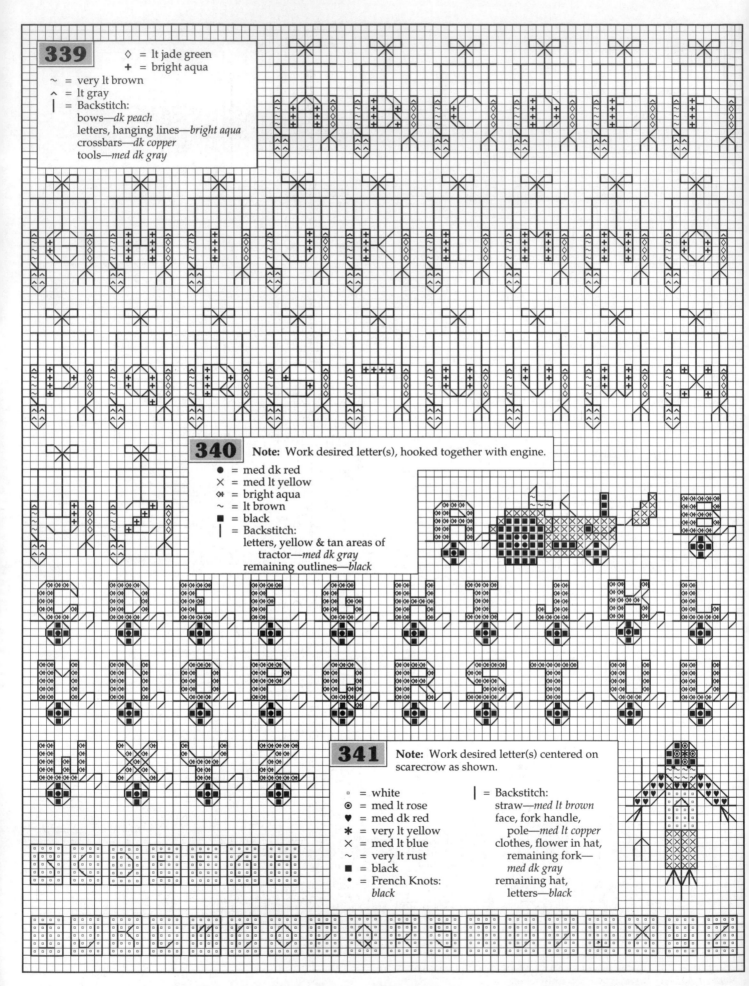

339
◇ = lt jade green
+ = bright aqua
~ = very lt brown
^ = lt gray
| = Backstitch:
  bows—*dk peach*
  letters, hanging lines—*bright aqua*
  crossbars—*dk copper*
  tools—*med dk gray*

340 Note: Work desired letter(s), hooked together with engine.
● = med dk red
× = med lt yellow
✳ = bright aqua
~ = lt brown
■ = black
| = Backstitch:
  letters, yellow & tan areas of
  tractor—*med dk gray*
  remaining outlines—*black*

341 Note: Work desired letter(s) centered on scarecrow as shown.
□ = white
⊙ = med lt rose
♥ = med dk red
✳ = very lt yellow
× = med lt blue
~ = very lt rust
■ = black
• = French Knots:
  black
| = Backstitch:
  straw—*med lt brown*
  face, fork handle,
    pole—*med lt copper*
  clothes, flower in hat,
    remaining fork—
    med dk gray
  remaining hat,
  letters—*black*

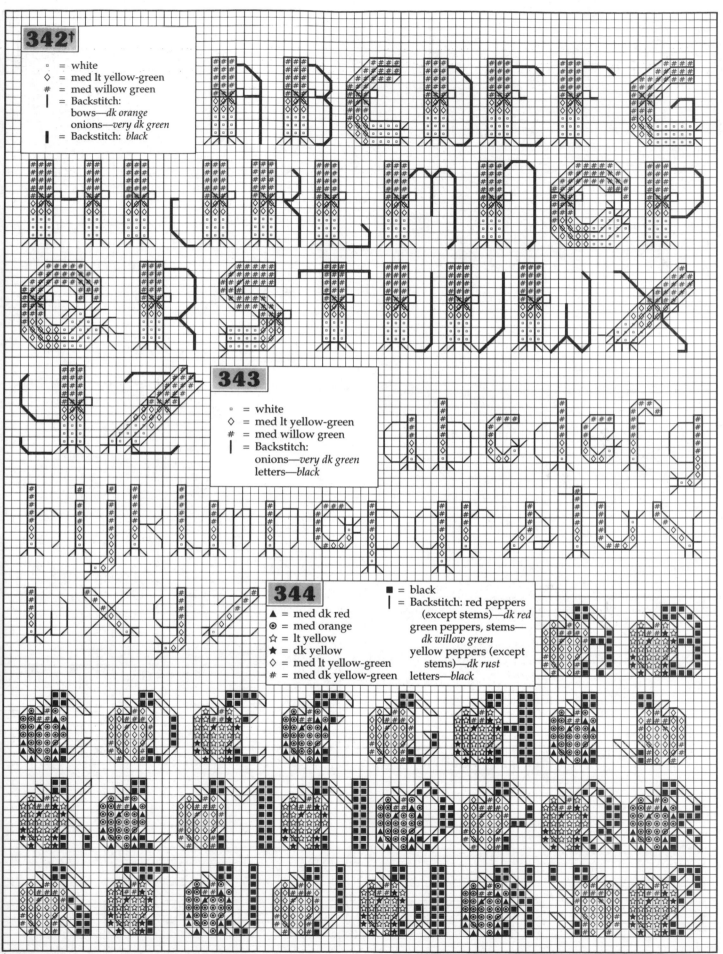

342†

- □ = white
- ◇ = med lt yellow-green
- # = med willow green
- | = Backstitch:
    bows—*dk orange*
    onions—*very dk green*
- | = Backstitch: *black*

343

- □ = white
- ◇ = med lt yellow-green
- # = med willow green
- | = Backstitch:
    onions—*very dk green*
    letters—*black*

344

- ▲ = med dk red
- ⊙ = med orange
- ☆ = lt yellow
- ★ = dk yellow
- ◇ = med lt yellow-green
- # = med dk yellow-green
- ■ = black
- | = Backstitch: red peppers
    (except stems)—*dk red*
    green peppers, stems—
        dk willow green
    yellow peppers (except
        stems)—*dk rust*
    letters—*black*

†**Note:** #343 is the lower case for this alphabet.

175

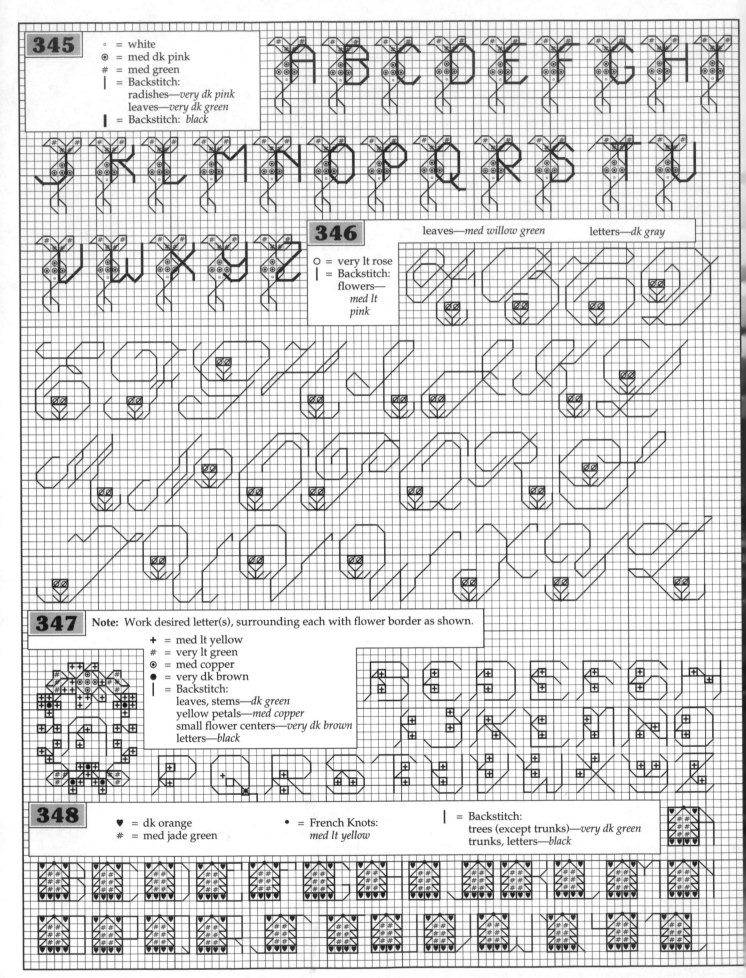

345
▫ = white
◉ = med dk pink
= med green
| = Backstitch:
  radishes—*very dk pink*
  leaves—*very dk green*
▮ = Backstitch: *black*

ABCDEFGH
JKLMNOPQRSTU
VWXYZ

346
leaves—*med willow green*   letters—*dk gray*

○ = very lt rose
| = Backstitch:
  flowers—
  med lt pink

347   **Note:** Work desired letter(s), surrounding each with flower border as shown.

+ = med lt yellow
# = very lt green
◉ = med copper
● = very dk brown
| = Backstitch:
  leaves, stems—*dk green*
  yellow petals—*med copper*
  small flower centers—*very dk brown*
  letters—*black*

348
♥ = dk orange
= med jade green
● = French Knots:
  med lt yellow
| = Backstitch:
  trees (except trunks)—*very dk green*
  trunks, letters—*black*

176

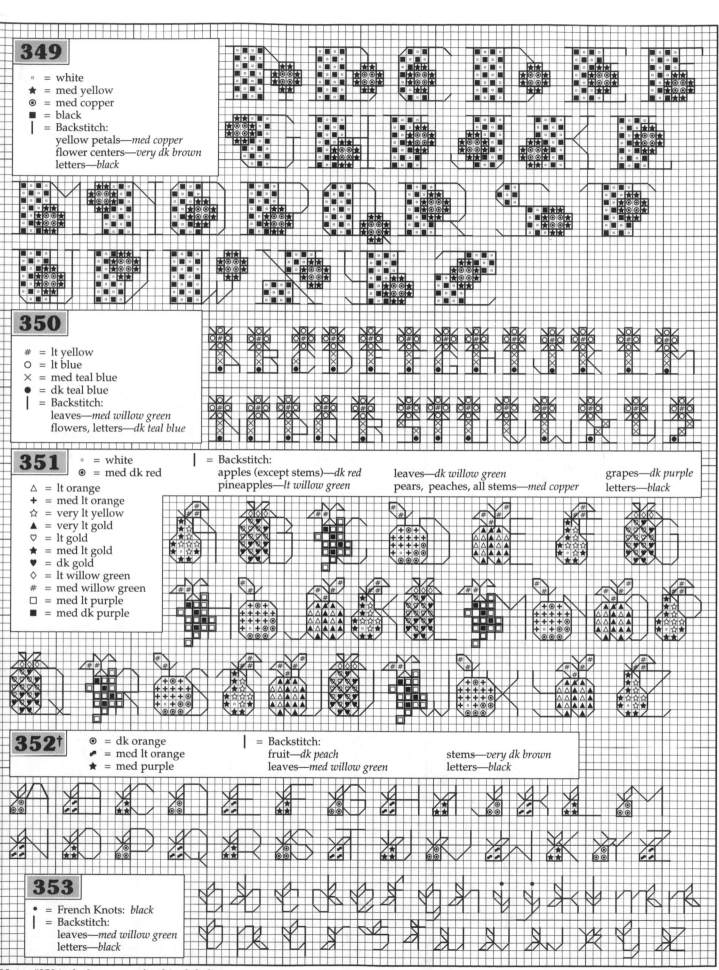

349

- □ = white
- ★ = med yellow
- ⊙ = med copper
- ■ = black
- | = Backstitch:
  - yellow petals—*med copper*
  - flower centers—*very dk brown*
  - letters—*black*

350

- # = lt yellow
- ○ = lt blue
- × = med teal blue
- ● = dk teal blue
- | = Backstitch:
  - leaves—*med willow green*
  - flowers, letters—*dk teal blue*

351

- □ = white
- ⊙ = med dk red
- △ = lt orange
- + = med lt orange
- ☆ = very lt yellow
- ▲ = very lt gold
- ♡ = lt gold
- ★ = med lt gold
- ♥ = dk gold
- ◇ = lt willow green
- # = med willow green
- □ = med lt purple
- ■ = med dk purple

| = Backstitch:
  - apples (except stems)—*dk red*
  - pineapples—*lt willow green*
  - leaves—*dk willow green*
  - pears, peaches, all stems—*med copper*
  - grapes—*dk purple*
  - letters—*black*

352†

- ⊙ = dk orange
- ✎ = med lt orange
- ★ = med purple
- | = Backstitch:
  - fruit—*dk peach*
  - leaves—*med willow green*
  - stems—*very dk brown*
  - letters—*black*

353

- • = French Knots: *black*
- | = Backstitch:
  - leaves—*med willow green*
  - letters—*black*

†**Note:** #353 is the lower case for this alphabet.

354 **Note:** #355 is the lower case for this alphabet.

□ = white
✦ = med lt pink
◣ = med dk pink
○ = very lt rose
~ = med lt peach
☆ = very lt yellow
✳ = very lt gold
◇ = lt jade green
◆ = med jade green
△ = very lt turquoise
▲ = lt turquoise

✕ = lt blue
⧼ = very lt purple
★ = very lt copper
= med copper
∧ = very lt brown
∞ = lt brown
⊙ = med lt brown
⊠ = very dk brown
♡ = very lt gray
⊌ = med lt gray

• = French Knots:
   pink shirts—*med dk pink*
   green shirt—*dk blue-green*
   yellow shirts—*med dk brown*
   eyes—*med dk gray*
| = Backstitch: pink letters, clothes,
   & flowers; apples; watering
   can design—*med dk pink*
   turquoise letters & clothes—
   med dk turquoise
   carrot tops, leaves, stems,
   tendrils, grass, green clothes—
   dk blue-green

blue letters—*med blue*
purple letters & flowers—*med dk purple*
remaining carrots, yellow flowers,
   remaining clothes, hats,
   tomatoes—*med copper*
dirt, rake (J), shovel handles (D, Q, T),
   pitchfork (W)—*very dk brown*
brown rabbits (except mouths &
   whiskers), basket, pot, seed bag,
   pitchfork—*med dk brown*
gray rabbits, mouths, whiskers,
   shovels, watering cans—*med dk gray*

355

| = Backstitch

• = French Knots: *med blue*

c, d, g, h, k, l, o, p, s, t, w, x—*med dk turquoise (2 strands)*

a, b, e, f, i, j, m, n, q, r, u, v, y, z—*med blue (2 strands)*

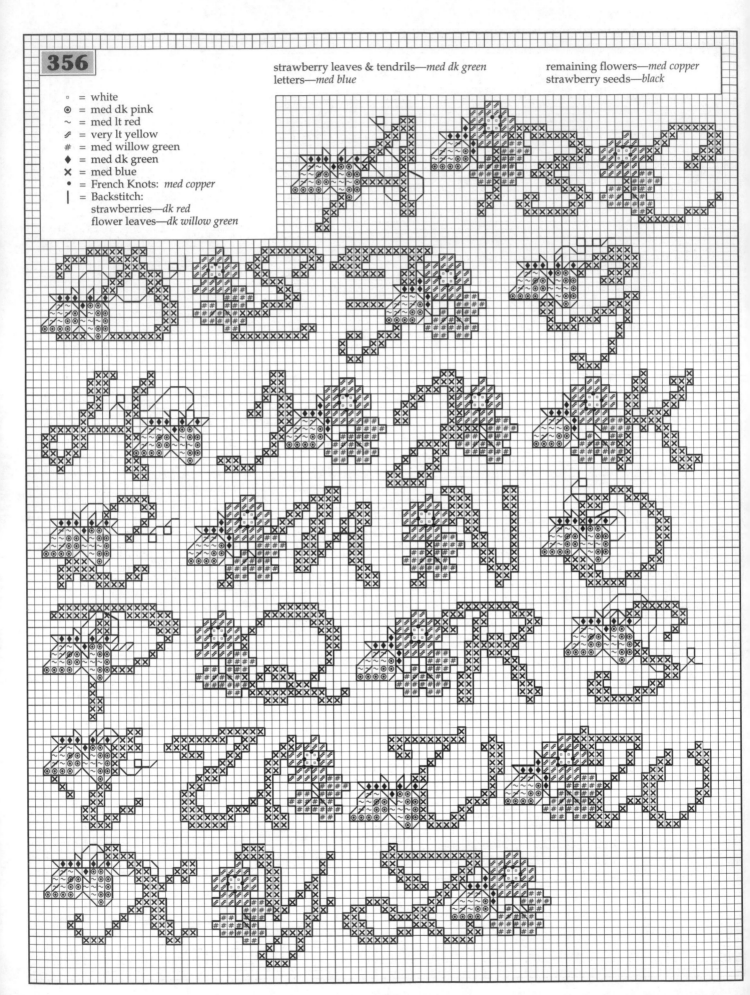

356

○ = white
⊙ = med dk pink
~ = med lt red
𝒮 = very lt yellow
= med willow green
♦ = med dk green
✕ = med blue
• = French Knots: *med copper*
| = Backstitch:
    strawberries—*dk red*
    flower leaves—*dk willow green*

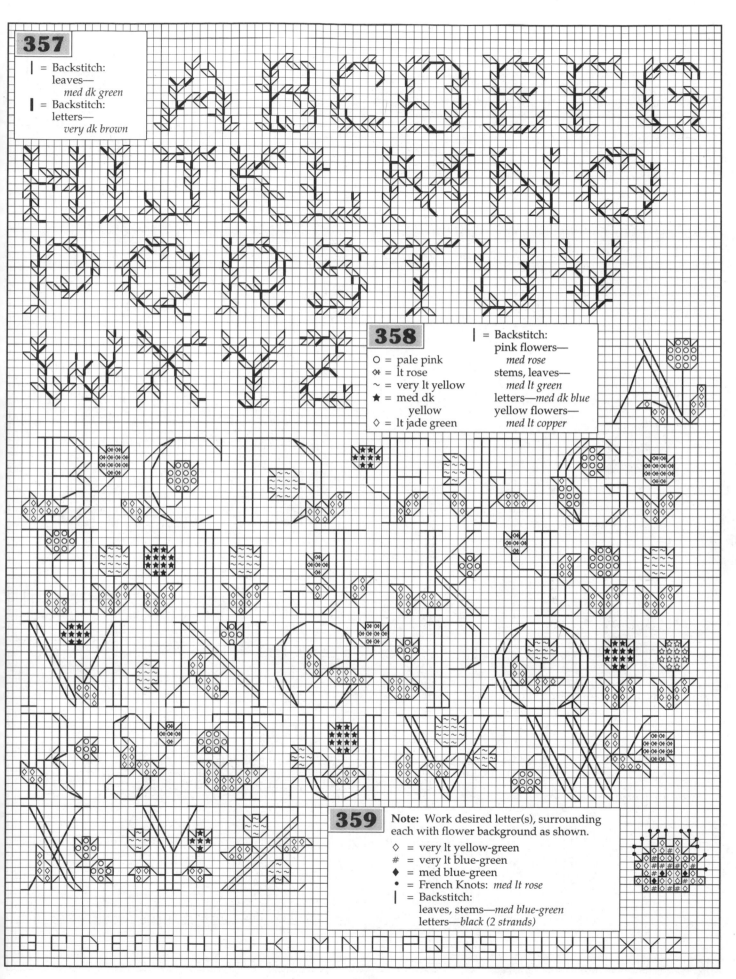

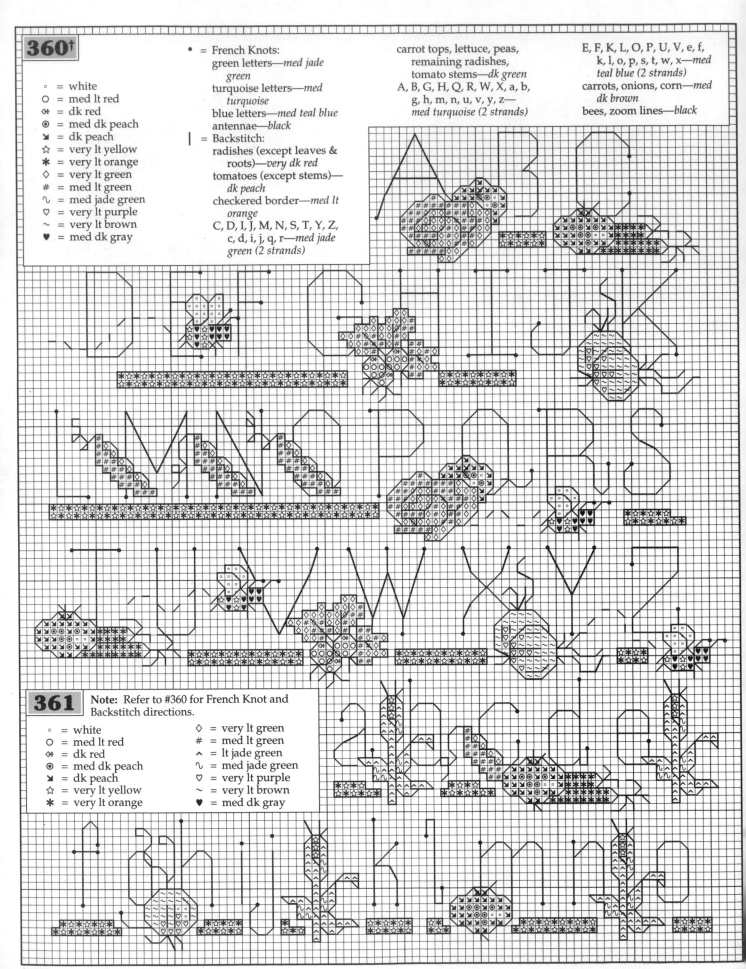

360†

• = French Knots:
- green letters—*med jade green*
- turquoise letters—*med turquoise*
- blue letters—*med teal blue*
- antennae—*black*

| = Backstitch:
- radishes (except leaves & roots)—*very dk red*
- tomatoes (except stems)—*dk peach*
- checkered border—*med lt orange*
- C, D, I, J, M, N, S, T, Y, Z, c, d, i, j, q, r—*med jade green (2 strands)*

carrot tops, lettuce, peas, remaining radishes, tomato stems—*dk green*

A, B, G, H, Q, R, W, X, a, b, g, h, m, n, u, v, y, z—*med turquoise (2 strands)*

E, F, K, L, O, P, U, V, e, f, k, l, o, p, s, t, w, x—*med teal blue (2 strands)*

carrots, onions, corn—*med dk brown*

bees, zoom lines—*black*

□ = white
○ = med lt red
⊕ = dk red
◉ = med dk peach
◣ = dk peach
☆ = very lt yellow
✳ = very lt orange
◇ = very lt green
= med lt green
∩ = med jade green
♡ = very lt purple
~ = very lt brown
♥ = med dk gray

361 **Note:** Refer to #360 for French Knot and Backstitch directions.

□ = white
○ = med lt red
⊕ = dk red
◉ = med dk peach
◣ = dk peach
☆ = very lt yellow
✳ = very lt orange
◇ = very lt green
= med lt green
∧ = lt jade green
∩ = med jade green
♡ = very lt purple
~ = very lt brown
♥ = med dk gray

†Note: #361 is the lower case for this alphabet.

182

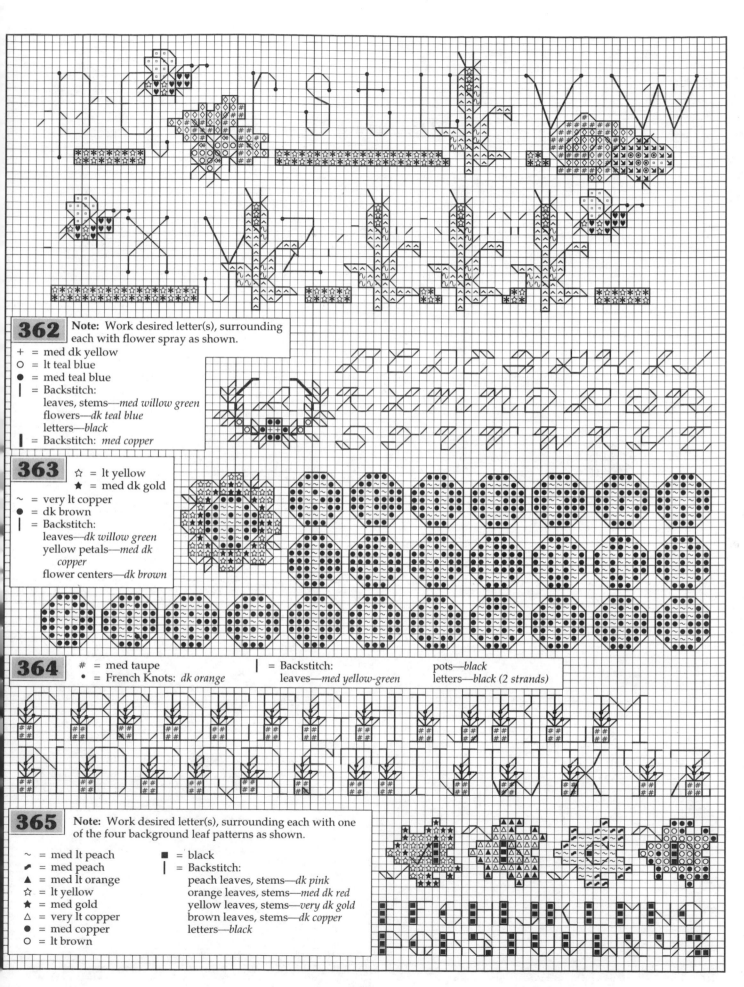

362 **Note:** Work desired letter(s), surrounding each with flower spray as shown.

+ = med dk yellow
○ = lt teal blue
● = med teal blue
| = Backstitch:
    leaves, stems—*med willow green*
    flowers—*dk teal blue*
    letters—*black*
| = Backstitch: *med copper*

363 ☆ = lt yellow
★ = med dk gold
~ = very lt copper
● = dk brown
| = Backstitch:
    leaves—*dk willow green*
    yellow petals—*med dk copper*
    flower centers—*dk brown*

364 # = med taupe
• = French Knots: *dk orange*
| = Backstitch:
    leaves—*med yellow-green*
    pots—*black*
    letters—*black (2 strands)*

365 **Note:** Work desired letter(s), surrounding each with one of the four background leaf patterns as shown.

~ = med lt peach
↗ = med peach
▲ = med lt orange
☆ = lt yellow
★ = med gold
△ = very lt copper
● = med copper
○ = lt brown
■ = black
| = Backstitch:
    peach leaves, stems—*dk pink*
    orange leaves, stems—*med dk red*
    yellow leaves, stems—*very dk gold*
    brown leaves, stems—*dk copper*
    letters—*black*

Master Color Key

The generic color names in this book represent the following numbers listed by brand. Most color groups have seven values beginning with very light (very lt) and ending with very dark (very dk). The symbol selection is different for each alphabet, but the names are consistent throughout the book. For example, in any color key, for a symbol specified as very lt pink, choose Anchor 50, Coats 3151, or DMC 605; for a symbol specified as med dk pink, choose Anchor 29, Coats 3047, or DMC 309.

	Anchor	Coats	DMC		Anchor	Coats	DMC
white	1	1001	blanc	med dk peach	11	3111	350
ivory	386	2386	3823	dk peach	13	3013	347
pale pink	271	3280	819	very lt orange	323	2323	722
very lt pink	50	3151	605	lt orange	328	2324	3341
lt pink	55	3001	604	med lt orange	329	2327	3340
med lt pink	40	3153	335	med orange	330	2330	970
med pink	57	3063	602	med dk orange	332	2332	946
med dk pink	29	3047	309	dk orange	333	2329	608
dk pink	59	3019	326	very dk orange	334	2334	606
very dk pink	44	3073	815				
				very lt yellow	301	2289	745
very lt red	24	3281	776	lt yellow	305	2295	744
lt red	31	3127	3708	med lt yellow	297	2294	444
med lt red	33	3012	3706	med yellow	298	2298	725
med red	35	3152	3705	med dk yellow	302	2302	743
med dk red	46	3500	666	dk yellow	303	2303	742
dk red	47	3047	321	very dk yellow	304	2314	741
very dk red	22	3021	814				
				very lt gold	311	2305	677
very lt rose	73	3173	963	lt gold	891	5363	676
lt rose	74	3003	3354	med lt gold	890	2876	729
med lt rose	75	3282	3688	med gold	306	2307	725
med rose	76	3176	3731	med dk gold	307	5307	783
med dk rose	77	3088	3687	dk gold	308	5308	781
dk rose	65	3065	3350	very dk gold	310	5365	780
very dk rose	78	3089	3685				
				very lt yellow-green	259	6250	772
lt fuchsia	85	4085	3609	lt yellow-green	253	6253	472
med lt fuchsia	86	4086	3608	med lt yellow-green	254	6001	3348
med fuchsia	87	4087	3607	med yellow-green	255	6256	471
med dk fuchsia	88	4088	718	med dk yellow-green	256	6267	704
dk fuchsia	89	4089	915	dk yellow-green	257	6258	905
				very dk yellow-green	258	6268	904
very lt peach	6	3006	754				
lt peach	8	3868	353	lt willow green	261	6266	989
med lt peach	9	3008	352	med willow green	267	6267	469
med peach	10	3011	351	dk willow green	268	6268	937